W9-DEO-696

Radical social work and practice

Contributors

Ron Bailey
Roy Bailey
Bill Bennett
Mike Brake
Myra Garrett
John Hart
Bruce Hugman
Charles Husband
Phil Lee
Marjorie Mayo
David Pithers
Elizabeth Wilson

Radical social work and practice

Edited by Mike Brake and Roy Bailey

SAGE Publications ● Beverly Hills

Copyright © 1980 by Edward Arnold (Publishers) Ltd

First published 1980 by
Edward Arnold (Publishers) Ltd
41 Bedford Square
London WC1B 3DQ

Published in the United States of America 1980
by Sage Publications Inc.
275 South Beverly Drive
Beverly Hills California 90212

ISBN 0-8039-1559-4 (hardcover)
ISBN 0-8039-1560-8 (softcover)

Library of Congress Catalog Card No. 80-83276

FIRST PRINTING, this edition

Printed in the United States of America

Contents

1

Contributions to a radical practice in social work

Roy Bailey and Mike Brake

The question is often asked, somewhat sceptically, 'what is radical social work?' More often than not the questioner is not really expecting an answer. The question is posed as a sure way of changing the subject. Clearly, it is difficult and it certainly does not lend itself to an easy answer. However, before we get too worried that maybe there is no such thing as radical social work and that maybe we are all chasing shadows, we should remember that just about the same nervousness and anxiety is created by the question, 'what is social work?' Most of the people we know who are either engaged in the process of teaching social work students, or employed as professional social workers, steer clear of the question. The hesitation is often with good reason: after all, anyone who confronts it and attempts an answer leaves themselves open to attack and criticism

In the brief introduction to our first volume (Bailey and Brake 1975) we made it clear there were no easy answers. This remains our position. However, what is clear is that we have raised an issue which has found its place quite unambigously into professional debates and into most, if not all, professional courses in Britain and the United States. If translations and publication in Sweden and Norway are anything to go by, then in those countries too radical social work has established itself as a legitimate object of debate and consideration. It is no longer possible to dismiss critical questions from students about the general purposes of social work or about a particular practice. Social workers, *like other workers*, are trapped in a social structure which severely delimits their power and hence their ability to initiate significant change. Social workers, *unlike other workers*, confront daily, as their job, the victims of an economic and political structure that creates poverty and humiliation. Social workers and clients alike are bemused by forces beyond their control but to which we are all subject. The very weight of the institutional arrangements that bind us results in our hesitancy to make any grand-sounding claims for radical social work as a framework for practice that might resolve anything. Nevertheless, this is the task that radical social workers set themselves.

The issues of social work remain ideological. Theories and practices in social work are not detached propositions and techniques. The criticisms are not of case-work or working with individuals, not of group work or working with the family, not of youth work or working with and within a community: the criticisms are directed at the purposes to which these theories and methods are put. At the same time social workers are not above criticism by claiming that the consequences of their action were not intended by them. Most if not all our actions result in consequences either in addition to our intentions or in spite of them. We cannot abdicate responsibility for the consequences of our actions even if we did not initially desire or anticipate the results. No matter how well meaning a social worker, a criticism is justified if, as a result of dealing with a client, that client remains unaware of the public dimension of his or her problems. The problems and difficulties that are associated with a person becoming a client should be identified and located within some structural and political process. This is not to enable anyone, client or social worker, to avoid or deny responsibility for their personal decisions and choices, but rather to make it clear that their decisions and choices were made in circumstances not of their own choosing.

This criticism remains even if a client ceases to be a client. For example, a person about to have the gas or electricity cut off after failure to pay the necessary bills goes to a social worker, who with the best will in the world understands the problem and how it arose, can use his or her influence and persuade the appropriate authority not to take the action. This, coupled with social security payments, may 'resolve' the client's problem. The 'client' becomes a person again, albeit not quite the same person that he or she was before. The social worker can feel pleased with a job well done. For the client, however, the problem was experienced as personal and remains so. Other people, however, were and are facing the same problem. Circumstances out of their control, and common to many individuals and families, are rendered private and personal. (For discussion of this issue, see for example Mills 1959, Pearson 1973.) The very commonality and public nature of the conditions that create the poverty leading to a denial of fuel are not exposed. The social worker knows about it, of course, but so should the client. Introducing the client to others in like cir- cumstances, or at least offering the introduction, assists in no small way in sustaining the individual's self respect and potentially makes him or her aware of wider problems associated with the production, distribution and consumption of fuel. It may further contribute to the arguments concerning the Right to Fuel as a social service. Social work as an institutional process can simultaneously assist people and render them less able to help themselves. Social workers cannot avoid criticisms of their practice by pleading that a consequence of their action was not their intention, indeed was nobody's intention. The focus on the public and collective nature of private and personal difficulties is left to the social worker. Each particular case has to be handled within the context of the sensitivities of both client and social worker. For radical practice, however, such connections should be taken for granted as dimensions of daily practice.

Radical practice is more than dealing with clients. The possi- bilities of doing much in the way of creating the conditions for real structural change are severely limited in the day-to-day working with clients, whether conceived of as individuals, groups, families or communities. Assisting in a positive fashion, trying to sustain mutual respect and self-respect, and trying to locate a client's position and problems within wider social groups and political processes are all important moments in a radical social worker's task. So too is the awareness of the social worker's own position within the structure, and the recognition of the many things they have in common with clients themselves. For example, government policy decisions may freeze local authority employment, which potentially throws newly-qualified social workers onto the unemployment queues where they find them-

selves alongside others who might well have been, in different circumstances, their clients. The crisis facing capitalism is translated
into the consciousness of professionals and the middle classes in
ways that have long been commonplace for significant
proportions of the working class. Indeed, it is likely that one talks
of the crisis of capitalism only when the uncertainties and insecu-
rities that are normal experiences for social work clients are
experienced by middle-class professionals. Only then do we read
of the 'current crisis of capitalism'. For many the 'current crisis'
has been with them for as as long as they can remember.

Working within a union and hence within the context of
organized labour is important. Strengthening the collective social
workers' voice within the labour movement is of considerable
importance. After all, which other workers have first-hand
knowledge of the consequences of the workings of our economic
system for an increasing proportion of the population?

The director-designate of the Child Poverty Action Group is
recently reported as saying, 'It 's going to be particularly hard on
the unemployed to have a government which thinks they are
already too well off and even workshy' (*Community Care*, 19
May 1979, 2). The review of supplementary benefits currently
being considered (DHSS 1978a) at once recognizes that an
increasing proportion of the population is going to be needing
and claiming assistance; it also begins a process of amending the
regulations which will undoubtedly create greater hardship for
those least able to bear further difficulties. Working within the
trade union movement is of growing importance, not only to
protect the interests of social workers themselves, but equally, if
not more importantly, to inform the movement of the great
hardship and suffering being experienced by those who find
themselves the victims of a harsh and exploitative system. Social
work has an accumulation of experience and information that is
of critical importance to the labour movement. Social workers
must make connections with the trade union and labour movements as a whole, and it must inform those movements of the
harsh consequences of capitalism. No group of workers know
better than social workers of the appalling consequences of an
economic system that, as it faces crises of its own construction,
creates more and more hardship for more and more people, and
simultaneously is forced to cut the very welfare resources that

make at least some contribution to an amelioration of that hardship.

In recent years the changes that have taken place, and are continuing, serve to focus the attention of all social workers on the dilemmas they face. The reorganization of social services into large departments within the structure of local authorities continually threatens to bureaucratize and depersonalize a personal service. Massive cuts in welfare resources in education, in the health and hospital services and in housing, coupled with the failure by many authorities to fill vacant posts in attempts to economize, has resulted in social workers carrying heavier and heavier loads with insufficient time to concentrate on many important problems which demand time above all else. The structure of social work as an occupation and a career has resulted in social workers leaving 'the field' and moving into an administrative machine. This is regarded by many as an unsatisfactory career process. To be committed to the social work task and to obtain rewards means ceasing to practise social work. The rights and wrongs of these changes and experiences are less significant than the resulting unrest among social workers, be they radical or not. The long industrial dispute at the end of 1978 and continuing well into 1979 was an expression of frustration with social work, with inadequate resources, with the structure of social services and with the operation of the union to which most social workers belong. The strike action united and divided social workers. It raised important questions about the nature of the work and the plight of clients. The consequences of the action will be far-reaching, not only for clients but, very importantly, for the development of the profession itself.

Since the implementation of the Seebohm Report at the beginning of this decade, the social services have grown extraordinarily fast. The drive to train, educate and prepare people for the social work task has been associated with the investment of considerable sums of money. To social workers, who experience ever mounting caseloads and seemingly intractable problems, such an observation may seem a denial of their experience. Yet this money will certainly be referred to again and again during the coming debate on the future of social work. The longest strike of the winter of 1978/79 passed with little attention by the media and hence the appearance of little effect on the lives of most of 'the people'. After all, the real effect was on those who are in danger of being cast into the bracket of the 'undeserving', and they are not in a position to influence either the media or public consciousness. The issue will be raised as to whether social workers are really necessary.

Arguably, a radical practice of social work and an overt admission by social workers of the political processes in which they are inextricably involved is not, in our terms, merely desirable, but in their terms urgently necessary. If 'It's alright for you to talk' was the expression that possibly enabled social workers to avoid some difficult questions in the seventies, then 'Whose side are you on?' is the question that must re-emerge and be confronted in the eighties. The need to obtain some security from the trade union movement was never more important. Social workers committed to a radical stance must involve themselves in their union branches and work on behalf of their union in those places where they have access, in trades councils and in social services committees of the local authorities.

They should not, however, lose sight of their day-to-day work as social workers with clients. A radical social work can be practised with clients and considerable help can be given to people who, at that moment, arguably need it most. To practise radically is to present oneself with considerable difficulties. It is not enough to have 'in one's head' a theoretically-refined view of the class structure of our society and possibly, as a consequence, sympathy for and sensitivity towards clients and their problems. From different or indeed incompatible world views, similar sentiments may be expressed.

The difficult questions are concerned with practice as socialists. These we suggest are the critical issues. What if anything are the *distinctive* modes of social work practice from a marxist and a socialist perspective? The task for those engaged in the issues from a position of sympathy is to raise and hopefully to answer such questions.

Social workers, like the rest of us, are entering a period where profound changes in the occupation structure of our society are likely to occur, coupled with cultural and political change. Problems and severe hardships will persist and intensify. New problems will confront us. We haven't yet learned how to deal with existing ones. We have to translate our theories of society into a practice that at once helps and assists the victims of our system, and simultaneously, contributes to the creation of conditions which will transform that society into a socialist democracy. The idea that our task is not to understand the world but to change it is crucial to social work practice and, at the same time, a central dilemma for that practice.

Since we have introduced the issues concerning radical social work and, with others, helped to legitimize and popularize the term, a considerable debate has grown up within social work concerning the political function of welfare, and the practice of radical social work. These range from the cautious liberalism of Halmos (1978) to the openly marxist practice of Corrigan and Leonard (1978). Social workers have become aware of their historical role in the political economy, and in the politically important issues involving the debate and struggle between conservative and social democratic political traditions (Pritchard and Taylor 1978). There has been a response both in the practice and teaching of social work. Statham (1978) suggests that radical social work needs to draw upon already existing radical alternatives in society, and suggests the practising social worker needs to be involved in these. The importance of feminism has been emphasized, and the relation social work has to domestic labour and the social relations of reproduction (Wilson 1977, Mayo 1977). The increasing influence of urban management on the everyday and family life of the community has been indicated as an increase in the powers of the local state (Cockburn 1977). The debate has been raised in the professional journals. The importance of social workers developing a power base through the use of their trade unions to influence departmental management concerning client's needs (Davey 1977) has been suggested. The relation of the social worker to the prevalent ideologies in the social relations of production (Wardman 1977) and the need for social workers to join 'with all those who are exploited in an organized mass movement' (Simpkin 1979) have been raised, and the dangers of an abstracted radicalism which loses sight of the client definition of the situation has been warned against (Tasker and Wunnum 1977). These sorts of discussion were unheard of a decade ago, and the nature and practice of radical social work seems to have been taken seriously by social work students and basic grade workers. Despite the difficult contradictions facing social workers in a capitalist economy with a welfare system, and despite the serious public spending cuts as a result of the crisis in capitalism, the defensive cynicism of the profession has been absent and there has been an optimistic and comradely support. It is within this context that this volume attempts to look at models of practise in a radical paradigm, or the experience of social workers trying to practise in this framework.

Welfare state workers in particular are only too aware of the present crisis in capitalism (DHSS 1978b). The apparatus of the State approaches welfare in a very different way from that adopted in a period of economic growth and full employment. Historically, during the pre-war period the demand for money wages was held down by a period of mass unemployment, but the post-war period of full employment meant a shift in power which gave the trade unions a lever to gain money wage increases which were greater than productivity increases.

The tradition of monopoly conditions in the market protected profit margins for the employers. The 'affluent' 1950s were a period when investment in industry was low and when output was low; this resulted in a serious decline in profit, which led to a struggle for the existing resources between capital and labour. The multinationals evolved as a dominant force, able to switch investment and plant from sector to sector, and even to another country if faced with militant trade union resistance. During the post-war period there arose increasing State intervention in production, nationalizing heavy industries (coal, power, steel, and the railways), and taking an increased share in maintaining and developing services which became part of the 'social wage' — health, education and social services (as well as attempts to control consumption and demand in the economy). The development of the welfare state was, Saville argues (Fitzgerald *et al.* 1977) a combination of working-class struggle and the requirements of industrial capitalism for a more efficient environment in which to operate. There was a distinct need for a highly productive labour force, and a recognition that welfare was the price to be paid for political security. The welfare state was trying to operate in an economy which had too high profits extracted in private industry combined with too little investment, leading to the crisis in profitability in the 1970s. One result, which has serious consequences for social work, is increased unemployment and the cutting of public expenditure. This has affected future development and the existing resources of the public sector. We have seen the lack of nurseries, the failure to improve housing stock, and the closure of hospitals, with the multiply-deprived inner-city working-class community particularly affected. Areas such as London's Dockland show the example of a traditional industry developed during the imperial economy of the last century, benefiting from little reinvestment, then being phased out when unprofitable. The once thriving shipping and docking industries were replaced by warehousing, requiring only a small labour force, with the loss of thousands of permanent jobs. The skilled workers left the area to the unskilled, the very young and the elderly. Such areas were promised redevelopment 'in the near future' and so were left to become run down. Now because of public expenditure cuts, housing and schools have not been built, health and personal social services have been overstretched and such districts have shown a high incidence of disease, poverty and delinquency, all made worse by chronic unemployment. To save money, there has been an appeal to community care, which has meant that sections of the elderly, the handicapped and the mentally ill have been dependent on the 'reserve army' of voluntary female labour, appealed to under an ideological concept of their nurturing nature. Such neighbourhoods have been the traditional homes of immigrants for decades, and one consequence of the crisis has been an ugly increase in racism.

The welfare state faces contradictions arising from its need to reproduce not only the forces of production — the accumulation of capital, increased profit, stock, plant and the actual labour force — but also the relations of production. The welfare state's influence on the former was initiated by the pre-war introduction of national insurance schemes and the building of council houses, and was extended by the post-war national health and State education schemes. These services were gained by working-class organised militancy, but at a pace largely set by the bourgeoisie. The State is provided with a healthy, efficient and competent workforce in a quiet political atmosphere, and the workforce has gained genuine material benefits and democratic rights by collective action. Cockburn (1977) has interestingly argued that the reproduction of the relations of production is also a potential arena for struggle. The State has developed specific local forms of power through the local State — the increased city managerial teams and their elected officers. The influence of these on everyday life and socialization into labour is far reaching. Not only has welfare definite progressive elements, it also possesses repressive features, as for example, the use of the benefits system to induce labour discipline, or the cohabitation rule to police the morality of single mothers. Cockburn suggests that this extends to the covert requests to teachers and social workers to regulate behaviour. It is important to note first that social workers and teachers come from different organizations and traditions than those of social security officers, and secondly that the role of the former is conceptualized more readily as being on the pupils' or clients' side than on that of local government officers. Finally, the teaching and social work professions have radical elements in their history, and operate in a completely different organizational tradition with different organizational goals. Nevertheless, if this tradition had been absent, one could see the teaching and social work professions being used more overtly as agents of social control. The city is, for Cockburn, a form of organization ideally suited to the collective reproduction of the labour force in partnership with the family. The difficult task of managing scarce city resources and of making unpopular increases in local rates and taxes palatable led to corporate management encouraging community organization and community development. The community was encouraged to participate in local affairs, but on the terms of the urban managers. Where the community workers in a locality have become involved in conflict with urban management the conflict has often been moderated and handled by a style of management that has the added bonus of displaying and reinforcing apparent democratic control. Community action is a spur into modernity for local authorities, which can be used to manage unrest in urban areas. This unrest is not always containable, as can be seen from the Community Development Projects documents (funded by the Home Office nationally and the local authority), whose analysis of the inner city set it not in a bourgeois pluralism but firmly in class struggle. Cockburn suggests that there are three areas of possible action concerning the reproduction of the relations of production. These are the local State workforce, the clients of the various social services, and the area of privatized reproduction or family life. The struggle in the industrial workplace is paralleled in the struggle for conditions in housing estates, schools, streets and for better conditions for the impoverished family. This concept extends the terrain of the class struggle from the workplace to the home, and necessarily involves the public services and their workers. To organize only in the workplace leaves out half of the actual experience of exploitation. The extension of this struggle opens up an arena of great importance to social workers, and involves the conditions of the wageless, the sick, the old and the unemployed. Following on Davey's (1977) suggestion of developing a power base through strong unionization, social workers can involve themselves as welfare state workers in the local political economy. They can provide information about resource allocation and defend community needs. This may bring them into conflict with their own management, with senior bureaucrats and elected officers, but they may drive an important wedge between groups which are too often politically indistinct from each other in their conservatism in the corporate management structure of the city. During scarcity and decline, the demand for managerial efficiency and control will increase, and what needs to be resisted is the replacement by technocratic efficiency of the humanistic morality essential in social work.

The crisis and possible decline of the political economy in which social work operates presents the profession with its own contradictions. There is a very real possibility that social work's traditional role of mediation between the rich and powerful and the poor and deviant may become replaced by an insistence on its social control function. The resistance to this can only come collectively from the profession itself. There may well be a crisis in the ideology of social work which needs to take note of attempts to manipulate social work to assist the state rather than its citizens. The extension of the state's participation in society means that the opportunity of social control through ideology has increased and that ideology needs to be given more emphasis in analysis. Marx in a famous passage reminds us (1939, 39),

> ... the ideas of the ruling class in every epoch are the ruling ideas .... the class which is the ruling force in society is at the

same time its ruling intellectual force. The class which has the means of material production at its disposal has control at the same time over the means of mental production, so that thereby, generally speaking the ideas of those who lack the means of mental production are subject to it ....

Gramsci in particular developed this concept to suggest hegemony, wherein ruling classes in society control the legitimation of the social structure, not by the coercive means of force (which remains in the background) but by ideology, and the acceptance (but not necessarily the approval) of ruling class ideas, not the least being that the ruling class rules. One element of bourgeois hegemony is, as Corrigan and Leonard suggest, that social workers should not even conceive of their work as being related to working class struggle. At this moment in history the appeal to a 'common interest' is the strongest since the second world war, as the national press 'union bashing' reveals. Social work has an important role to play not only as a key sector within the welfare state, but also as an important counter argument to welfare state ideology. In this way it can radicalize concepts of social change in the welfare state system.

One difficulty that arises for social workers who wish to develop a radical form of practice is that they need to develop their political and social analysis of the role of their profession and its historical development. Having understood that the problems which their clients experience are fundamentally related to the political economy, and faced with difficulties like structured unemployment, what can they do for individuals to relieve their exploitation and pain? The rest of this article will attempt to deal with this.

Implications for the practice of a radical social work

Because of the nature of social work practice and the tradition of its training, social workers constantly appeal to the pragmatic practice of their day-to-day case load, asking for a recipe to help them deal with it. It is not possible to give a recipe for individual cases, but what is important is not so much the techniques used, but the analytical framework in which they are practised. There is a place for social work techniques traditionally used, such as casework, group work or community work, but these need to be used by a social worker who has analysed his/her relation to the State and has developed some form of political understanding of his/her role. The place to do this is during training, and the use of political and moral philosophy, social policy, sociology, economics and psychology is of primary importance in this. (At present the social work postgraduate courses in Warwick University in Britain and Carleton University, Ottawa, Canada, see Moreau, M. 1979 (and presumably in other places) are making serious attempts to evolve this basis for radical social work practice.) The practice of social work needs to be divided into two forms of activism — collective action and individual practice

1　Collective action

It is important to avoid the individualism evolved from the heritage of social work training. Basically, and ideally, the notion of a collective de-hierarchized practice of teams, and of teams and consumers, is important. This is not to say that the one-to-one situation is to be abandoned, but that the notion of the individualism of social work practice and decision-making needs to be resolved by more collective action. It is extremely difficult to work radically without involving the team, and other welfare state workers. Ideally collective work involves the consumers in policy decisions. The commonsense view is that most social work consumers are too damaged or 'inadequate' to be involved. One method of practice is to organize the team so that a few regular meetings are arranged to discuss policy (and also frank inter-personal team dynamics), and that — separately at first — meetings are held with client groups and teams to assess what the former feel their needs are individually and in the community. The community has got considerable resources, as any community worker or voluntary worker finds out. There is no reason why consumers and workers should not work towards the breaking down of the professional hierarchy as community projects do.

The second area of collective action is that of welfare state trade union politics. The social worker not only needs to build up trade union consciousness within his/her own section, but also needs to develop links with other welfare state trade unions. This trade union base can be used to develop an informed opinion concerning the needs that welfare services consumers feel they need. This means that this base can be used to improve the position of basic grade workers in the corporate management of local authority services. Following on from this, representation can be forcefully made about public expenditure cuts, and strong resistance encouraged. The trade union can be used to improve conditions both for the worker and for the consumer.

The third area is involvement in community issues, particularly community politics. It is certainly important, as Statham (1978) suggests, to develop involvement in radical alternatives which are occurring *outside* social work practice, as they will have relevance for that practice. They offer alternative views of reality, and emotional and ideological support. An obvious example is in the area of sexual politics, either in feminism or gay liberation. There are other groups involved in class politics, fighting racism, or sexual politics. Feminism is important because of its useful insights into the political importance of women in servicing the economy. Cockburn quotes the council's use of the family (i.e. women) to keep their children from getting into care and being a burden on the rates, of defining squatters only as a family, and as such qualifying for rehousing if they begot children, as well as labelling families who were administrative problems to the council as 'problem families'. Wilson also suggests that the welfare state can be seen as the state organization of domestic life, with the woman acting as unpaid domestic labourer to service the wage labourer, and the wage labourer being motivated by his dependants' relation to him to work regularly and hard. Statham has suggested that there is, for example, an alternative to the traditional family which can be used to explore the alternatives to ideological concepts of the family. Involvement in these alternatives means that their example can be used in influencing the practice and theory of social work. Again the development of groups such as the Gay Social Workers Group or the Gay Probation Officers Group has had important effects on the consciousness of gay people at work and on alternative concepts of sexual orientation which challenge heterosexual hegemony.

The fourth area of collective action is involved in the decentralizing and democratizing of team work. It is important to develop a mode of operation which counteracts hierarchical structures in the team. One important element is to set aside weekly an allotted time to discuss what the goals of the team are, and to what extent these have been prevented by intra-group dynamics and by organizational problems. This is essential if the team is to be developed in any collective sense. It also saves time in the end, because it can be used to delegate work, and to prevent the endless meetings that often bedevil social work. The actual work of the team needs to be community-based as far as possible, and obviously this raises problems for a team with statutory duties. This latter point is an important area for collective decisions. In attempting to gain a community-based social work, the social worker needs to know the area, rather in the way of the old 'patch system'. This a system of dividing up an area into neighbourhoods with a group of workers attached to this patch. The group work from a local sub-office in the neighbourhood, and one important element is the use of sub-office premises for community purposes. The benefits of this localization, Thomas and Shaftoe (1974) suggest, are that the worker gains an intimate knowledge of community resources and sees the multi-faceted view of the consumer group in the neighbourhood, and that this acts against a pathological or inadequate view of consumer groups. The worker is able to develop a more informal relation with the client, which has the advantage of breaking down the impersonal bureaucratic face of social service departments, and also provides the worker with more information about community needs. This is important in developing the role of the social worker in an educational role concerning resources and benefits. It also assists the worker to build up contacts between isolated cases sharing the same problems and exploring with them what they require as a solution. It is important for the worker to develop networks and contacts, using such diverse resources as sympathetic voluntary workers, clergy, trade union organizations and the local trades council. The sub-office can become a meeting place, community centre and resource centre offering advice, information and legal aid.

One advantage is that the team can be involved in broader community issues through contacts. For example, several youth workers have formed a group of workers with youth against fascism aimed at combating racism and the National Front's attempt to recruit young people. A similar group has been formed by feminists against sexism in youth work. These have links with broader based political movements involving the Jewish Board of Deputies, the British Council of Churches, the Anti Nazi League, trade unions and the trades councils. Other issues can be organized around homelessness, fuel for the elderly and similar campaigns.

An important area of collective work is welfare rights and advocacy, although this should not be seen as the only area of work for radicals. It is important that consumers understand their position, and this means assisting them to get all the benefits they are entitled to, and helping them agitate in the community for more. Schragg (1977) suggests that hiding the availability of benefits is one of the most important mechanisms that the State has to reduce demands made on it, and that fighting for these benefits is an aspect of political struggle for social work. The social worker should not be manipulated as a buffer between the client and the bureaucracy which has the power to grant benefits, but should use this situation as a political lever against the State. Schragg suggests that one strategy is to document the social cost of concrete resources, and provide evidence to the State that it might for example be wiser to invest in perhaps nursery resources which will release people for work at a reasonable level of wages. In Britain the A code (a Department of Health and Social Security guidelines code containing details of the rights of supplementary benefits claimants and the strategies open to officials) is carefully kept secret from anyone except supplementary benefits officers. The present political climate is obviously aimed at labour discipline, and is characterized by attempts to drive people to work at menial tasks, the wage for which compares unfavourably with welfare benefits. The prevailing ideology means that these jobs are eulogized by those who do not have to perform that labour, and who extoll its dignity as preferable to living on welfare benefits. This reactionary backlash will have to be resisted as the crisis deepens and as the economy is geared to even more public sector cutbacks. Social workers need to resist this and to maintain this position — that welfare is paid for by the working class and as such remains a right for the poor.

2 Working with consumers in individual practice.

No matter how collective team work is, the social worker is always

faced with the one-to-one situation. Whilst it is essential to collectivize problems, it is worth noting that it is important not to use
individuals or groups of the most vulnerable sections of society in
confrontations against the state where they can be destroyed. This
practice is cruel and dangerous. A radical political perspective
and a radical concept of psychology need to be used as an
analytical base to build from, and not used to manipulate the
powerless in a confrontation in which they lose considerably, and
which leaves the social worker unscathed. Any confrontation
needs powerful allies in the community and in organized labour.
Any political campaign for change needs long and careful preparation, otherwise social work becomes a substitute for political
work. It is important to politicize social work, but this is different
from being involved in political activist movements. This is not to
suggest that social workers should not develop issue-based groups
as far as possible with the intention of developing self-help groups
and pressure groups. A radical, political framework such as
socialism can be used to sensitize the social worker to the actual
definition of the situation by the client, and also to sensitize the
client to problems due to contradictions in the system. This is
particularly true in the area where the client has lapsed into self-
blame, as with racism or unemployment or depression in women.
In work with families, for example, it is necessary to understand
how the reproduction of social relations of capitalism involve
family members in everyday oppression. Corrigan and Leonard
make a pragmatic attempt to deal with family dynamics within
this framework to gain an insight into all the members of a family,
and this makes a valuable starting-point for social workers and
social work students. This means that traditional techniques such
as casework, group work and family work, and such traditional
humanistic concepts as the autonomy of the client, are given a
new meaning and a new dimension when affiliated to a radical
socialist perspective. It is important to retain the client's perspective, including how the client sees the worker, and one
important lesson is, to see their relation to the wider social
structure, and not to romanticize them, which helps neither client
nor the worker. It is important to make a distinction between
radical work and the radicalization of consumers. The consumers
of social services are not the vanguard of the revolution, and they
mostly hold a mixture of reactionary and progressive views. They

are the least likely group to be involved in progressive action, but at the same time they must not be written off. They often have a very realistic appraisal of their situation and what they feel the social services should provide. Radical social work is not an evangelical campaign, and many people who seek help are at a moment in their lives when they are too brutalized or desperate to be reached. The danger is that this may provoke a cynicism in the worker, which has its basis in despair over the difficulty of the situation, and eventually a contempt for the consumer. It is essential that this is resisted, which is why involvement in an alternative movement in the wider society is important. It is essential to work through people's feelings of depression, aggression or despair with the aims of helping them at both an individual and a collective level. This means starting with their definition of the situation and their values, and then trying to extend these into a wider understanding of self and of society. It means trying to understand and work through the roots of depression or hostility, and using this to prepare the person to become whole enough so that they can engage in struggle against their situation individually and then, perhaps, collectively. Society has developed a competitive ethos for scarce resources which accepts that there must by definition be casualties. Consequently failure is personalized by the most dispossessed and powerless groups. Consumers need to be helped to understand their position, and their feelings, and given insight into their motivation. Care must be taken that this does not become a form of social control, or used as a substitute to meeting material deprivation.

Radical social work needs to develop an organizational context which provides a space to collectivize practice as far as possible. For this reason we suggest that the libertarian socialist tradition may have much to offer for a basic democratic structure. Within this space there must be room for work with individuals which is based on a radical theory of being, involving a socialist analysis both of the political economy and of human nature. Social workers are caught up in a contradictory role, as implementers of state aid which they are powerless to change as individuals, and a mediators against the extreme forms of injustice of this aid. Social workers need to use their training courses to develop analysis and to work out strategies which will genuinely enable them to be activists on their consumers side. Schragg has commented on the necessity to bring together clients with common needs and problems to engage in collective action on their own behalf. An important step too is to break down the isolated individualism of the problem to collectivize it, to draw on resources among the consumers, and to initiate a campaign to resolve that problem. The basis of this problem is a political analysis, preferably developed in training and continued during practice, which can assess the consequences of different forms of action and practice. The solution lies not in a recipe book for individual problems, but in developing through practice ways of working which will give support to social change and which will genuinely affect the lives of consumers.

2

Feminism and social work
Elizabeth Wilson

One important aspect of the development of the women's liberation movement has been its development of a *theory* of women's oppression. Feminists active in social work and related fields such as law have contributed to this theory, especially in their analysis of women's relationship to the State. They have argued that the way in which women are defined by the State as being (1) mothers, (2) dependent on a man, and (3) within the privacy of the family, is not only of central importance to women, but also of central importance in understanding the bourgeois State generally. There is a further dimension to the situation of women in relation to the State in that many State employees at many levels are also women. Amongst these are many social workers.

Feminists, marxists and analyses of the State in industrial capitalism

It is generally agreed that with the rise of industrial capitalism came increasing State intervention in the economy and in the sphere of private life, as the State began, however reluctantly, to take over tasks previously carried out by the family, such as education, and as industrial society brought about a greater differentiation of roles both within the family and in the workforce. Marxists, from Marx himself and Engels onwards, have been interested in the relationship of capitalist society to the family, and Engels believed (Marx and Engels 1970) that industrial society would entirely erode the family as it was in the nineteenth century; instead of that we find today increasing State concern with and intervention in the family, and recent feminist and marxist analyses have sought to understand whether these interventions are attempts to shore up, undermine, or extend the family. Is the development of State intervention a case of the left hand not knowing what the right hand is doing? Is it part of a master plan? Or is it perhaps the expression of a contradictory tension?

Right-wing critics have tended to see State intervention in family life as the advance of socialist totalitarianism. The mainstream of sociology has for the most part interpreted it from within a functionalist perspective — the State responds to the 'needs' of society, the family fulfils certain basic 'needs', and so on (an approach that cannot explain why and how 'needs' are defined, and by whom) — while on the left and amongst 'radicals' generally there has been much debate and disagreement as to the meaning of State intervention and the nature of the family.

Feminists are therefore primarily interested in the State in its welfare and social policy aspects, and feminist theories of these aspects have developed alongside a more general debate in recent years amongst marxists as to the nature of the bourgeois State. The State plays today such an important role in controlling the economy, the environment and local community, and the family, that it becomes of urgent importance to understand it. Anyone interested in changing or modifying society, even in fairly modest ways, is bound to come up against the State, and its political importance is therefore obvious. Feminist struggles have especially had to concentrate on the State since, apart from equal pay, they have been struggles not engaged at the point of production, but around facilities in the community or as part of state-provided health, education and other social services.

Some marxists, and along with them some feminists (Cockburn 1977), have tended to see the capitalist State in very conspiratorial terms. For them the political struggle is *against* the State, to smash it, and all aspects of the State are seen as more or less coercive. On the other hand is an approach owing much to the Italian communist, Antonio Gramsci (Gramsci 1971), which emphasizes the importance of 'ideological hegemony', of the ways in which the State induces the consent of the oppressed. In its less thoughtful versions this view can lurch towards the idea that the state itself is neutral and that the main problem with it at present is its *control* by the bourgeoisie (Woddis 1976). In its more creative versions, however, this approach more fully takes account of the complex nature of State provision, of its ambiguity. It also stresses the importance of class struggle in changing and modifying State provision of all kinds. Paul Corrigan, for instance, in an interesting article on the welfare state (1977), has emphasized this aspect.

Corrigan's article, however, also revealed the limitations of this view. He started from a criticism of the French marxist philosopher, Louis Althusser, as a source of some of the more conspiratorial approaches to the problem of the State. He suggested that Althusser, especially in his well-known essay on Ideological State Apparatuses (1971), had fallen into a 'left functionalist' position; that is, for Althusser the development of State intervention was somehow 'necessary' to capitalism — a position similar to that of sociological functionalists, except that where they interpret society's 'response' to shortcomings in the system as benign, the 'left functionalists' interpret it as malignant, as an attempt to buy off unrest, or patch up bits of the system to make it work better for them.

Corrigan suggested that it would be more accurate to acknowledge the role played by working people in their struggle to shape health, housing and education provision, for example, to their needs. It is significant, however, that he failed even to mention the part — a crucial one — played by women both as recipients and as meditators of State welfare provision; and he rather strangely failed to discuss the whole ideology of welfare intervention which has borne harshly on women. The place and role of women as defined by the welfare state in fact raises difficult questions about class struggle, and its limitations, in this area.

The Althusser essay has been influential, often subliminally, amongst feminists, and it is true that feminists have tended to see their opression as a form of conspiracy. (The most recent *name* for this conspiracy is 'patriarchy', when this word is misused to mean a timeless, universal and transhistorical oppression of all women by all men (Edholm *et al*. 1977)) Yet this is not surprising, since the ideology of women's opression is so widely accepted, and seems so natural, that it is often experienced subjectively as a conspiracy. The Althusserian approach was also popular amongst feminists because Althusser named the family as an ideological institution, whereas more marxists had traditionally seen the family as non-problematic, and had accepted the bourgeois view of it as a sphere of 'natural' relationships outside the boundaries of capitalism.

At certain periods class struggle has represented what might be interpreted as a loss rather than a gain for women. So far as the social security system is concerned, the Beveridge Report envisaged a rigidly traditional role for the wife and mother — and it did represent a concession to the unions, a gain in the class struggle. Similarly the Factory Acts: the working class fought for these acts in what may be seen as a struggle for family life and to get women and children out of the workforce and back into the home, and while this was progressive at some levels, it did also tend to confine women more rigidly within the home. In a recent article, Jane Humphries (1977) has restated the view that those nineteenth-century struggles represented an advance for the 'working-class family' without appearing to recognize that the interests of the separate members of the family may at times be in conflict. She made the good point that the family as a private area represents the desire of people to have some area of their lives that is not dominated by market values and profit motive; yet this does not address the problem of State interference in family life. It also ignores the fact, noted by many empirical sociological studies of industrial family life (Dennis *et al.* 1956), that a master-employee relationship crept into marriage, and that for many years the working class man referred to the housekeeping allowance as 'wages for the missus' — wages that were, moreover, a source of conflict between man and wife.

At certain times, women have participated in a class struggle for necessary social services. For instance, in her oral evidence to the Royal Commission on Population (1949), one of the representatives of the Standing Joint Committee of Working Women's Organizations said:

> I think the development of the social services in this country has come largely from the prodding and pressure of women, who have a very high sense of responsibility, and our own

Committee has played a very great part in the development of these services, because...when this Committee was formed in 1916 one of its first campaigns was for the passing of the Maternity and Child Welfare Act, which was passed in 1918. One of the big campaigns that we carried out in the early twenties was for the nursery school, and that came from women who took a very high view of their responsibilities as mothers of families and as housewives in the home.

But on the other hand it was women alone (Abbott and Bompass 1943) who spoke out against the Beveridge Report with its backward-looking definitions of the dependent wife.

An explanation, then, solely in terms of the importance of class struggle does not actually deal with women's special oppression. In two recent articles (1978, 1979), Mary McIntosh has gone beyond the conspiracy theory/class struggle dichotomy by looking at the whole problem of 'needs'. She argues that in capitalist society the wage system does not and *cannot* meet the various needs of individuals. One group of persons — the bread-winners — earns a wage which then has to be redistributed amongst the rest of the population (the majority) who are not wage-earners — children, non-working wives, the old, sick and unemployed. In some areas the State has stepped in to facilitate the redistribution, but within the nuclear family especially State intervention other than in the form of family allowances is still regarded as impermissible.

The analysis of the family has been an important part of the contribution of feminists to theories of ideology and theories of women's oppression. This specific contribution started from the idea that 'the personal is political'. Far from being 'natural' and unproblematic, family relationships create and sustain the dependency and inferiority of women. Not only is their domestic and child-rearing work in the home belittled and ignored, but it is also a handicap when they take paid work outside the home. Some earlier feminists — and one or two feminists are beginning to fall back into this position today — simply argued that the status of women's work in the home should be raised and that child care should be regarded as the important job that it is. This is not enough however, for as long as men are excluded from full participation in child care, and as long as older children and men expect to have a wife/mother/servant taking responsibility for cleaning up after them instead of taking responsibility for their own mess, patterns of servitude will be sustained. Within the privacy of the family the 'head of the household', normally the man, acts effectively as the agent of the State in enforcing certain kinds of behaviour on his wife and children (Dahl and Snare 1978). Most individuals don't, of course, experience family life in this way, and much of the hostility towards the women's movement has come about because this kind of statement has been seen as a generalized attack on family life and loving relationships. The situation can be illustrated by looking at divorce. So long as a couple is happily married both partners tend to look on it as a personal, intimate and unique relationship; only if it breaks down and they seek divorce do they fully realize the extent to which marriage is a public affair, defined by the law and involving certain sorts of behaviour, and with inbuilt inequalities.

The feminist analysis has stressed the *ambiguity* of the family, and in so far as stress has been laid on the negative aspects of the family as an institution, this has been in part a reaction against the ideological stress on family life characteristic of the 1950s; in part because the family as at present constituted operates against the achievement by women of independence and fully adult status. Feminists have also sought to understand why capitalism saw an elaboration of family life rather than its withering away. It is argued that domestic work performs an important role in the reproduction of capital (in the contribution of unwaged domestic labour performed by women) and that the family as consumer is an important feature of the economy which would be threatened by (for instance) socialized laundries or canteens. Secondly, the family is the place where personality is created and structured. Children could be brought up in different ways without psychic damage, but the very intense and limited relationships of the modern nuclear family create particular kinds of personality with tremendous needs for dependency and gratification, perhaps well suited to modern capitalist society with its constant production of titillating material goods and its stress on relationships, especially sexual relationships, as a 'free area' of pleasure and satisfaction to offset the aridity of 'work'. This is in fact a third area in which the family plays an important role, and the wife, particularly, plays an important part in 'tension management' — in making the life of the male worker more tolerable. For him, and for children, the home and family may be seen as a source of satisfactions to offset the difficulties and cruelties of life outside, as a refuge from capitalism; a locus of personal warmth and of emotionally satisfying relationships; the place where sexual relationships happen (but where they are also most stringently forbidden by the incest taboo); and where children are loved and cared for. Finally, the 'responsibilities' of his family drive the male wage earner to work, so that the family acts as a powerful work incentive in our society.

Feminists have laid stress on the overwhelmingly ideological role played by the State in its interventions in the family. Social work and social security are especially important here, which is why social workers should not ignore what the women's movement has to say about the family. Although there are some signs of change, social work has traditionally sought to reinforce the most conformist types of family pattern. In attempts to prevent juvenile delinquency and family breakdown the solution has usually been seen in a return to more traditional patterns of family life — a more 'mothering' mother, a more authoritative father, when perhaps the adoption of more flexible relationships would have been more rewarding. Just as the cohabitation rule is *more* oppressive than marriage and brings out very crudely the State assumption that there is a necessary connection between a sexual relationship between a man and a woman and an economic relationship (which puts it not too far from prostitution), so the ideology of social work has emphasized traditional attitudes more strictly than the surrounding society, perhaps because social work deals mostly with fringe groups (although at one time or another many individuals may experience mental illness, be unemployed or in a one-parent family). And despite the fact that it deals with marginal groups, social work clearly expresses a concern central to our society: the maintenance of family life in the face of disintegrating or atomizing influences that may naturally tend to undermine, loosen or at least change it.

The State and the family are then of interest both to feminists and to social workers. I have suggested that neither a theory of the State that regards it as coercive in all its operations, nor one which emphasizes class struggle fully explains the way the State operates, and that it would be more fruitful to look at what people 'need' materially. This is an oversimplification, but does *not* imply a biologistic or absolute 'subsistence' concept of 'need'. Needs are always socially determined. We should see the State as attempting to juggle between these 'needs' and the wage system that cannot fully satisfy them. Both feminists and 'radical' social workers (a vague term, I know) are critical of some of the ways in which the redistribution of the wage occurs, and are struggling against it, or to change it.

Social work — itself, by the way, an important aspect of the modern welfare state — can in no sense be seen as the outcome of class struggle. There has never been any demand by working people for welfare provisions to be administered in this way, and indeed there has been a traditional hostility in the working class to 'the Welfare' both in factory and community. This does not imply that individual social workers are powerless to stretch their role, and their support and practical help can be very important. As an *institution*, however, it has been created from above and not by the people.

I have dealt summarily with the feminist analysis of the reproduction of labour both in terms of domestic labour (Himmelweit and Mohun 1977) and of welfare intervention because these have been discussed at greater length elsewhere; and because I want to look in this article at some of the similarities between 'radical social work' and the women's movement, and the difficulties both have met in struggling to bring about change in the intimate sphere of personal relationships.

'White-collar groups' in our society: Women

The 'class struggle' approach to welfare provision is bound to be inadequate in adressing the problem of women since it regards women as either simply lost within the working class, or else oppressed by some entirely separate (and indeed nebulous) structure, the patriarchy. It therefore fails to confront the ambiguous position of the modern woman in relation to the class structure. Orthodox sociology has tended to define a woman's class position in terms of her husband's or father's — his or their class position determines hers, implying that she is the appendage of either or both. Sociology also defines the individual's class in terms of status, in terms of work and salary, rather than in terms of his relation to the means of production (i.e. whether he is a capital-owner or a wage-earner). Orthodox marxism defines the individual's class position only in terms of his or her relationship to the means of production, and has therefore tended to ignore the problem of women. Engels saw the solution of the 'woman question' as the mass entry of women into the labour force, since only this could end their anomalous status as privatized domestic slaves. Wally Secombe (1973) more or less restated this position in a contribution to the 'domestic labour' debate, seeing little place for women's struggles except at the workplace, and he tended to define women as a problem for the working class and working-class advance instead of seeing traditional definitions of working-class struggle as a hindrance to women. He spoke of the existence of family violence, yet his analysis could not account for and failed to predict the rise of the movement to help battered women, which occurred even as he was writing.

Since neither bourgeois sociology nor traditional marxism has adequately come to grips with the ambiguous, confusing and complex class position of women, some feminists (Comer 1977, Delphy 1977, Barreff and McIntosh 1979) have sought to resolve this difficulty by assigning all women to a single class — the class of women. This is a crude and unsatisfactory solution, for the only basis on which all women could be said to belong to a single group is on the basis of their biology. The argument uses a rather strange analogy with marxism; the marxist analysis is said to deal with production, while this analysis deals with reproduction. Women are united by their biological (not social) reproductive capacity. Yet the whole thrust of the women's movement has been to get away from the idea that 'anatomy is destiny' and that women's lives are to be determined by their biology. Reproduction is social rather than biological — this is what crucially distinguishes human beings with their language and cultural institutions from animals. We are living through a transitional period in which women are no longer defined solely by their reproductive capacity, but are not as yet fully integrated into the labour force. No final theoretical position is possible at this stage. The question of class is however relevant to the women's movement since it is often seen as 'middle-class', and to examine this criticism is to shed light on the position of social workers as well as women.

The women's movement is composed of individual women who

come from varying backgrounds but who have themselves mostly received further or higher education — students, teachers, legal workers, social workers — women, that is, in the 'ideological' sections of white-collar work. This is a relatively small and privileged group who, subjectively at least, experience their life as containing elements of choice and freedom. Most women in the movement have been fully exposed, through education, to the dominant culture in its more sophisticated aspects, with its cult of personal relationships and of the fulfilment of the individual 'personality'. The dominant themes of our culture are a sort of mirror image of the individualism engendered by competition and exploitation; they are the existential themes of angst and loneliness, but as a corollary of these, liberation and fulfilment by means of personal life-style and personal experiences, sometimes of a mystical kind, sometimes through therapies or forms of 'creative' self expression, sometimes through travel and adventure. Simone de Beauvoir (1953) pointed out 25 years ago something that is still true today, that women especially are expected to express their personalities by creating a life-style; rooms, houses, interiors, their own appearance, dinner parties, even children, are expected to express this personality of which lifestyle is but the extension.

Certain of these themes of bourgeois culture have been taken over into the women's movement so that at its core lies a contradiction — on the one hand the recognition that collective action is necessary, and a spontaneous socialism which understands that within a society dominated by the profit motive women's liberation cannot fully be achieved; on the other hand a bourgeois belief in the primacy — and the possibility — of personal and individual solutions. The valid slogan 'the personal is political' is then too often interpreted as meaning that the purpose of feminism is the immediate liberation of individuals. This in turn often leads to the belief that changes in lifestyle will in fact turn out to be the solution to the problems women face. Lesbianism may then become the solution to the oppression of male/female relationships, collective living the answer to the fragility of the unsupported nuclear family.

The drawback to such individual solutions is that they cannot of themselves bridge the gap between public and private. Thus, it is not enough to say, 'we must get out of the couple and abolish jealousy and possessiveness'. It is necessary both to recognize the support the couple gives many people, and also see that it is not the individual relationships that are wrong so much as the State definition of marriage as *the* personal relationship, a definition that affects all men and women, married or single, gay or straight, at the level of pay, housing and tax; and that the institution of marriage as we know it creates situations in which jealousy is bound to arise out of economic dependence, resentment, loneliness and so on.

Politics has nonetheless bridged the gap between public and private in some of the campaigns of the women's movement. The women's movement started from the important idea that 'the personal is political' and with the practice of consciousness-raising in small groups. Consciousness-raising is a political activity. Women talk about their experiences and thereby come to understand that their problems which seemed personal to them and part of their individual inadequacy or neurosis are actually a part of the way in which women are defined and oppressed. Group support and strength, gradually formed, leads to more outgoing political activities as well as continued mutual support. It is a way of creating solidarity and of learning to value oneself and others. Because the early consciousness-raising groups revealed that many women shared problems to do with child care, sexuality, violence, both campaigns and self-help groups gradually got under way. 'Self-help' can be defined as alternative forms whereby people organize collectively to help themselves over particular social problems (Gordou and Hunter 1977-8 : 23); rape crisis centres would be one example. These grass-roots organizations offer an alternative to the standard help offered by the welfare state — which has often signally failed to help women — and while not revolutionary, they reach towards democratic, non-hierarchical forms of organization.

One good example of the combination of individual and collective help with political campaigning is the women's aid movement in Britain, and this movement also illustrates two major inhibiting factors in the struggles both of feminists and of radical social workers — the fear of reformism, and the difficulty of combining individual help with wider political objectives. The fear of reformism — reformism being the belief that reforms taken through Parliament in constitutional fashion to become law will change society fundamentally and are sufficient in themselves — haunts feminists and some sections of the Left, and reformism comes to include forms of campaign as well as ultimate goals.

In the campaign to help battered women the danger of reformism has been perceived by feminists as coming from social workers who have involved themselves in the issue. Many have of course not involved themselves, seeing wife-battering as yet another form of neurotic relationship for which 'treatment' of both parties is the answer. Some who have entered the campaign have not accepted the wider feminist analysis of the institutionalization of violence and unequal male/female relationships within the family, and for this reason have sometimes seen refuges as simply temporary marriage-mending or marriage-broking agencies and have been less concerned to fight for long-term 'second-stage' housing, or to assist those women who wish to get council housing in twos or groups; nor have they seen the relevance of helping women towards self-reliance, or why it might be better to exclude men from participating in the running of refuges if their presence undermines women's independence and self-reliance. Still less are they drawn towards ideas about changing. the institution of marriage or making it easier for married women to work or get trained for decent jobs. Rather are they likely to advocate better preparation *for* marriage for school leavers, and to endorse contraception as a way of preventing women who are 'tóo young' or 'too inadequate' from having babies rather than as a means of promoting women's independence within more equal sexual relationships. To these, fertility control is indeed seen as an instrument of the control rather than the liberation of women, and as a way of preventing poor child care amongst the promiscuous young of social class V who are still so regrettably inclined to have large families.

I must emphasize that by no means all social workers active in women's aid hold these views — I am talking about a tendency, not about individuals. On the other hand, some feminists not involved in women's aid have been highly critical of the whole enterprise as being reformist, seemingly perceiving all attempts to help battered women as middle-class social working. This misses the vital point that the struggle around the issue of battering was initially to get the problem recognized as being a problem at all.

This was not reformist, but a victory against sexism and traditional definitions of women. Then the struggle to set up refuges and run them on non-hierarchical lines was a victory against State inertia and/or State coercion. Finally, battered women were not just done good to, but are themselves actively involved in the campaign. While these achievements may seem piecemeal and tactical, and while the goals for feminists can never be just a few changes in the law (although considerable struggle was involved in getting the by no means adequate 1976 Domestic Violence Act passed), these changes can be used as a further platform for a higher stage of the campaign. Also, and perhaps more importantly, any improvement brought about in the position of women by reforms that increases their sense of their rights, their dignity and their potential strengthens all women.

I have barely touched on the whole difficult question of reformism; and although I have tried to draw an optimistic picture of the possibilities of campaigning, I am aware that this leaves unresolved the problems of many individuals. This brings me to the second problem, of individual happiness. The general position of battered women may have improved, yet there are still many battered women who cannot get to a refuge, or who feel they 'deserved' to be beaten, or that even if they did not deserve it, some women *do* deserve it. Similarly, many women who have been raped or had abortions feel that they are the guilty ones, and turn inwards in depression. There are indeed many women who have thought of themselves as feminists, who have campaigned for women's liberation, and yet who have wanted nothing so much as to find a happier personal life, have secretly longed to experience a Great Love, have crawled back into the safety of marriage with relief. Everyone wants to be happy. Everyone wants to be safe.

'White-collar groups' in our society: Social workers

Social workers too are preoccupied with this problem of the relationship of individual change to political change. Their class position too is similar to that of many feminists and similarly uneasy. Relatively affluent white-collar workers who have quite often left a working-class background by way of education, yet not part of an academic elite, nor a profession, employed to 'help the powerless' yet employed by the State, they are torn like many women between radical ideas and a conviction of class injustice on the one hand, and personal, privatized solutions (Pearson 1973) on the other. Social workers are presented with the 'choice' (widely discussed in the literature and in social work education) between 'trying to effect social change' and 'helping the individual'. An assumption is commonly made that these two activities are mutually exclusive. This way of posing the individual against society is fundamental to bourgeois thought (de Beauvoir 1953); but, faced with the daily problems of the job, even 'radical' social workers seldom have time to question this sacred opposition. Yet it is not that help for the individual is inimical to social change (all political activists and movements have combined social aid for individuals with political campaigning); and social change cannot be brought about unless individuals feel that the politics will answer their individual needs (Jaggi *et al.* (1977) give a detailed account of this process in action). But the problem that faces social workers who are concerned with social change is the rather brutalized and atomized nature of the groups with whom they have for the most part to deal; groups whose rebellion against their conditions of life often comes out not as rebellion but as personal disaster in the sphere of private life. Social workers deal every day with freakout and failure, as has been said often enough (Cohen 1975). But social work has never thrown up an adequate strategy for dealing politically with these personal problems. Some have concentrated on trades union work; some have done what they could at the level of individual support or advocacy and welfare rights work; others have felt helpless faced by the enormity of the gap between their understanding of the structural change that is needed and their powerlessness to change life in the inner city or the isolated estate. Although, too, social workers may be well aware that ultimately the malfunctioning economy is responsible for their clients' problems, yet at the immediate level it is not clear that rehousing will help a depressed housewife (help, that is, in terms of curing her depression, although she has a right to adequate housing whatever her psychic condition); or that a better job will stop a man beating his wife; or that employment will seem more attractive to delinquent teenagers than a life of carefree petty crime. After a while behaviour takes on a momentum of its own. And what is required is perhaps not just a place a few rungs up the ladder of affluence, but some altogether different kind of life.

Radical social workers of today have not on the whole turned to the reformist solution, although social work has been historically associated with reform. While many support liberal abortion laws, while many hate the iniquities of social security, while many would like to see more nurseries, more playgrounds, more refuges, few become campaigning reformers because their training so sensitizes them to see all problems in individual terms that reformism comes to seem irrelevant or even 'collusion' (collusion, that is, with the client's attempt to locate his personality problems in the world outside his own head). They have been trained to appreciate, not collective solidarity, but individual differences and emotional nuances, and it is not surprising if, feeling hopeless about getting clients off social security or rehoused, they turn to the sphere of the personal and try to improve relationships.

To increase a client's sense of his own worth is valuable, yet to concentrate on relationships at the expense of giving any energy to changing the 'system' reinforces the split between public and private. I am arguing that the two are bound up together. A 'happy relationship' only exists in some social context from which it cannot be divorced. Also, defining their own work as being to do with relationships, many social workers see women's refuges and claimants' unions as merciful solutions to their own overload of cases and thus turn them by default into extensions of the social services. Thus, presumably without meaning to, social workers often find themselves party to the co-option of the alternatives, killing (even if with kindness) their radical potential.

Alternative therapies: Personal solution or radical gain?

Some social workers, in an effort to reconcile radicalism with individualism, are drawn towards radical therapies. And here is another point of convergence with the women's movement.

I have already spoken of consciousness raising as a political activity. Therapy is a form of consciousness raising *about oneself*. Alternative therapies based partly on Reichian and gestalt theories have flourished during the past ten years or so as part of the 'alternative scene' that our society has thrown up as an attempt to compensate for the aridity and loneliness of much of metropolitan existence. But encounter groups just as much as the straightest Freudian analyst perceive the solution to personal problems as being inside our heads, and easily perpetuate the false dichotomy of outside/inside.

Social workers have borrowed techniques from these therapies, techniques which sometimes seem to make communication more contorted if anything; and the two strands, of alternative therapy and of consciousness-raising leading to self help, have met in the practice of the women's movement, where feminist therapy has become quite popular and is sometimes posed as an alternative to consciousness raising. I have no space here adequately to discuss the issues raised by recent writings (Humpty Dumpty 1978, Red Therapy 1978) on this subject, but I will mention one quite personal reaction.

It may be that the question 'is radical therapy political?' is the wrong one; but one of the main questions raised for me by the concept of 'red therapy' or 'feminist therapy' is: to what extent are these relationships or should these relationships be distinguished from 'ordinary' relationships and from social support? Do they distinguish some individuals as 'emotionally disturbed' or as suffering from neurosis; or are all comers offered an emotionally enhancing experience with the question of 'symptoms' or malfunction being regarded as itself a bourgeois mystification? If the latter, why are friendships felt to be so unsustaining that this other more special thing is needed? Should we rather be devoting more effort and care to friendships?

This raises one further and important question for political groups, including the women's movement. Should not these be offering their activists the sort of support some claim to have found only in 'therapy'? It is a serious criticism of revolutionary parties that they do not in practice do this (Doris Lessing's *The Golden Notebook* (1962) has one of the best accounts of this failure). It is an even more serious criticism of the women's movement if it too is failing to give women support, since it is based on the ideal of collective solidarity and love, in the widest sense, among women.

The question of the relationship of therapy to politics is an unresolved one; but in the case of the women's movement, women have perhaps expected too much from it. The movement was expected not only to change women's lives but to be a way of life. Yet it could never solve all women's problems. It could only be and has only been a beginning. Perhaps women are only beginning to realize just how difficult and slow a business it will be to bring about social change. But the flight into therapy need not be a retreat if women bring the personal support and strength they find there back into the movement.

Conclusion

I have raised a number of issues briefly and superficially in an attempt to draw them together in a way that suggests connections between feminism and social work. I cannot offer detailed suggestions of ways in which feminist social workers can help their clients, nor can I hope to offer general solutions; but only end with the plea that activists continue to try to keep the political and the personal together.

Feminists and social workers have a common struggle over the whole nature of State welfare provision, particularly where the State defines women as the dependants of men, whether this be expressed in the cohabitation ruling, or child-care arrangements. Social workers do seem to be increasingly aware of the nature and extent of the problems faced by women. Feminists are demanding adult status for women and a life in which work and child care are not in such dire conflict. Social workers, in recognizing and supporting feminist demands, are perhaps at last acting in the spirit of that 'client self-determination' they were always claiming to espouse.

3

It's just a stage we're going through: the sexual politics of casework
John Hart

Although writers on radical social work have addressed themselves to the personal problems of people who are seen as socially and economically oppressed, there is a danger that such concerns will be assessed and dealt with as separate from structural criticism and action. Ragg (1977, 140) writes:

> There remain, however, lacunae in the theory of radical casework. They are, I think, filled in a personal approach. People may, through no fault of their own, find themselves in emotional distress, more or less acute, and want help. What radical casework has to offer to such people is incomplete,

Milligan (1975, 110) appeared to legitimize such a split between casework and political stance in the counselling of gay people:

> The purpose of political action is to defend and extend the freedom of homosexual people to enjoy their sexuality. On the other hand, the object of counselling must be to render individuals capable of living, loving and working in a hostile environment. Political struggle and counselling depend on each other.

It is important to note that this was quoted with approval by Wright (1977, 6) in his consultative document aimed at defining the content of CQSW (Certificate of Qualification in Social Work) courses in a climate which he saw as undesirable: 'it is not uncommon to hear people who might be expected to know better say "social work? — what is it" .... this has become a trendy negative stance and it is about time it stopped.' Wright's approval of Milligan's specific statement has to be seen *in the context of the omission of the last sentence* and his view (10) that 'Action to change social policy ... is political action and outside the daily responsibility of the social worker.'

The implication here is that political views are the private property of an individual social worker and have the status of a personal response to living in a society that is characterized in liberal writings as unjust, unhealthy, unequal, and unlikely to change within the author's life chances. Pearson (1973) writes:

> Social work as a career becomes for some a limited solution to the problem of mass society. But, unwilling or unable to extend the diagnosis of his ills and their prescribed remedy to his clients, and searching in his professional life for the differences between himself and clients rather than the shared features of their lives, the social worker's solution remains privatized.

However, the whole notion of radical social work implies a working towards certain ideological achievements, and hence there should be a valuing of contributions towards social change that *individual* workers and clients can make in the meantime. This process is what Cohen (1975, 92) described as 'the unfinished': either this is what workers are about in all their duties and tasks between the hours of nine to five, or else they are using their social influence to maintain the present equilibrium of social policy in society.

It would be wrong to see a division between personal distress and wider social concerns as being exclusive to radical social work. In the recent past there has emerged both in North America and Britain a complaint that theory taught in academic institutions was out of touch with the field. This criticism has been levelled at panaceas like psychodynamic casework theory which did not help the individual worker and client faced with all the pressures of the public welfare services. The fact that radical theory and action is now said not to account for 'emotional distress' is a complaint of a similar order. However, in terms of a practical working out of theory in practice, we have to face the fact that, whilst psychodynamic casework practice had an ambivalent reception from employers and clients, radical casework practice can be assumed to have a less enthusiastic reception, at least from central and local government agencies.

In terms of the possibilities of building on practical experience of radical intervention on a personal level, there has, since the creation of a social work career structure suitable for (especially male) graduates, been a long-drawn-out process of co-opting experienced caseworkers into probation or social service administration. The inexperience and organizational naivety, in relation to welfare agencies, of social work teachers in academic institutions has, alongside this co-opting, ensured that few role models are available for the new social work practitioner. In summary 'the unfinished' is likely to be under-achieved for some time to come. Meantime, the work in progress consists of:

(a) relating casework with individuals suffering psychosocial conflict to the social and economic structure within which they are oppressed;

(b) helping clients with their individual problems in a way which does not weaken their political awareness by a turning of the problem into an individual fault or deficit;

(c) helping social workers to see such individual work as part of structural change;

(d) helping social workers understand their own personal politics and the relationship of these to the clients' situations;

(d) recording such transactions in order that the possibilities of radical casework can be legitimized for clients, workers, teachers and employers.

This brief outline of the problem is to introduce a contribution to the theory of radical casework by means of a lengthy excerpt from an interview I recorded in 1977 as part of a study of social work and sexual conduct (Hart 1979). The transcript is a very personal account of the experience of Hazel who gave me her permission to use the material. She is now in her forties, having been a social worker for over twenty years. She was first a child care officer and is now a middle manager in a social service department.

She discusses her training; her casework relationship with two women clients; the way her course(s) prepared her for casework; her own 'personal problems'; her *evolution* from a 'personal problem' orientation to a political analysis of both her own and her clients' positions as women in this society.

As we shall see, one of the essential questions involved in radical casework is that of *distance* — between helper and helped, theory and practice, ideal and achievement. What may appear as biography is also public issue, for Hazel is gay and I want to dwell on this aspect at some length, developing a theme that social workers who are sexual outlaws or outcasts are day by day confronted with reminders of their own deviance and faced with the necessity of defining the distance they wish to maintain between themselves and other deviants who become the recipients of social work. During training courses gay social workers have found their integrity threatened by psychiatric or psychological teaching about the 'causation' of homosexuality. Within organizations the threat of dismissal is ever a possibility. The National Council for Civil Liberties Report of a Survey of Local Authority Social Services Committees (1977, 18) quoted a Director of Social Services who 'would not "be prepared to condone the employment of homosexual women and men in posts in this Department which carry a responsibility for the care of people and especially the care of children"'. In addition, as we have noted, writers such as Milligan (1975) have little to say operationally to gay social workers employed by the major social service organizations. This may be especially important if the worker's own analysis of his/her sexual orientation includes a political definition of their situation, and *coming out* and carrying on is seen as central to that person's professional work as well as their personal integrity. In the NCCL Report another Director of Social Services is helpful in giving his reasons (24, 25) why 'a caseworker who did not conceal her or his homosexuality would be subject to discipline or dismissal "not because it was homosexuality, but because it would be unprofessional practice"'.

The position of the lesbian social worker carries additional problems of self-definition, as Gagnon and Simon (1974, 177) observed: 'we generally neglect the degree to which the lesbian shares all the problems of a woman in the society prior to usual age of marriage, some of the problems of the single heterosexual female later in life, and some problems of the single person in a married society, whether that person be male or female, heterosexual or homosexual.' In addition, views such as those of Munro and McCulloch (1969, 157) still have echoes in social work education corridors: 'Most lesbians are content to keep their homosexual inclinations hidden from general view and it is only the most psychopathic among them who make a show of their abnormality.'

Openly gay social workers, therefore, do pose a threat — to theories of sexual pathology and corruption, of gender role and of family life, and perhaps most important, to the distance placed between helper and helped in social work's professional culture. The radical casework possibilities of the situation are theoretically intriguing. What of the *practice*, which in radical casework can only be evaluated in terms of the costs and benefits to the individual worker and customer, although the aim and consequence will be a contribution also to structural change? How will this worker, who has been both helper and helped, bridge the personal and the political?

Hazel talks about her training

I did two courses, one in child care in which it was known that I have had psychotherapy but when I was asked at interview why, I said I preferred not to say and this was accepted and I was accepted on the course, because the tutor was a very nice man who didn't like intruding. I then somehow felt dissatisfied with this over the next three or four years and felt I hadn't been able to integrate my own personal experience with my work experience. I then applied to join a mental health course feeling that this time I would tell them about my psychotherapy and being a lesbian. I was interviewed by a psychiatrist, a supervisor and by a tutor and said that I was a lesbian and the psychiatrist during the interview put me through a classical-type examination, in the nicest possible way; asked about family relationships, why I was a lesbian, what had the treatment achieved and why I thought I was a lesbian which still at that time was seen in terms of family dynamics. I was accepted on the course and the subject was never referred to after and I got really very steamed up about this, because I wanted it to be something that would get talked about and it wasn't. I felt I didn't know what they thought about it, though I did know they had accepted me on the course. I said to my tutor who hadn't been at the interview, did she know I was a lesbian and she just said,

"Oh yes, she had heard about it but so were a lot of people, so what." That was the end of the conversation. So again, in terms of personal integration that course wasn't very helpful either but at least I was very pleased with the fact that I'd mentioned it at the interview. In more general terms on neither course was sexuality talked about except as part of the sociology or psychiatric lectures but there was nothing more vital than that. I can't remember any discussion about how one talked with clients about sexuality, it just came in the general lectures so it was very little preparation.

'In the past, my idea was that being a lesbian was somehow a sort of psychological failure in me, I always felt that because I hadn't achieved sexual maturity, I wouldn't be able to help heterosexual couples to achieve sexual maturity and somehow I would block them off because I was blocked off. I think for many years when I was practising as a social worker, I wasn't having sexual relationships myself, I went through a period of psycho-therapy and my sexuality, sexual behaviour seemed to go into abeyance somehow for a number of years. What I felt always for clients was very strong, warm, protective feelings. I could use the word maternal but that's very traditionalist, but certainly very warm protective feelings. I also think that I empathized a great deal with my clients and that I directly related that to my own personal situation — that of a lesbian from thirteen onwards. I obviously suffered quite a lot as a result of that and thought it gave me quite a lot of identification with deprived and depressed groups. In a way the worst you could say about that was that it was a kind of projecting out of my own situation. But it had a positive side in that it seemed to work a lot of the time. It certainly gave me strong feelings of commitment to my clients. No doubt, it had weaknesses too, possible over-concern and over-protective-ness at times. So that in very general terms the fact that I was a lesbian seemed to have a strong connection with the fact that I was a social worker.'

Two clients

'One or two cases come to mind. I'm thinking particularly now of a case that threatened me very much as a gay person. It was a teenage girl who had been in care all her life pretty well. I think she was abandoned by her mother when she was quite young and she'd been through the usual situation, starting off in residential care and then went into a foster home where she spent quite a number of years and then things began to break down pretty much, she was fourteen or fifteen, and I took over the case shortly after the foster home situation had broken down and Pat was living in domestic service (this was over ten years ago) a living-in job in the Midlands. Though as a child she had been reasonably settled, she really began to break out increasingly in her teens and this job broke down after a while because she wasn't acting very responsibly and she wasn't very satisfactory. She then got herself another job in Scotland and I can remember going up to see the people who were going to employ her to satisfy myself that it was a reasonable place for her to go to. It was a very upper-class sort of set-up and I wasn't very happy about that. The man was a doctor and the house stood in its own grounds and was very beautiful, but Pat thought she wanted the job and so took it, and again, that didn't last long either and letters and phone calls came from her employers. She was unsatisfactory and she just wasn't doing the work she was meant to be doing and she began to go off for the evenings and things like that.

'Then eventually she came back to Bradford and met her mother again (at her own request and I organized it) whom Pat hadn't seen since she was a child and by this time was married and had two younger girls but Pat went to live with them for a time but became increasingly unsettled and over the next year or so Pat behaved in every conceivable way — she took drugs, drink, she took to normal sexual promiscuity and she really was extremely difficult and extremely worrying. And into all this she began to throw in the fact that she was in love with me and began to write love letters to the office and at that time I worked in an office where all the personal mail was opened by an administrator and it was treated as something of a joke by the admin. officer and he would say "Here's another letter telling you how much she loves you" and I would just smile and laugh. But this really made me acutely uncomfortable. Not really because I felt under any kind of threat that I might be sexually attracted to her myself, luckily as a social worker this has never been a very real threat; it could be an element in the background but it's never something that's been difficult for me and that's probably because of the kind of role I have as a social worker and also because of the disparity between myself and my clients in terms of general sort of interests and background. But I think I found this threatening because obviously it got at what I was concealing and for that reason it made me feel uncomfortable and because I suppose in some very covert way I did feel threatened and didn't know how to handle it. When I was with Pat the way she would behave with me would be to become extremely moody and silent and if I was taking her for an interview or an appointment she wouldn't get out of the car and would just sit there. She would become depressed and just sink into herself and then again, just sort of threaten suicide or say she was depressed and miserable and half of the time she had nowhere to live so in general terms she was very difficult to know what to do with, and through all this was her feelings for me and continuation of writing letters to me. Never at any time did I talk to her directly about this or if I did, I think it might just have been to imply that it was a sort of dependency thing but I never talked to her about this in terms of it being a lesbian thing at all, because she was at the same time being fairly promiscuous with men. I just saw it as being a deprivation and I also saw it as just yet another thing she was throwing at me to make me afraid or anxious. I think in the end I went on a course and Pat just drifted off into the general scene in town.

'Several years later she did turn up again and I saw her three or four times, often at two or three year intervals. She would turn up out of the blue where I worked and just say could she see me and then disappear again. But over that time she had three children, all of whom were from quite casual relationships and each of these children she didn't keep. They went into care somewhere or other but the last time I saw her she was settled into — she was only about twenty-five — thinking that she was a lesbian and she had lesbian relationships, not particularly satisfactory ones but by the last time I saw her she had met a women she had a strong attachment to who was married and had gone to live with both of them in their home. Again it was in the Midlands and she got a job in the country doing some sort of farm work and was getting a lot of support from living with this couple. I was a bit worried about the husband being jealous of this relationship because although it wasn't sexual because she didn't want to upset the marriage, she was nevertheless obviously attached to this woman and was seeing it as a lesbian attachment but also wanted to keep the thing as happy as possible without rocking it. I think she'd been there about seven or eight months and I didn't ever see her again but she had told me a lot about herself and how she thought about herself and had decided and accepted that she was a lesbian and had by that time given up casual relationships with men. I still didn't acknowledge that I was a lesbian but came in a way pretty near to it and I am sure if she turned up again, I would do so now but I don't think she is likely to.

'I haven't said anything about my aims. I think my aims in that relationship were just to get her some kind of focal point to hang on to because I knew a lot of teenagers who were pretty unstable and you couldn't do more than offer them some kind of stable relationship and some kind of possibility of making contact with you so at least if you were that sort of person they would ring up, no matter what the situation was, it always seemed to me that that was the best you could offer because any attempt to get their life organized was pretty impossible with that sort of background.'

. . .

'I am picking out again another case with a homosexual element which hit me quite a lot. This was an unmarried middle-aged woman who lived with her daughter. She had had hospitalization for some kind of psychiatric breakdown many years previously but had lived a very secluded life with her daughter for a number of years, she hadn't gone to work and her daughter came the way of social services because she wasn't attending school, she was in a rather tight situation with her mother and just stopped going to school. Her mother had no other complaints about her but the girl was brought to court. I was a senior at the time and a social worker in my team took on the case. This woman, I think, was very angry about the supervision and the interference in her life. She was a seemingly rather quiet, rather stolid small woman, but she became increasingly rather dependent on her social worker and in the end accused the social worker of having a lesbian interest in her and got a very fixed idea about this and began to complain about it to me and then also to the area officer. She had the idea very firmly fixed in her head and was quite sure that the social worker was lesbian. Then she came to see me and began to suggest that she thought I was too. She said she could see it in my eyes and also said things like I'd been kind and that meant I was a lesbian because I had been kind to her.

'That became a tremendously difficult case because at one time she was ringing me where I worked and the switchboard counted as many as a hundred calls a day asking to speak to me. At the beginning we would try and deal with this and take the calls but they came so often that I had to ask for them to be cut off. She went to see the area officer but she just found he reinforced our position and she didn't get anywhere with him and she kept saying she was going to write to her MP and get a court order and so on. About the girl; she had now left school and although she wasn't working, there wasn't much we could do about her. We didn't at the time think we should remove her from home and in fact I think the girl found a boyfriend and got engaged fairly soon. But the mother just went on becoming increasingly difficult and again I felt this as a very threatening thing — because she was accusing me of being a lesbian. I never did deny it but then neither did I actually acknowledge it. I dealt with it in fairly traditional casework terms — I'd ask her questions like, "What would you feel about it if I was, and so why does it matter?" It was just a very difficult situation, she also began to ring me at home — she got my number from the telephone directory and it was all incredibly difficult. She told me a great long story about when she was in hospital twenty years earlier and was quite sure a nurse who attended to her was a lesbian because of the way she looked at her. It was always to do with the way one looked at her, the expression in the eyes that she could tell. In the end I think it only got solved when I left the borough, I also moved home and she didn't pursue me and never managed to find out where I lived. I thought about going ex-directory but I hate the thought of that so I didn't.'

Hazel talks about her own responses

'It was the mixture of her own psychiatric problems and her obsessive personality with the lesbian bit thrown in. The tension was almost certainly partly that in each case I thought I was being less than honest with the people. With hindsight now, though it might have made it even more difficult to handle, if they'd known I was a lesbian at least there wouldn't have been those layers of emotion in me that I was sort of covering over. In a way I was increasing the fantasy. If they'd known I was a lesbian, they wouldn't have been bothered by the fantasy of not knowing whether I was or not and it would have got rid of that and would have made it, I hope, a more workable situation. And for them as well as for me. The girl I described to you probably didn't think lesbianism was a bad thing even when she was quite young but the woman obviously thought it was quite a bad thing. If she had known, I don't quite know what she would have done with the information. She might have taken it elsewhere, perhaps that would have mattered then more than it matters now, but again, it would have been a more honest situation. It would have been a reality situation to have worked with. So yes, I think there must have been some guilt that I wasn't telling them the truth and in a way being less than fair to them because they were enduring a burden, partly as a result of feeling they were lesbian and I was not letting them off the hook.

'I think generally as a social worker there is always a degree of tension in situations like the first example where you feel responsibility; where there are children at risk, or teenagers leading very unstable kinds of lives. I have always felt a lot of tension in relation to cases. Certainly there was additional tension often put on by the sheer practical fact of her homelessness. There always is with a young person who is homeless or not living in very satisfactory circumstances, but yes, there was the additional tension of her feelings for me which I think were pretty strong. And yes, I suppose the tension I felt was; was she going to make a physical advance to me, was she going to break down completely because she was in love with me and I wasn't responding in the way she might want me to. My whole view about homosexuality has changed so much. I don't think at the beginning that I had any conscious feeling that I ought to have been telling her because at that time I took a fairly traditional, developmental view about homosexuality as a gap in my personal development, or a deficiency. So I wouldn't have thought it would have been helpful consciously to have told her. But there must have been part of me that felt perhaps a bit dishonest in not saying anything about my situation because in a way I was increasing her problems because in addition to everything else, she was also having these strange emotions about me and if I'd said "Well lots of people do and I have these feelings too". ... '

'But what's happened over time is that your whole method of operating, your whole view of relationships has changed?'

'Certainly my whole attitude to gay relationships but also to heterosexual relationships as well has changed quite a lot in the last five or six years. My attitude to the traditional roles of husband and wife has altered a great deal. At one time I would have thought that a woman who wasn't happy looking after children and was depressed about it had somehow failed to come to terms with her maternal role and this might have been due to failure in her own relationships with her mother; failure in acceptance of her womanhood and femininity. I would have seen it in those kind of developmental terms. Whereas now I am likely to see it as a woman's role in society. Expectations placed on women to be in the home and look after children. Often in the case of clients without the wherewithal to do it — without housing, money, the possibility of self-help play groups. So that my whole way of looking at that situation in marriage would certainly be to relate the woman's feelings to the wider society and social expectations rather than to her maternal development. I would certainly look at the husband, instead of assuming that the man goes out to work and maybe occasionally helps with the washing up and putting the children to bed. I would look for greater flexibility and not let the man sit at home to be waited on. So that would be an enormous shift.'

'We have talked about the sorts of cases where you have held back for important reasons; have there been other cases where you haven't discussed sexuality through your own choice although you thought it was important?'

'I suppose it really sounds very feeble now, with hindsight, because I know that for some social workers who do talk about sexuality with clients, they find that their clients are ready to do so and that it's obviously very helpful for them to do so. I suppose I hid behind the fact that people didn't ever bring it to me directly and I also hid behind a view which I guess is pretty puritan that somehow what was important was people's emotional relationships; the personal dynamics, and that their sexual behaviour followed from that. And that if for example, there was a married couple, and often if there was marital disharmony they wouldn't talk about sex necessarily, they would talk about how he or she behaved in terms of their general behaviour or general personality. I felt that if those things got worked on, then somehow whatever sexual disharmony there was would also work out better. So it was that sexuality was just the mechanics of the business and not the real thing about people. I've only recently come to feel that if you get the mechanics right, it might help you in other ways.

'I still tend to find it rather difficult to feel that sex is an enormously positive thing to be developed in its own right. I still find the thing of perfecting sex so that orgasms get better and better goes a bit against my grain and that's a lot to do with my rather puritan view about self-indulgence and seeking one's own physical satisfaction and somehow to put yourself first and look for your own sexual satisfaction even if you're looking for your partner's at the same time is somehow a selfish thing to do. It's all tied up with that.'

'Can we think now about moral judgements and come up with some examples?'

'I've always found this a slightly curious thing about my moral judgements in relation to social work, and clients, and in relation to my personal life. I was brought up in an orthodox Catholic background and accepted broadly the view that sexual relationships were only permissible during marriage. In social work from quite early on I never had those sort of feelings. The disapproval that I would feel in my private life never seemed to operate in a social work context and if I had for example a fifteen-year-old girl who had a sexual relationship with her boyfriend and was fairly happy about that, I never felt myself disapproving. I was able to accept that as her situation and to accept her morality and to take my view of her morality from her own feelings about it, to use a cliché — in a non-judgmental way. I don't feel I was denying to myself my disapproval. And even for a pretty — I hate the word but 'promiscuous' — teenager, a girl who had sex fairly casually, again I didn't feel personal disapproval about it in relation to clients. I accepted co-habitation in heterosexual relationships one came across, very much as taking it from where the clients stood and accepting it and working from that, and if they were unhappy about it, OK, I would recognize what was making them unhappy about it but if they seemed to see it without any great moral dilemmas then it didn't worry me either; and this was quite different from my personal life, where I acted much more traditionally towards friends who behaved outside the norms and to my own breaches of sexual conduct, according to my traditional upbringing. Obviously that's altered quite a lot now, well enormously in my personal life because I no longer view my own sexual behaviour in the way I used to. But there's still a bit of difference between how I view my personal sexual behaviour and clients'. I've never quite been able to account for this sort of split but I would like to carry over the sort of attitude I had to clients very much more to the personal sphere and I don't know why it operated like this quite.'

'So you have this rather split view about morality but now you're saying it's coming more together and the kind of judgments you make for clients, you're making for yourself. So the clients have had a liberating influence?'

'It might be a background that's affected me but I haven't seen it like that. What's accounted for the personal shift in my views is the whole gay liberation movement and also because it's still something I am trying to work out and still is important to me and, as I'm very affected by it, the gay Christian liberation bit, which has some quite strong voices saying things. The whole gay liberation thing, both Christian and non-Christian, has had a much bigger effect on my shift and particularly a personal relationship I have had in the last four years with the woman I live with. Consciously that's what moved me in a different direction. But certainly there must be some relationship between how I operated with clients and where I've reached now.'

Towards a new definition

'I would think the positive thing about being gay — it's something that has typically been seen by society as a handicap and something to struggle against. It can be turned in very personal terms to positive account, in terms of happy personal relationships and that in itself must have some spin-off for people in other situations where they may feel handicapped in some way or other. I'm being careful here because I'm not saying that homosexuality is a handicap that can be turned to more positive account, I'm saying it's not even a handicap, it's only a handicap because society views it so. In more general terms I think it does force, both for oneself and for everyone else, a thinking through of sexual relationships generally and sexual expectations between men and women and the kind of role which it's expected that they should play and I certainly think it forces people to look at that in their own personal terms, whether they're happily married or unhappily married or single or whatever. It throws all that in the balance and makes them rethink.'

After such an articulate description of the memories, stresses and achievements of a personal political conversion directly affecting the role of a social worker in statutory social service, any analysis of this woman's responses will inevitably reduce their richness. I hope readers will use the transcript as a supplement to the following discussion.

In my view a major theme emerging from these excerpts from the interview is the dynamic state of ideological positions and the effect of this on social work interventions. This is emphasized by having the rare opportunity to hear from someone who has been in touch with clients for over twenty years. Clearly a political conversion has been undergone by Hazel from a psycho-pathological view of herself and her clients to a feminist conviction. And yet, as with all conversion experiences, the process is never complete, even if the conscious recognition of a change in personal definition is time-capsuled. Hazel still feels a gap between personal and professional moral evaluations, despite an identification with the gay and the women's movements. At the time of the interview she still has not felt able to come out with a client she had known at a certain distance, for over ten years.

Given this *process* what can we learn, from her descriptions, of any changes in the basis and outcome of client/worker encounters? She had herself been evaluated on a scale of healthiness derived from psychodynamic psychiatry. Although it was allowed that individuals might not achieve 'heterosexual maturity', this was the goal and any falling short was the subject of searching inquiry to ascertain if the prospective social worker had achieved a degree of personal awareness. This involved showing insight into one's psychological deficiencies. Having achieved this the worker could be assumed to be in control of herself and by implication not in danger of identifying too closely with her clients. Here the idea of role distance is modelled by separation, in the worker's own mind, of her individuality, defined as a personal problem, from the professional tasks and duties of her as a *social worker*. Further, Hazel gives us a glimpse of the importance that was attached to what was seen as the chief means of communicating between workers and clients. This was described as the 'professional relationship'. Of course social work like other professionalizing groups attempted to model its activities on established professions like medicine. However, the nature of its clients always made this a less than perfect achievement. As Ferard and Hunnybun (1962, 3, 4) so clearly stated,

> At the one extreme is the client who in the main is self determining ... [able to] carry his responsibilities adequately: he is unlikely to come to the agency .... At the other extreme is the client who is a somewhat childlike person who has to depend on others for help in time of need: he is probably a frequent visitor to the agency .... it may be that he is his own worst enemy in that, for reasons deeply buried in his mind, he tends to behave in ways that serve to promote and perpetuate his misfortunes and that nullify attempts made by others to help him.

Any meeting with these sort of clients could not be one of equals. The frequent visitor to the agency was characterized as difficult to help, resistant to good intentions and not in control of his behaviour. The 'relationship' which caseworkers were enjoined to achieve in these circumstances was a corrective, parenting one for the childlike client. In brief it was asymmetrical. The relationship was primarily *used* rather than experienced or enjoyed. There were formidable technical demands on the caseworker. The interaction between worker and client had to be filtered through an analysis which searched for psychological symbols in the overt content of the communications. A response had then to be made to the client in a way which met his core anxiety which was seen as the threat of loss of good [parental] relationships. This response by the worker was also intended to be 'egosyntonic' so that the client would feel able to work on his problems *within* the relationship rather than act them out. Acting-out behaviour was viewed in casework terms as the id breaking through the reality-testing barrier of the ego; and the caseworker had to strive to contain, discourage, interpret, that is to control such manifestations of immaturity. As can be seen from this simplified overview of a complex way of seeing relationships which were intended to be 'therapeutic' for the client, the value of *control* was central to the encounter. The worker had to be in control of both his or her own responses and those of the person sent for or seeking help.

In Hazel's first case example, the fact that the girl was already sexually 'acting out' would have provided little encouragement to the worker to discuss the lesbian element in their relationship — 'was she going to make any physical advance to me, was she going to break down completely because she was in love with me ... '. This was related to the client's lack of control but Hazel's view of her own identity saw homosexual feelings as immature and therefore to be controlled or hidden. Apparently around that time Hazel's own sexuality was 'in abeyance' during a period of psychotherapy. In this climate it is easy to see how sexual expression and orientation were devalued. As Hazel stated, 'somehow what was important was people's emotional relationships ... '. Sexual behaviour was either an aspect of marital counselling or the acting out of personality problems and therefore to be controlled by the worker in order that the 'deeper' problems could be reached. These problems were defined as those of family interactions and the purpose of the casework relationship was to redirect behaviour inwards to considerations of the appropriateness of that behaviour to certain ideal forms of family life. Hence the wide discussion in the 1950s and 1960s of 'transference', in which the worker was seen as becoming possessed of aspects of the client's early experience of parent figures. The casework relationship was provided to talk out dissatisfactions with family life experiences. Diverse sexual expression meant physical satisfaction, self-indulgence, and above all a threat to family life.

But it was in the fifties, with affluence and more babies that the ideal of marriage, stressing a sexually satisfying relationship gained currency, particularly since sex was discussed more openly in that and the subsequent decades. This ideal had two important functions: it represented a criterion for normality applicaþle to all social classes and it also constituted an important discipline on the working population. If the social criterion for responsible adulthood is being a provider for the family and if the family itself provides man with a private world where he has dignity and control then disciplined production and disciplined consumption have powerful allies.   (Pearce and Roberts 1973, 67).

The attitude of social workers, among other professional groups, in the recent past to pregnancy and childbearing in the married as being normal and desirable and in the unmarried as being evidence of personal pathology has been contrasted by Macintyre (1976). In the 1970s an organization known as 'The Responsible Society', which claims to have been founded by social workers among others, described its beliefs as, 'We believe that the basic unit of society is the family which is founded on marriage. A lasting and happy marriage forms the best environment in which children can develop the uniquely human capacities for affection, generosity and creative imagination.'

As it seems likely, and as is demonstrated in Hazel's case, that both workers and clients would have experienced some unsatisfactory aspects of family life, it is obvious that professional distancing was a prerequisite of the worker meeting the recipient of casework. To have moved closer would have entailed the risk of mutual recognition of social criticism *and the possible acting out of that recognition.* This professional socialization was achieved by a selection process which emphasized the importance of a knowledge of one's personal family dynamics and then by the training course itself, and was later reinforced by supervision in fieldwork. The concern throughout was with self-awareness. Also it is my impression that many gay social workers have undergone, as did Hazel, behavioural therapy or psychotherapy in relation to their sexual orientation, with a resultant further dilution of any political analysis of their situation.

Hazel shows herself to have been uncomfortable with the

dishonesty of her responses, but her identification with clients remained at an emotional level. This in itself is not to be devalued. She describes clearly the influences brought to bear which have provided a feminist identity for her and the practical consequences, although this as we have noted has to be seen as a process rather than an entity. The operational consequences of such a personal redefinition do not just refer to coming out in cases like the first one, where the girl had accepted her own sexual value. Hazel also tackles in the second case the implications of dealing with 'the mad'. All the gay social workers I interviewed expressed reservations about coming out on every occasion, and the most frequent reason given was not knowing what the client would do with the information. Hazel faces this, wishes to treat the woman as still capable of responding to honesty even if she has been assessed as psychiatrically ill. Here she is envisaging a work situation where, having faced the challenge of very real threats to her own livelihood, she could through her own integrity make an honest response to a woman whose behaviour had placed her in danger of being disqualified from such moral considerations.

One of the comments Hazel makes ties in with my discussions with social workers concerning the lack of content or later usefulness of teaching about sexuality on qualifying courses. Concepts such as grief, loss, mourning are regularly covered but these are events which usually have happened in the past or are likely to occur in the future. Hence some distancing is possible. Sexuality is a part of every encounter between teachers and students, social workers and customers, administrators and staff. A certain reluctance to include sexual content on the curriculum involves not just a failure to provide information but rather an avoidance of a discussion of social work values and ideology at a very practical level.

If one moves beyond the psychosexual developmental ideas of the psychodynamic school, then social work enters the real world of the 1980s without consensus, the only certainties about 'right' sexual behaviour coming from fundamentalist groups who are always awaiting evidence of new threats to family life when they can successfully use existing laws to ensure that other groups are reminded of their status as sexual outlaws. What should social work education be about in such uncertainty? Should welfare rights extend to sexual rights and involve children and older persons in care? When social workers spend much of their working lives maintaining the myth of idealized family life as the unit of their operations, to look for a while at sexuality is to expose the falseness of attempts to evaluate people against a model of desirable family life which has been implicit in training workers and adjusting clients. In Hazel's first case her client and she were both in similar positions in flight from heterosexual, nuclear family norms, and in search of new identities as women who chose to express love and share their lives with other women. Because of the social work culture of the time, Hazel was unable to help the younger woman along the road to a personal definition of herself as a good person who could give and receive loving feelings. The missing element was the familiar one in social work — that of reciprocity which could have resulted in a challenge to existing social institutions within a casework relationship.

Sexuality is but one part of the encounters which occur between helpers and helped; but it can serve as an example in other social work situations where the problem is to make respect for persons a reality. This can only be achieved if social workers carry their own political analysis with them into the arena of personal distress. This involves looking at the roots and processes of our own socialization, seeing this as work in progress, sharing our analysis with the customers, and filling in our lack of understanding from their teaching. It is by this process of opening up the mystique of the 'professional relationship' that the customers can be given more power to decide whether in fact a worker/client experience is what they want, and with that particular social worker. There can then be a working together on the compromises which may be necessary towards some mutually agreed aims.

This focus on the sexual politics of casework does highlight the falseness of divisions between the designated handicapped and non-handicapped in social work practice. The interview with Hazel shows the continuity of a movement towards wholeness on a professional, political, personal and inter-personal level.

The political aspects of sexuality are often ignored in favour of who does what, where, how and with whom. This is perhaps the reason for the obsession with the sexual acts of homosexuals. An example is the assumed physical threat to children in care from gay social workers. This is a diversion alongside the very real possibilities of gay people not just achieving a tolerance for their difference but actively advocating alternative life styles and providing for their clients as Hazel recognizes in her concluding remarks, a variety of alternative models outside those often expected of both men and women struggling to achieve competence in roles for which they have neither the material provision nor the personal motivation. Such an advocacy may well imply not just recognition of other sexual orientations and lifestyles but acceptance of the possibilities of an increase in these as people become aware of such possibilities in their own lives.

Such a moral operation involves a *getting alongside* people which will directly threaten some definitions of professional practice and role distance in casework. There will, therefore, be conflict between social workers and some employing authorities. Like Hazel we may all need intimate personal relationships to change our world views but, also like her, we need group definitions to defend and extend our individuality.

Hazel's story shows the *long interdependent process* of personal and social structural change; and, although not a pure example of radical casework, her struggles illuminate both reasons for the past failures and future promise of helping individual personal problems and at the same time achieving social change within one very visible area — sexual politics.

Gay people have particular problems in relation to security of employment. They share with other social workers the common task of where to place themselves in relation to individual distress in offering casework help. What they can ask from customers and colleagues is solidarity in defining themselves as gay workers within organizations. What they can offer is a continual reminder of the invalidity of divisions between personal distress and social structures, and between day-by-day interventions and ideological aims.

4

Culture, context and practice:racism in social work
Charles Husband

This article represents an attempt to present a particular perspective within which social work practice with members of ethnic minority communities may be examined. It does not aim to offer detailed accounts of the 'appropriate' social work methods which ought to be employed in working with ethnic minority clients. Among the reasons for this are my lack of personal practice experience and a conviction that it is too soon for prescriptive statements to be made about social work methods in this area. This latter view is founded on an awareness of the recency with which social work practice with ethnic minorities has emerged as a significant issue for analysis in social work, and a belief that the current expertise in this area rests with those grass-roots practitioners who have grasped the significance of our society being multiracial. It is these individuals who in their work have begun to question the relevance of traditional social work provision, and of their personal professional skills, for an entirely new client population. It is they who are developing practice expertise through faltering innovation, through personal reflection, and through incipient networks for sharing and comparing this expertise. Given the structure of social work practice and social work education, it is also the case that these are the individuals who typically are least likely to have access to a professional audience. Moreover, their professional training will have induced in them, ironically, a conception of innovation proceeding via the written word from 'experts', rather than arising from practice. This reification of the expert was made painfully explicit at a recent conference on multiracial social work where conference members, who shamed most of the conference staff with their years of practical experience, anxiously awaited the provision of 'experts' who could offer definitive statements on practice with ethnic minority clients. It is this assertion, that currently the emergent expertise in social work practice with ethnic minorities lies diffused throughout a relatively small proportion of social workers, which more than anything shapes the nature of the analysis to be offered here. I hope to do no more than provide a broad framework which may aid the compilation of data and the formulation of hypotheses on social work practice with ethnic minority clients.

There will be two continuing threads to the argument developed here. One is the centrality of the structural position of the black communities in Britain for an understanding of their social work needs, *and* of the social work provision made available to them. The other thread is the powerful dynamics of ethnic identity which has considerable significance for individual behaviour and institutional policy in an inequitable multiracial context like contemporary Britain. An adequate comprehension of the significance of these variables can only be attained by employing a historical perspective. With this in mind it is preferable, therefore, initially to outline a theoretical account of the generation and maintenance of social identity in an inter-group context. For our purposes this will be specifically related to a brief historical account of race in British culture. This will then provide a logical and useful background for considering the structural location of the ethnic communities in Britain.

Personal identity is not the product of some micro-chip technology implanted at birth, but rather is an ongoing product of an individual's interaction with his or her physical and social environment. Therefore, in coming to comprehend social identity, that entity which is so frequently the explicit or implicit focus of social work intervention and professional reflection, we must employ a theoretical framework which adequately taps this reality. Currently such a theory is Tajfel's (1974) statement on social identity and intergroup behaviour. For Tajfel the individual exists within a rich social environment in which there are a multiplicity of social groups, some of which an individual will come to perceive as groups to which they belong. Thus social identity is seen as being derived from an individual's group membership. But since there are a multiplicity of groups, this membership is not a once and for all attachment. Rather there is an active and continuous social comparison of the membership groups with those other groups which are a discernible part of the social environment. Nor is this social comparison a neutral activity: it proceeds in such a way as to sustain, and enhance, the distinctiveness of the membership group. This distinctiveness is itself structured inasmuch as the comparisons will proceed in relation to criteria and values which are already established and significant for the membership group. For our purposes this theoretical statement opens up several very relevant questions: not least of which are those concerned with how social groups come to be defined, and how the values along which social comparison takes place are established.

A historical approach to answering some of these questions in relation to the emergence of 'race' and colour as significant criteria for determining group membership is fundamental to our understanding of social work with ethnic minorities. For the purposes of this article, the focus will be upon black minorities, wherein I include West Indian and Asian individuals, since they currently constitute the largest (although not homogeneous) minority client groups. From the vantage point of a historical perspective it becomes apparent that distinctions based upon skin colour have a long and remarkably consistent existence within British culture. We know that in Elizabethan England, at a time when the first black slaves were being brought into England, there already existed within English culture a stereotypical perception of black persons as inferior, bestial and over-sexed (Jordan, 1969). Indeed the historic antecedents of these beliefs have been outlined by Hunter (1967) in an article which demonstrates the necessity of prevalent colour prejudice for the success of Shakespeare's *Othello*. Lines such as 'an old black ram is tupping your white ewe' were not idly thrown into some attitudinal vacuum. Black sexuality and miscegenation, then as now, were a focus of acute concern to the white audience. The tremendous embeddedness of British attitudes to colour and to persons *ascribed* different racial identity is illustrated in the content of an edict of Queen Elizabeth I, which in 1601 declared:

Whereas the Queen's majesty, tendering the good and welfare of her own natural subjects, greatly distressed in these hard times of dearth, is highly discontented to understand the great number of Negroes and blackamoors which (as she is informed) are carried into this realm...who are fostered and powered here, to the great annoyance of her own liege people that which covet the relief which these people consume, as also for that the most of them are infidels having no understanding of Christ or his Gospel: hath given a special commandment that the said kind of people shall be with all speed avoided and discharged out of this her majesty's realms.   (Walvin 1971)

Here we have at the beginning of the seventeenth century an official response to the growing black population in England. Note the social comparison which actively seeks to distinguish between the English in-group and the black out-group. These blackamoors are illegitimately benefiting from relief which, being infidels (not proper Christian English people), they have no right to consume. Even in the seventeenth century black people were being labelled as a burden on society. The historical comparison is vividly made in looking at the uproar surrounding Asians entering Britain in the 1970s (cf. Evans 1977).

Equally, the response of repatriation to this 'threat' does not require elaboration in order to make the continuity with more recent times explicit. Indeed it is this historical continuity which is so important. From the earliest days of British involvement in slavery, relations between white British society and black people, whether in Britain or overseas, have maintained skin colour, and the racial categorization which has overlaid it, as a potent basis of social identity. It also has been a categorization wherein the assumed inferiority of black in relation to white identity has remained intact (Hunter 1967, Davis 1970, Kiernan 1972). The exploitative relations between white Britain and black societies necessarily generated ideologies which legitimated the nature of these relations. Although the basis for the legitimation may have shifted from biblical reference to 'scientific evidence', the fundamental function of maintaining the belief in white superiority has not varied. Again the contemporary manifestation of this potent cultural legacy can be found in recent studies of white British attitudes to the current black presence in Britain (Community

Relations Commission (CRC) 1976, Marsh 1976). Not that we need rely only on what people believe; their actions may speak louder than their words. The continuity of racism is amply documented in contemporary British society, most powerfully perhaps in the *Political and Economic Planning* study of racial discrimination (Smith 1977), but also in relation to police behaviour (Humphry 1972, Demuth 1978), and Government legislation (Dummett and Dummett 1969, Humphry and Ward 1974, Moore and Wallace 1975).

Having established the encapsulation of racist assumptions within British culture, and having identified the current racist behaviour which is characteristic of multiracial Britain, we will hardly have advanced our comprehension of social work in this society if we maintain a static and simplistic account of this situation. Britain as a geographic and political entity, and 'British' as a social identity, a membership group, are not naturally occurring phenomena. The creation of Britain as a state has only been achieved through military conquest and cultural imperialism: through the subordination of the Irish, Welsh and Scots to the English (Johnson 1975, Hechter 1975). As a consequence of this enforced emergence, British identity has, throughout its existence, had potentially disruptive forces within it; recently manifest in, for example, Scots and Welsh nationalism (Brown 1975, Webb 1978, Williams 1978). Given this potential for internal divisiveness, British identity has been nurtured through highly visible social comparison with out-groups. For example, wars against European opponents have reinforced national identity by submerging regional and class identities in a united opposition to the external enemy (cf. Postgate and Vallance 1937). A similar process of enchancing the in-group has been achieved in comparing the in-group (white British nationals) with 'aliens' who have settled in Britain. This has been the case with, for example, Jewish, Irish, Chinese and West Indian immigrants (Garrard 1971, Foot 1965, Holmes 1978). Thus contemporary 'British' culture represents a product of centuries of focused social comparison which has maintained a unique sense of British status in relation to 'aliens' in general, and 'blackamoors' in particular. What is important is that we should grasp that this process has *not* resulted in Britons perceiving themselves as superior bigots. Such an outcome would be contrary to the empirical literature subsumed in Tajfel's theory. Social comparison operates in such a way as to maintain and enhance positive in-group identity, and ideologies therefore develop in order to counter any intrinsically negative consequences of intergroup behaviour. Thus for example the racist beliefs which emerged to legitimate slavery sought to maintain the valued liberal humanism of post-enlightenment England against the reality of the brutal treatment of slaves. This was achieved by defining the slaves as less than human and thereby maintaining intact the valued perceived humanism and civilization of English society. Thus a continuing complement to British denigration of out-groups has been an emphasis on the inherently superior civilized culture of British society (Lyons 1975, Jordan 1969, Kiernan 1972). Within British identity, images of balance, fairness, rationality and tolerance, amongst others, can be found variously interwoven. Indeed, Chibnall (1977) has identified these images as being clearly represented within the dominant values of the British press. The significance of this apparently paradoxical but psychologically sound fusion of beliefs in the intrinsic inferiority and appropriate subservience of others with equally strong acceptance of tolerance and fairness as quintessential British values will become more apparent after we have briefly reviewed the structural location of ethnic minorities in contemporary Britain.

The structural position of black communities in Britain

The current black population in Britain is very largely a consequence of postwar immigration; for after the war Britain was faced with a desperate shortage of labour which it sought to resolve by drawing upon the reserve pool of labour in its colonies and ex-colonies. Thus black labour came to fill the vacuum in the British labour supply and, as Peach (1968) demonstrated for the West Indian migration, the inflow followed the demand in the British economy; and labour went to those areas in Britain where the indigenous labour was insufficient or unwilling to fill the vacancies. This last point is very important to an understanding of the position which the black population came to occupy, both geographically and economically, in Britain. In the postwar boom a significant proportion of the white labour force exercised their options in a period of labour shortage and industrial development to move out of the essentially undesirable dirty and physically hard jobs into the more attractive and better paid areas of industry. Thus it was in essence to these jobs in heavy industry, textiles and the service industries, which were subject to a flight of white labour, that the black workers came. Such were the selective pressures of white job mobility and discrimination against the black worker (Daniel 1968) that in 1969 a major review of race relations, *Colour and citizenship* (Rose *et al.* 1969), was able to demonstrate a remarkable concentration of the black population within a relatively small number of conurbations, and their employment within a narrow range of jobs. Indeed, there was clear evidence of geographical and industrial concentration of different ethnic groups within the black population itself. Thus selective forces within the employment market, and the social networks and cultural values of the migrants themselves, resulted in the emergence of ethnically distinct communities within the major conurbations of Britain. (For accounts of this process of migration and settlement, see Rose 1969, Allen 1971, Wright 1968.) The location of the black labour force within already over-crowded conurbations where they occupied the largely unskilled and low status jobs resulted in their also occupying very poor housing in the inner city areas. Consistently with the white British response to the black community in employment, discrimination in housing ensured that the housing disadvantage suffered by the black workers was greater than would have arisen from their economic disadvantage alone (Burney 1967).

Thus, from the outset, not only is the emergence of black communities in Britain shaped by the market forces of labour supply and demand, but suffused through every aspect of the influx and settlement of black persons is the exploitative relations between white and black which we have already noted as being characteristic in British history. Not only did employers, trade unions and workers collude in actively discriminating against black workers, but society at large noticed nothing untoward in the peculiarly skewed distribution of black labour into low-status and low-paid work. Not only did estate agents, council employees and slum landlords discriminate, but 'nice' people were concerned lest 'the area might go down'. Throughout the early 1960s active discrimination among the few in positions to direct the fate of specific black persons was nurtured in the passive racism of the white population as a whole. Together these forces effectively isolated the black communities within specific areas of our cities and within specific niches in the employment market. The pattern of black settlement and employment outlined by Rose in 1969 is today the context in which, with industrial recession, we can observe the screw being turned tighter.

That discrimination in employment is a continuing feature of the labour market, and in housing, has been amply demonstrated in the relatively recent PEP survey (Smith 1977). This survey demonstrated in field studies discrimination against West Indian and Asian workers both in manual and white-collar jobs, and Ballard and Holden (1975) have demonstrated that black university students born and educated in Britain are, when compared to their indigenous counterparts with similar qualifications, at a great disadvantage in finding employment consistent with their qualifications. The PEP study showed that whilst only 8 per cent of West Indian and Pakistani men are doing non-manual jobs, the proportion for white males is over 40 per cent; and for those with qualifications up to degree standard 79 per cent of white males are in professional or management jobs compared with only 31 per cent of similarly-qualified black males. Even when there are black and white workers in the same industry, conditions of employment tend to disadvantage black employees: for example, almost a third of black workers work shifts, more than twice the percentage of white workers who do so. Whilst it is true that the black workforce have developed their own support networks within the employment market (e.g. Brooks & Singh 1979; Saifullah Khan 1979), these strategies tend to operate *within* the situation of structured discrimination. The black workforce during the period of industrial recession has remained particularly vulnerable to unemployment, as indicated in the statement: According to figures released for the eighteen month period up to May, 1975, unemployment rose 65 per cent for the general population, but 156 per cent for minorities, and 182 per cent for young West Indians (CIS/IRR 1976, 33). A view supported by a CRC (1974) report which indicated that black youths (and especially West Indian youths) were twice as likely as their white counterparts to be unemployed.

In focusing upon the employment situation of the black

communities I have been seeking to indicate how in a critical sense they have been forced into a pathogenic environment of poor housing and low-paid, low-status work. Now whilst we can accept Cross's (1978) statement, 'There is no doubt that ethnic minorities share some disadvantages with their indigenous counterparts in areas of urban deprivation, we must also take particular note of his review of the evidence relating to employment, education and housing which demonstrates that there are discriminatory forces uniquely impinging upon ethnic minorities which ensure their particular disadvantage. Indeed Hall *et al.* (1978), in speaking of the second generation of black citizens in Britain, regard the location of the black community within the labour market as sufficiently uniquely determined to speak of them as a 'class-fraction'. Thus for the practice of social work it is critical that comparable 'disadvantage' apparent in the personal circumstances of black and white clients should not be taken to indicate the operation of similar social forces, nor a comparable perception of their disadvantage. Only through an appreciation of the structural position of black communities can social work begin to comprehend the specific consciousness of the black client. I am not here speaking of an awareness of cultural variation, in an ethnographic sense, between say Hindu, Muslim, and West Indian families. The 'isn't it fascinating' travelogue anthropology which abstracts the cultures of ethnic minorities from their location in Britain as a class society is positively racist in effect, since it denies the unique experience of black minorities in a racist society. We have already noted Tajfel's formulation of the process of identity maintenance, and in a racist society such as contemporary Britain ethnic minorities constantly have their ethnic identity brought to consciousness. In the labour market they are not potential employees, but Asian or West Indian workers; in interaction with the police they are not citizens but West Indian or Asian 'immigrants' (Humphry 1972, IRR 1979), and their extended family outside Britain are not 'kin' but potential immigrants who must be 'curbed'. Thus a sense of ethnic identity, though not a permanent feature of minority consciousness (Saifullah Khan 1979; Wallman 1975), is a perspective which frequently informs the black person's perception of life in Britain. It is not the disadvantage *per se* which shapes the black person's experience of life in Britain, but more particularly their awareness that this disadvantage is uniquely unjust, it is racist. This has implications for the growing political consciousness of the black communities whether it be among West Indians in Handsworth or Chapeltown, Sikhs in Southall, Bengalis in the East End of London or Gujeratis in Leicester. Social work delivery systems must recognise that they are operating in a context where black community groups, and individuals, are already highly suspicious of what they rightly perceive as 'white' institutions, and indeed can sustain this suspicion with illuminating descriptions of a variety of racist mechanisms exposed in case lore (relating for example to trade union duplicity in discrimination, and tokenism in effete race relations legislation) and the enervating blandness of official reiteration of faith in the values and functioning of British liberal democratic institutions. Social work institutions should not conceive of black clients as passive victims of a racist society. It is in seeking to comprehend the nature of the black response to this racism that knowledge of the specific cultural values and practices of ethnic communities is vital.

This argument is seemingly coming close to stating that ethnic identity and racist processes will always be crucial elements in the etiology of any ethnic minority person becoming a client of a social services agency. In an immediate sense one can clearly conceive of many instances where this would not be the case—for example postnatal care, conviction for assault or a request for part three accommodation. However, it is difficult to conceive of an instance where the social and physical environment of the client would not be modified by their ethnic identity. Thus post-natal care may be particularly crucial given the housing conditions of a black family; an assault may in an objective sense have been without adequate provocation, but perhaps not when viewed from the sensibilities of a black person for whom experience has shown insults and threat to be an ever-imminent possibility. There are instances where cultural differences *per se* are important, in for example child-rearing behaviour, sexual norms, or the somatic presentation of psychic distress. Here knowledge of cultural variation would be critical in determining appropriate intervention with a client, and the client's member-ship of an exploited minority, subject to discrimination on racial grounds, *may* not be pertinent to an adequate comprehension of their needs. However, even in instances such as these, awareness of the racial disadvantage they suffer as members of an ethnic minority may be appropriate to developing an adequate form of intervention for the client. For example Bagley (1971) has demonstrated that with a West Indian sample where 'chronic environmental distress' was shared by both a schizophrenic and a control sample, it was higher levels of goal striving which distinguish the patients from the control sample. Now here both samples equally experienced the type of chronic environmental distress which we would associate with the ethnic disadvantage suffered by West Indians in Britain. Is then knowledge of the racial disadvantage irrelevant to intervention? I would argue that an implication of Bagley's finding is that where, for example, young West Indians have high levels of goal striving, continued good mental health may be facilitated by their being conscious of the extent of the racist barriers operating in this society, and by being assured of the 'normality' of their relative failure. Given the extent to which ideologies are complex, and not monolithic entities, it is quite possible for members of minority groups to be aware of the racism they suffer, and yet still respond to the heavily socially-reinforced values of material acquisition and personal success. I would argue that any social work agency involved with such youth would have to faciliate the black youth's critique of white society. In work focusing upon black youth in the United States Gurin *et al.* (1969) showed that criticism of the discriminatory society was associated with positive innovatory strategies and political activism directed toward advancing black status. In Britain, if social work intervention is concerned with the integrity of the client, then in instances such as the example above, and generally in this racist society, the basis for social work intervention must be to seek to sustain and enhance the client's (ethnic) identity. This then requires us to ask whether the current delivery systems are capable of such disinterested commitment.

Social work institutional response

In asking whether social work agencies can be sufficiently disinterested to counter traditional modes of thought in order to meet the needs of minority clients, we are already presuming a consciousness of the existence of a new ethnically differentiated client population. At a policy level the indications until very recently were that this was a very naive assumption indeed. Jones (1977) in a study of statutory social services reported that most departments had not made a specific organizational response to black clients, such as keeping separate statistical records, undertaking staff training, or providing special treatment for black clients. This was a picture which was sustained in a report of the CRC (1977b) which stated: 'It was very rare for Social Services Committees to have even discussed the needs of minorities.' Indeed the report indicated that where some thought had been given to minority groups it was in the context of an ideology of assimilation inasmuch as the 'promotion of good race relations was equated with the provision of multi-racial facilities.' Thus in essence the black client has either been unacknowledged and thereby rendered non-problematic, or has been noted as existing, and then accorded 'honorary' citizens status and encouraged to make use of existing services. This latter perspective has been particularly represented by the liberal activist position which conceives of minority ignorance of existing services as the major factor blocking the provision of adequate social work services to minority communities and individuals. Perhaps given the essentially white staffing of social work institutions, and certainly the near monochrome at management level we should not find these reports of Jones and the CRC so surprising.

If we return to our earlier discussion of white British identity then we should anticipate that the emergence of a significant black population within Britain would stimulate culturally latent notions of white superiority and black inferiority. Indeed, throughout the 1960s we had ample demonstration of the definition of black persons as non-citizens, mere 'immigrants;' and through the mass media there was created a ubiquitous acceptance that Britain had 'an immigration problem' (Hartmann and Husband 1974, Critcher *et al.* 1977). The black population which had been the vital, and cheap, labour force of postwar expansion became the scapegoats for urban malaise and industrial decline (whilst still buffering white workers from unemployment and still servicing those areas of industry which remained unattractive to white labour (Sivanandan 1976)).

Throughout this period, too, we must remember that politicians and social pundits were making much of Britain's liberal and tolerant credentials as the mystificatory accompaniment to discriminatory immigration legislation and neutered race relations legislation (Husband 1975). Powellism and the rise of the National Front were after all only particularly gaudy litmus tests of the increasing significance racial identity had achieved for white Britain (Husband, 1978). 'Nice people' and the Labour Government were all concerned that there were 'too many of them coming in and they had to be curbed.' It is in this context that we must place the failure of social services management to identify the unique needs of black minority clients. Racism was becoming painfully apparent, and part of the response of white Britain was to vociferously reiterate our credentials as a liberal and tolerant society. An ideological commitment to our tolerant democratic credentials makes it exceptionally difficult to identify those processes in our society which actively generate social work clients. The refusal to acknowledge our national failure to maintain an equitable society is partially responsible at policy level for the failure to note the specific needs of minority clients. To the extent that such an ideology persists within social services personnel, conceptualization of minority client needs in terms of variants of personal pathology will always be more available.

John (1978) illustrates this perspective in relation to the social work perception of inter-generational conflict within West Indian families. He notes the tendency to see West Indian parents as strict disciplinarians who rigidly apply to their children the expectations they had at home. The solution to this failure of the West Indian parents is then seen to lie in the necessity for West Indian parents to 'understand that they cannot bring up children in England as they themselves were brought up at home'. This 'culture-lag' theory takes as given the 'unreasonable expectations' which the parents have for their children, thereby circumventing an analysis of the racist forces in education and employment which render parental expectations unreasonable. An additional benefit of this perspective is that it further allows the nonconformity and perceived problematic behaviour of West Indian youth to be accounted for in terms of *their* partial adherence to West Indian cultural norms and conflicting 'British' values acquired from their socialization in Britain. This conflict is itself then seen to be exacerbated by the already demonstrated inadequate parental control. This perspective adopts a liberal cultural awareness which tends to portray West Indian youth as the victims of culture conflict. It does not make possible the essential understanding of the interaction of culture and context. Yes indeed, West Indian youth do have access to a minority West Indian culture, but in order to comprehend their behaviour we must be able to examine the ways in which their culture is *actively* engaged in responding to the racism and disadvantage of their everyday experience. Quite clearly at present, for a very significant proportion of West Indian youth, the interaction of a minority culture and a racist context generates an enhancement of their distinctive black culture, perhaps most vividly apparent to the white community is the growth of Rastafarianism and its symbolism (Troyna 1978, Barrett 1977). Such a development is entirely consistent with Tajfel's (1974) theory of social identity and intergroup behaviour; for in their current structural disadvantage, the West Indian community has no access to the economic or political power which could change the conditions of their exploitation. However, they are able to mobilize psychological resources which sustain their sense of ethnic worth, and which also modify their response to the conditions of their existence. Of course, to white institutions operating within an ideology of tolerance and assumed equality such responses are seen as atavistic and unhelpful in creating a multiracial society. Indeed this response of white institutions to the black reaction to their experience of racism in Britain is well illustrated in the provision made for programmes with black community groups (John 1977, 1978). Here, as John shows, control of funding at national and local level operates in such a way as to obstruct any latently political programme and to encourage projects which pursue aims whereby they 'end up being little more than a substitute, albeit a black one, for the social welfare provisions of the local authority' (John 1978, 120). This evidence is itself consistent with the control function of Government urban policy in general as indicated by Bridges (1975). Indeed the role of the CRC and local Community Relations Councils was itself indicative of the dominance of white political interest within the 'race relations industry' (Hill and Issacharoff 1971).

A particularly telling example of a white agency's sensitivity to interventions which acknowledge, and indeed potentially promote, a distinctive black identity was recently available in an account of a probation officer's interaction with a black, West Indian, client. The probation officer was himself black, both in terms of his ethnic background and his consciousness, and his rapport with his client caused him to be brought to the Assistant Governor of the penal establishment where the client was detained: the probation officer describes the scene:

> 'I hope you won't be embarrassed but my men are a bit concerned about the letters you write to your lad. It's about this Ras Tafarian thing; we are trying to stamp it out in here but in your letters you mention something like JAH lives. The men specially brought your last letter to show me.' I remind him that I always send a copy to him. He acknowledges that. He continues, 'Well, when your lad gets your letters, it makes him feel a bit proud and this upsets things. You understand.'
>
> I reach into my file and retrieve my last letter. It is five sentences long. I read the sentence which upset his men — 'May JAH's blessings be with you.' 'It is OK if I say "May God's blessings be with you?" ' 'Of course, there is nothing wrong with that. These black lads read the bible very well, but they just read and see what they want to. I think that is a real pity that they are so narrowminded. Are you a Rasta?'   (Ramdhanie 1978)

In this instance the dominant ideology of generic practice, which as a consequence of the acceptance of the 'reality' of British tolerance and equality is committed to a suppression of ethnic distinctiveness, necessitates the *active* censure of an instance of 'deviant' practice; and in this respect is relatively rare. For within the probation service there is evidence that it is this ideology which, at least until very recently, has been normative. Among a few concerned probation officers there has been discussion of the likelihood that many black clients are being disadvantaged because white probation officers do not know how to work with them and share a muted agreement that 'young blacks do not respond well to probation.' In this way, by blaming the offender for the probation service's inability to conceptualize and develop new styles of working with black clients, the edifice of professional competence within a caring service remained intact. One anticipated possible consequence of this defensive rationalization has been that the probation service is contributing to the excessive number of black clients receiving custodial sentences through their reluctance to recommend probation. Indeed a confidential report by the Home Office Inspectorate on a large city probation service generated da:a which suggested that such speculation was justified. In the study on a sample of non-immigrant, English-speaking black clients, who were males under 30 years of age living in the city centre, it was found that out of 136 Social Enquiry Reports, probation was recommended in only 36 instances, and in 52 cases, no recommendation was made. It is the failure to make specific recommendations which is symptomatic of professional ambiguity. Although this data is no more than indicative it has since been supported by independent analyses in unpublished reports from three other probation areas. The Report of the Home Office Inspectorate itself noted that 80 per cent of the cases were said to present no cultural difficulties: in the words of the report, 'sample readers found this unconvincing.' Indeed the report went on to say — 'Colour as a factor in the individual's development and sense of personal identity was consistently underplayed, not to say ignored .... The client was repeatedly treated as white.'

Perhaps it is that in the Probation Service the conditions of referral make it particularly problematic for white personnel to seriously take cognisance of the ethnic identity of a client. For where the referral of a black client is in relation to alleged crime it becomes increasingly difficult to maintain a belief in British tolerance and freedom. First for black persons in general (Humphry 1972) and for black youth in particular (Demuth 1978, Institute of Race Relations 1979) the discriminatory practice of British law and the racist harassment of black youth by the British police has become too visible and well documented. Secondly, any competent social inquiry report upon a black youth would almost necessarily bring the probation officer into contact, at second hand, with the discriminatory processes of British society. The cumulative experience of preparing such reports would render acknowledgement of the political definition of crime inescapable. Where the location of the black community as a class fraction at the bottom of British society makes underemployment and unemployment inevitable, and where the members of the ethnic minorities experience social rejection and psychological assault from the white majority, then the survival strategies from within the black colony have to be considered within *that* framework. For probation officers who remain open to this reality, the problem will be negotiating this frame of reference within the courts and with senior mar · 3ement. It is likely therefore that normative pressures from wiuin the service and the broader cultural beliefs in 'British' values will conspire toward white probation officers submerging the significance of ethnic identity in their interaction with black clients.

In social service settings where we have already noted the dearth of specific policy for providing services to ethnic minorities, it is perhaps the unproblematic normality of many of the referrals which facilitates a submerging of issues of ethnic identity. For example, West Indian children and children of mixed parentage are overrepresented in care (Boss and Homeshaw 1975, Pinder and Shaw 1974) and the 'pathology of the black family' has frequently been invoked to make this phenomenon 'natural'. Yet, within this explanatory system, there is the passive racism which denies the relevance of those social conditions which cause parenting to break down. Similarly the unavailability of black families to foster children from their community is not perceived in terms of the specific disadvantages which debar the minority communities from meeting the requirements for being foster parents. Even within children's homes the concern to treat all children as equal, as children having common needs within the normal routines of caring, has constituted a passive racism in its denial of the individual child's ethnicity (Community Relations Commission 1977a).

Even when a social work department acknowledges the presence of a distinct ethnic minority within their area, it does not follow that the response will benefit the minority client. As I have noted above, it has often seemed to be the case that social work management has perceived the fundamental problem in providing services for minority communities as being a matter of communication. Whilst the production of leaflets, information and forms in the language of minority communities would facilitate their awareness of the services available, and improve contacts with local social work agencies, it would not guarantee that the service provided was then appropriate to clients' needs. For example, we have argued above that a necessary basis for interaction with black minority clients is a comprehension of the dynamic relation between the specific minority culture and the context of their life in Britain. Much of the argument above has pointed to the difficulties white British social workers are likely to encounter in achieving a conscious understanding of this context, and yet it is also the case that probably the majority also lack adequate understanding of specific minority cultures. Certainly it cannot be assumed that social work training will have provided the necessary basis of cultural awareness (Baker and Husband 1979). The awareness of black client culture is not only a necessary basis for efficient communication with members of that culture, it is also the basis from which social work can begin to seek out the specific *needs* of minority clients. Because they apparently share a common urban and economic disadvantage with many indigenous white clients, it cannot be assumed that they share common needs vis-à-vis social work agencies. To date too little has been done to establish an understanding of the specific needs of black clients, as they themselves define them.

One strategy has been to employ black social workers on the assumption that they will fulfil this function as a consequence of their shared cultural backgrounds. Of course there are many fallacies in this strategy, not least that in many cases the middle-class black social worker is as alien to his proletarian client as is his white colleague. A flaw in this strategy is the assumption that there is an Asian ethnicity as such, and therefore any Asian social worker is well equipped to work with any Asian client, or indeed that any black social worker can work with any black client. A good example of this flaw is provided by Rooney (1980), in which he discusses the 'Immigrant and non-white British Communities Project' in Liverpool which sought to recruit black social workers with specialist knowledge to provide a particular response to the social work problems of the black community. Rooney estimates the ethnic minority population of Liverpool to consist of approximately 4000 Asians, 9000 Chinese, about 8000 of Carribean or African origin and about 20,000 Liverpool blacks of mixed parentage. The people actually recruited to this project were according to a report of the Director of Social Services — '2 Indians, 2 East African Asians, 1 Pakistani, 2 Nigerians, 1 Somali and 2 British second generation West Indians.' Of these 'West Indians' Rooney comments that in fact in one case the father came from the USA and the mother from Dublin, and in the other the mother was from South Shields and the father from Nigeria. Thus a project intended to give particular attention to the large Liverpool coloured population recruitment was a classic example of the 'If they're non-white they're right' philosophy of client-worker matching. Not only this, the possibility of black social workers becoming identified as a relatively autonomous team was pre-empted by their being incorporated as part of the normal social service complement. The possible underlying rationales for this are lucidly spelt out by Rooney himself, writing as a social worker in Liverpool:

> The fear that may raise its head is of black staff, within a white organization, working solely with black clients. While there are rational arguments for and against such an idea the motivation appears to come from two sources. First a feeling that black social workers must be used to prove that white social workers can 'integrate', and secondly a fear that white social workers would be excluded, wouldn't know what is going on between black social workers and their clients, a fear that identification would be stronger with the client group than with the organization. This fear may be well-founded but it has to be confronted. The employment of blacks from alienated communities to work within their community is all about change, changing relationships, changing service, changing perception; and the organization must change. If it fails to allow the social workers to use their identification with their community to challenge preconceptions and prejudices, there just isn't any point in the exercise. But the resistance is strong and can express itself in an insistence that the black social workers must either provide a generic service to an integrated caseload (within normal priorities so there's little chance of innovation) or, and this is very common, anything different just isn't up to standard, it's an affront to social work professionalism and they should do it in some other capacity where they won't dilute standards.

Given the white social worker's professional anxiety toward work with clients from ethnic minorities, which is consequent upon their inadequate training for such work and the debilitating racism of their 'white' culture, then it is not surprising that they are equally ambivalent about working with colleagues from these communities. There is, however, a necessity for the recruitment of black social workers, firstly, for the benefit of white clients and British society as a whole. At least one Director of Social Services realized that he was one of the largest employers of the black community in the area, and most of these employees were in low-status service posts. Therefore, social work agencies should seek to counter the discriminatory practices in their own departments. Secondly, the employment of members of specific minority communities enables such workers, whilst working a normal case-load, to provide advice to white colleagues on culturally relevant aspects of cases they may be handling. This does not mean acting as interpreters. Constantly to assume that it is an appropriate use of a qualified social worker to require them to interpret for *your* case is itself denying the professional integrity of that worker. However, such a worker as a member of a team could contribute specialist knowledge for the benefit of all, and provide in-service training to white colleagues which would fit them to work with all their clients, black or white. Finally, in the current context of minority community life in Britain a black social worker, whose identification is with his or her ethnic groups, can assist in developing a service which is more directly relevant to the needs of his or her community. As we have seen, the question remains whether social service agencies will recruit such people, and when recruited allow them freedom of operation. Ramdhanie, above, demonstrated the sensitivity of the system to such modes of practice within probation, and within youth work I am aware of black workers whose survival requires their negotiating a 'professional' identity with management and a black identity with their clients. The danger in this strategy, which applies to black social workers in a variety of contexts, is that eventually the 'professional' performance may undermine the worker's credibility with his own community. At which point the worker either leaves, or becomes a compromised and marginal individual, always susceptible to retreating into a 'professional' identity. Within social services the recent report of the Association of Directors of Social Service, *Multi-Racial Britain: The Social Services Response* (Commission for Racial Equality 1978), marks a shift in the area of policy: here at least there is an indication of specific policies toward the recruitment of minority staff, and the provision of services to minority clients. However, it remains to be seen with what spirit these recommendations will be implemented. It may already be the case that within at least one authority it has been implemented in such a way as to suggest a token commitment, which has exacerbated the feelings of bitterness and frustration amongst those staff committed to establishing a competent multiracial provision.

Conclusion

In this chapter I have attempted to outline a perspective within which social work practice with members of ethnic minority communities may be examined. In particular I have focused upon the West Indian and Asian minority communities within Britain, often referring to them both as black clients. This is because to a very large extent they both occupy comparable positions of ethnic disadvantage with the racist society which is Britain. The term black is also intended to indicate the growing common consciousness of Asian and West Indians in Britain; a consciousness located in their common experience of racism. In this respect I have argued that the social and economic context of minority communities in Britain is fundamental to their needs as social work clients. However, I have also argued that a knowledge of the cultural norms of specific ethnic communities is a critical prerequisite for appropriate intervention with minority clients. In this sense there are no black clients; indeed no Asian or West Indian clients. The units of ethnic categorization which are appropriate for identifying a person's cultural affiliations are much more specific, and complex, than contained in such broad categories as West Indian and Asian. It is the individual's unique response to the context of their life in Britain from within the perspective of their culture which forms the dynamic which social workers must grasp in working with clients from ethnic minorities.

We have already noted the way in which white British social workers have within their own culture notions of racial identity which impede their comprehension of the context in which black clients must exist. In addition these same cultural values, in conjunction with habitual professional routines, render white institutions particularly resistant to comprehending the new demands which they must meet in order to service a multi-racial clientele. When we reflect upon the benefits which accrue to white Britain from economic exploitation and psychological scapegoating (Sivanandan 1976) of black clients, it would be naive to anticipate social work agencies innovating to the point of threatening this function. Indeed the evidence of policy in this area has been consistent with social work developing in relation to the ideological counterpart of this exploitation, a commitment to the 'self-evident' virtues of British tolerance and humanitarianism. Although there is evidence of innovation at the grass roots level, John (1978) has warned us that we must be acutely aware of the wider ideology within which innovation is being contained.

5

Radical residential child care: Trojan horse or non-runner?

Phil Lee and David Pithers

> Abolition of the family! Even the most radical flare up at this infamous proposal by the Communists.
>
> K. Marx and F. Engels,
> *The Communist manifesto*

Social work in the last decade has experienced a significant questioning of its traditional ethics, practice and training. Various contributors have provided a mainly theoretical critique accusing social work practice of tending to individualize essentially social problems, and have argued that such practices merely operate as a system of social control within capitalist societies by both directly 'blaming the victim' and indirectly camouflaging the precise nature of social problems. Much of value has been written (Bailey and Brake 1975, Jones 1975, Pearson 1975) but too often the critiques were overdrawn leaving social workers who wished to chart a radical path without a clear direction. The balance sheet of this period is now beginning to be drawn up, particularly for community workers and field workers (Clarke, 1979, Corrigan and Leonard 1978).

This same decade also witnessed the growth of personal lifestyle movements generating issues outside of traditional left-wing concerns. The most important of these are undoubtedly the women's liberation movement (WLM) and the gay liberation movement (GLM) both centrally concerned with questions of sexuality, personal life-styles and the nature of the family. These movements have had a constructive impact upon left-wing groups, obliging them to analyse such issues. Of course there has been mutual interaction between these two developments, and often those people moving towards radical social work have been involved in wider cultural and political movements. It is all the more surprising, therefore, that one area has received only cursory attention: child care. Residential child care has been virtually ignored. It remains like an island unwashed by any of this radical bravado, yet the questioning about sex roles, sexuality, the family and social control are even more relevant to residential child care than to any other social work setting. Why has there been this lack of radical analysis in residential child care?

We hope in what follows to offer some clues that suggest an answer to this question. We also hope to provide a concise, necessarily brief, dissection of the major radical contributions to critical thinking about the family and childhood. Finally, of course, we have attempted to give some guide-lines on the problems and possibilities of actually doing radical residential work. First though, we must place residential care within its societal context.

Radical residential child care? You must be joking

> I wanted to come into care and I kept on running away until someone took notice. I'm glad I'm in care. I don't want to go home.
> ('A Child in Care', in Page and Clarke 1977)

Residential care is not only that setting of social work practice least permeated by radical thought, it also represents an issue on which there exists a remarkable degree of political agreement. If one were searching for a feature of society almost universally condemned, across lines of class, interest and political outlook, residential care would have to be a very strong contender. Whether one is old or young, fit or handicapped, sane or not, it seems that the worst thing which can happen to you is to be 'put in a Home'. Unreflective acceptance of this fact transcends all the usual divisions. For the Right, residential care is either a poor substitute for the family or one more example of creeping socialism. By the Left it is regarded as one more agency of punitive control integral to the continuation of the existing bourgeois social order. Both views lack serious analysis and do not go far beyond the reflex response so typical of media coverage of residential establishments.

For a defence of contemporary practice, and then only in a limited sense, one has to look to certain of the more progressive residential practitioners. One such, Peter Righton (1976), neatly captures both the flavour of the general antagonism and the shaky credence with which the social sciences often feed it:

> Sociologists, for example, deliver blockbusters manufactured in the arsenals of Goffman and Garfinkel and designed either to blow holes in the concept of the total institution, or to expose the hidden iniquities which result from the subjection of residents to alien but taken-for-granted definitions of social reality. The howitzers of developmental psychology, whether they are Bowlby-type (now beginning to gather rust), or Rutter-type (gleaming with new paint) are trained on more limited targets: residential institutions for very young children.

Whilst the general standard of residential care is admittedly very low, we must resist generalizing present shortcomings into permanent features. Most of the social scientific work briefly alluded to by Righton suffers from being taken out of context or from falling victim to what has become a widespread truism for both Left[1] and Right: that life in the nuclear family, however unsatisfactory, is bound to be superior to life in a residential community. It is almost impossible to ask limited, optimistic questions about residential care: such as under what conditions, for which groups of people, for how long, might a period or permanence of group living meet needs and even wishes *better* than family life?

Such thoughts are difficult to entertain in polite society. Many of our radical friends and colleagues have choked on their lunchtime snacks as we have attempted to discuss with them our ideas for this article. 'You mean you're going to defend institutionalized care?'; 'It's just social control — enforcing middle-class child rearing standards'; 'How can you write a radical article about that — you must be joking!' have been stock responses.

---

1   The Left also has a tendency to swallow whole Goffman's simplistic critique of institutionalization (Goffman 1968). The words 'residential care' and 'institutionalization' become almost synonomous for certain critics. Tizard *et al.* (1975) point out how they overstate their case.

Some of our students, committed residential workers, have found our ideas difficult even to entertain, given the pernicious hold that the 'child-in-the-nuclear family' (Wilson 1977) has in our culture. So tenacious is this ideological grip and the belief that all residential child care is reactionary that the bare minimum of evidence is necessary to sustain it. Perhaps this article justifies itself simply by exploring arguments that put these assumptions to the test. Take this quotation from an educationalist with purported liberal inclinations (Holbrook 1971, 16):

> There are in the world some 2,000 million human beings all of whom could speak of how much a child needs his mother from 'inside' experience. There are also many works of art, including millions of depictions of the Virgin and Child, symbolising the human experience of the need for a mother.
>
> In what sense do the 'hard facts' of empirical experimentation seem preferable to the kind of human fact we all know from the inside about our need for a mother or mother-substitute? *Why not study the wretched children in institutions anyway?* Do not they provide evidence enough?   [our emphasis]

It does seem a little rash for us to try and contradict a view apparently held by 2,000,000,000 people from different cultures and radically different systems of child-rearing. Nevertheless, it is implicit in Holbrook's question that the evidence on the condition of children in 'institutions' is not available, and so ought to be studied. But, of course, his findings are already assured in his description of the children as 'wretched'. Conventional assumptions, as always, stand in lieu of evidence. There are many children in residential care at this moment, and many more who were in the past, who are far from wretched. Indeed, are there no wretched consequences to family love, is not parental power used in arbitrary and repressive ways, and are there not problems intrinsic to familial organization?

The pervasiveness of such ideas is so absolute that many residential workers can only refer to their jobs as offering concessionary family life, just as most social work theoreticians exhort them to. Jean Packman starts her book (1968, 15), essential reading for all residential workers in training, with the following passage:

Most children are brought up by their natural parents. Some are not so lucky.

The British Association of Social Workers' Children in Care: Charter of Rights states:

Children in care are entitled to a family life. The child who does not have an opportunity to enjoy the experience of family life is in a sense doubly deprived, and all staff dealing with these children will need to recognize this.

A lecturer in residential care at the National Institute for Social Work talks of children in residential care being nearly all products of total family breakdown: yet later, and predictably, he informs his readers that their 'needs are for intensive therapeutic care followed by reintegration into a family setting' (Paine 1976, 16). In short, we will return our flock from whence it came, but the second time around the family life the child returns to will be a few notches up the social ladder.

Of course, this general defensive sentimentalization of family life is not without purpose. Interesting examples are provided by the way in which the media portray the Royal Family (Burgoyne, n.d.) and the increasing attention being paid by social democratic politicians to what they see as a decline in 'the cohesion of family life' (Callaghan 1978). In a less elevated way residential care performs a similarly ideological function for the 'status quo' by buttressing utopian notions about the family. Thus, the predominant view of residential care operates according to a particularly distorted logic; if the family works residential care cannot work, residential care does not work therefore the family works.

The ultimate paradox of this antipathy towards residential care is that most radicals are no friends of the family either. In general terms it is condemned for many evils — producing a docile work force, restricting women's potential, repressing sexuality and generating 'mental distress' are but a few of the many. Most radicals openly, but abstractly, look forward to the day when the nuclear family will disappear, where people will not be stifled by monogamous relationships and where, surprise, surprise, children will be brought up communally.

Yet little of this theoretical distaste for the family generates any practical opposition to it. How will the change from the oppression of today to the ideal of tomorrow be realized? We hope to explore some of the conventional answers radicals have given to this question in the next section. But what we find incredible is that residential care, the collective care of working-class children who have had a disastrous experience of family life, receives little or no attention from those discussing alternatives to the family. The Left, while being only too concerned with the ideological role of the family (Althusser 1977), seems unable to locate residential care as a potential source of inspiration for realistic alternatives to it.

The radical 'Solutions'

> People who talk about revolution and class struggle without referring explicitly to everyday life, without understanding what is subversive about love and what is positive in the refusal of constraints, such people have a corpse in their mouth.
>
> R. Vaneigem,
> *The revolution of everyday life*

Why has residential care proven such a barren ground for the growth of radical ideas? We can best approach this question by looking at how different radical approaches have accounted for the existence of the family. We can broadly identify three principal positions.

Feminism

Feminism lays emphasis on male domination, or patriarchy, a phenomenon which is seen as socially enforced. Firestone, for example, emphatically rejects the marxist view that all class struggle originates in the 'economic development of society' and 'in changes in the modes of production and exchange' and urges us to seek 'the ultimate cause and great moving power of all historic events in the dialectic of sex.' She adds that marxism's failure was that 'it did not dig deep enough into the psychological roots of class' (Firestone 1972, 15).

The politics that flowed from such a position produced an exclusive focus on the family and personal relationships, e.g. consciousness-raising groups, and a search for entirely personal transformations. However, the equation of women's oppression with male power obscured more questions than it satisfactorily answered. For example, one development, radical lesbianism, advanced an attack on the family that urged women to break completely with their 'female role'. In short, until feminism was challenged by those marxists who took questions of personal transformation seriously it remained a diffuse credo, offering no systematic critique of contemporary child care other than that it should no longer remain the exclusive preserve of women. Childhood received no attention apart from being seen as an arena of crucial importance for a growing number of important studies of sex role socialization (Belotti 1975, Sharpe 1976, Chetwynd and Harnett 1978).

Marxism

It is not too difficult to ascertain why many feminists found it necessary in the 1960s to look to sources other than marxism for inspiration. Engels' seminal work incorporating Marx's notes (Engels 1962) was the orthodox marxist text attempting to situate the family, and the oppression of women, within the historical development of production. For Engels the rise of private property oppressed the female sex, not their traditional responsibilities for child-rearing and domestic duties. Woman's oppression arose through the creation of a separate sphere of private life — the 'family' — based upon the private appropriation of communal property. Through this emphasis 'the man seized the reins in the house also, the woman was degraded, enthralled, the slave of man's lust, a mere instrument for breeding children' (Engels 1962, 225).

Amongst the early marxists only a few isolated individuals developed a serious interest in the family, the position of women and childhood[2]. However, most contemporary marxists concede that Engels' work contained many flaws; despite this its influence

2 See, in particular, Reich 1972, Kollontai 1972 and Trotsky 1972. Of greater importance for our purpose is Vera Schmidt, who ran a children's home in Moscow between 1921-3 based on Reichian principles. We would have liked to have paid greater attention to this period, the infamous Bolshevik 'abolition of the family' experiment, but were wary of the paucity of objective sources. We hope to tackle these issues in depth in a forthcoming book.

remained unchallenged until recently. The political consequences of Engels' work were that women had to be enabled to take part in production and that private housekeeping, along with child-rearing, must be transformed into social industries. The needs of women were inseparable from the needs of the industrial proletariat. Children were simply left out of account as Sartre (1963, 62) has sarcastically noted:

> Marxists are concerned only with adults; reading them, one would believe that we are born at the age when we earn our first wages.

Another implication of Engels' argument is that socialism will not bring about the abolition of the family: rather, the functions currently performed by it will be socialized, leaving intact monogamy and the sexual division of labour. The legacy of this view, we will argue, is still with many marxist commentators on the family.

In recent years however a growing number of people have responded to the important questions posed by the feminists about personal emancipation and have attempted to apply marxist categories in answering them. We will refer to this third group as socialist feminists.

Socialist feminism

This tendency is united in a serious attempt to separate out different aspects of women's oppression and to clarify the precise role that both capital accumulation and other processes play in exploiting women as wage workers, mothers (reproducers of labour power) and occupiers of the feminine role.

The initial debates that emerged in this current clustered around those specific questions posed but inadequately answered by the feminists. Of central importance was the question of women's work in the home as housewives (including child care). The exclusive concern of the feminists with being a housewife led to the demand for wages for housework (see Dalla Costa and James 1973) whereas the intervention of socialist feminists shifted the scope of analysis towards what Gardiner (1975) has described as 'an emphasis on the role of female labour in the family in maintaining and reproducing labour power.' This controversial issue has become known as 'the domestic labour debate', and pursuit of the issues related to it gave rise to two sets of questions.

First were the questions relating to women's role in production where marxist categories had direct applicability (reserve labour army, the production of surplus value etc.) and second were those appertaining to women's role in childbearing and child-care. Increasing attention was directed to how the state managed this problem of mediating its ideological insistence on women as the sole caretakers of children while simultaneously encouraging married women to work during labour shortages. As Elizabeth Wilson (1977, 158) remarks, commencing on the post-war Labour Government's commitment to full employment:

> This period then saw the development of a contradiction between the need to expand the labour force, and the need to raise the birth rate and tangling with this were new anxieties about the emotional well-being of children. Women have been the battle-ground of this conflict within capitalist society ever since, for what has been attempted is to return the mother as, in practice, the individual solely in charge of the day to day care of children and yet at the same time to draw married women, the last remaining pool of reserve labour, into the work force. These demands are not fully compatible.

The socialists accurately perceived how this dual role of women constituted a major contradiction both for capitalism and for the state, a contradiction that has to be managed (Bland 1978, 52). It is indeed possible to account for the growth of the Women's Liberation Movement itself partly as an outcome of the management of this contradiction. Braverman explains this neatly (1976, 120):

> ... household work, although it has been the special domain of women, is not thereby necessarily so central to the issues of women's liberation as might appear. ... On the contrary, it is the breakdown of the traditional household economy which has produced the present-day feminist movement. This movement in its modern form is almost entirely a product of women who have been summoned from the household by the requirements of the capital accumulation process, and subjected to

experiences and stresses unknown in the previous thousands of years of household labour under a variety of social arrangements.

Such insights allow us to explain how four of the seven demands of the WLM are directly concerned with negotiating this very same contradiction. Similarly the political demands that emerged from within socialist feminism were for women's equality primarily at the workplace, as their theories directly led to the conclusion that (Bland 1978, 60):

> Capital can only retain these advantages of cheap labour power — unpaid labour in relation to the reproduction of male labour power, and cheap female labour power — so long as women continue to labour in, and have prime responsibility for the home and child-care.

The vital issue therefore was to fight for practical programmes that erode women's prime responsibility in these fields. For our purposes this has tended to mean a concentration on the demand for more and better day-care facilities for children. The original WLM demand for twenty-four-hour nurseries seems to have been entirely abandoned. Childhood again, as such, has received very little attention except for a recent edition of the radical psychology magazine Humpty Dumpty (Comer 1978)

Is an alternative to the family possible?

> The problem is not, why does the family disintegrate? The reasons for this are obvious. The question which is much more difficult to answer is, why is this disintegration so much more painful than any other revolutionary process?
>
> W. Reich,
> *The sexual revolution, 158-9*

All these radical schools examined above are characterized by a general but uneven critique of different aspects of family life, in particular (Bruegel 1978, 5):

(a) privatized form of reproduction;
(b) monogamous sexual relationships;
(c) stable life-long coupling;

(d) distinct sex roles;
(e) hierarchical familial power structure.

In practical terms though, concern has tended to focus on those aspects of family life that prevent women from competing equally in the labour market. The rest remains largely rhetorical. Childcare is recognized as a crucial issue because it centrally affects family life, relations between the sexes, the structure of the labour force and the socialization of children; but there has been little systematic encouragement or thought about alternatives to nuclear family care. This is exemplified by the failure of all three schools to study the one major 'living' alternative to nuclear child rearing: the Israeli kibbutzim (Bettelheim 1971). This despite the wealth of evidence kibbutzim supply countering the 'supposed' effects of maternal deprivation and their clear commitment to limit competitiveness and rampant individualism. There is a similar failure to take seriously communes and collective living experiences (Statham 1978).

The theoretical shortcomings are reflected at the level of practice. The campaign around the rights of one-parent families is a useful illustrative case. Mothers in Action, the most militant of the campaigning groups, explain their politics thus (Frost 1977, 79):

> ... by arguing against the Children Bill it looks as if we were insensitive to the needs of children, but this is an incorrect assumption; it is precisely because we were sensitive to their needs that we drew attention to the injustice of providing a means for children to be removed from their families without balancing this with provision for them to remain there. We felt that if children had the right to be removed from families where their welfare was clearly going to be a long-term risk, they also had the right to remain in their families if their parents showed concern for them, but lacked the means to express it. There is at work, mostly unseen, the ideological view that a one-parent family is not a 'proper' family; if this is so, we would point out that if society were organized differently one would not even have to think about such things. Children would grow up in social groups large enough to provide a variety of adult models and relationships as a matter of course, and the presence or otherwise of their biological parents would

cease to have the pathological importance it has today. They would also be a lot healthier emotionally.

As we later hope to demonstrate, we are sensitive to this position; but it has to be recognized that radical critiques of the family are liable to concentrate on no more than one or two of the five attributes listed above. The Mothers in Action campaign is clearly undermining (c) and (d) above, and this is important; but surely the crucial attribute, in a sense the fulcrum around which the other four revolve, is (a), the privatized form of reproduction. Their campaign actually reinforces, structurally and ideologically, nuclear child-rearing. They recognize this retrospectively and propose alternatives 'if society were organized differently', but in so doing merely repeat the fallacy of the unbridgeable gulf between present practice and future goals so common in radical writing about the family. We can also find a similar gap in the campaign for lesbians to be mothers despite its explicit attack on (d). It must become a central concern of the radical social work movement to be clear about how the amelioration of short-term hardships actually translates into long-term revolutionary strategy.

At this point we will probably be accused of ultra-Leftism, of trying to promote arguments about future struggles prior to the correct stage for their advancement being reached. We offer only one defence. This is the same argument used by all revolutionaries concerned with changes in everyday life when confronted by those dogmatists who assume that all forms of liberation will be guaranteed by a change in the economic mode of production. We are arguing that if revolutionaries believe in the importance of collective child-care it must be discussed and developed now.

Thought must be applied to these questions urgently, for we suspect that it is not just the lack of serious theoretical attention[3] that leaves the Left vague about collective child-care: real doubts exist as to the efficacy of such proposals. This quotation from the

3 Another manifestation of this is the lack of contributions by marxists to important empirical debates such as the controversy surrounding the importance of the first five years of life. It has been most left to behavioural psychologists (Clarke and Clarke 1976) to supply evidence to challenge the dominant belief that this period exerts a disproportionate influence on later development. There seems to be a general disdain within marxism towards contributing to such empirical issues.

marxist Reiche (R. Reiche 1970, 155), commenting on the commune movement, confirms our suspicion:

> One of the classic functions of the family is impossible, or very difficult, in the type of Commune outlined here: the upbringing of children. Brückner's statement that 'one cannot approach the socialization process in a spirit of dilettante experimentation' is of the utmost importance. No more satisfactory model for the early socialization of children exists in any of the highly developed capitalist industrial countries than averagely successful family upbringing (whether the success be the result of accident or design). The necessary conditions are: normal and loving parents, moderately favourable subsidiary factors such as secure economic circumstances, reasonable living conditions, satisfactory division of roles between the parents, and time for the mother to devote herself to the child.

Arguments such as these dissolve much of the radical vitriol against the family. Bookhagen *et al.* (1973, 140) point out that it is as if Reiche has forgotten his previous trenchant critique of bourgeois family life in which:

> ... 'normal' families are incapable of loving and the existing family structure can only be maintained in the presence of extreme constraints on all its members. In the material sphere, this pressure is brought to bear through the irrational dependency of wife and child. The erotic and sexual desires that are constantly aroused by the promises held out by consumption cannot be satisfied in an institutional framework that is based on mutual dependency.
>
> Material and psychic dependency prevents the total disintegration of the family as institution from producing a corresponding increase in the number of divorces. Instead, the majority of married people make life hell for one another. It is the children, above all, who are affected by the pressure. The average nuclear family produces clinging, unstable, individuals who have a fixation on infantile needs and irrational authority-figures. The fact remains despite the parents' good intentions or their child-rearing practices.

Such a resumé would be accepted by many socialists, yet when it comes to paying attention to child-care the ills of the family either seem to magically disappear or are discussed as effects of 'the family under capitalism' rather than the institution itself. Memories of Engels' rather genteel conception of the family under socialism immediately spring to mind. We are again confronted with an apparently unbridgable gulf between radical goals and contemporary practice. Corrigan and Leonard's recent book (1978, 135) — itself paying little attention to residential work — offers a similar view 'which urges social workers to build on the progressive elements in the family and not to over-emphasize the ideologically oppressive functions.'

Similar concerns, though less overtly expressed, can be found in the general underplaying by the WLM of their original demand for twenty-four-hour nurseries. This passage from Charlton (1974, 169) leaves little to doubt as to why:

... Unfortunately, the wording was ambiguous and many people took it to mean that the same children stayed there for 24 hours a day.

Socialized child care is a crucial concept for the women's movement and the left to introduce, but in the form of a demand isolated from the support of a total socialist system and simply plonked onto an alienating capitalist one, it created formidable contradictions as we discovered when we tried to launch a national campaign around the demand.

Again, we do not wish to minimize the enormous difficulties to which Charlton correctly draws our attention, quite the reverse, but equally such difficulties should not mean we compromise our goals. Socialists examining child-care too often allow the 'happy family' to be smuggled in as the 'normal' and only one through the back door of nuclear child rearing.

Social control?

To answer fully our original question about why residential work has been bypassed by much progressive thought, we have also to look at the history and present practice of residential child care. This will necessitate examining the most difficult question of all — just what is radical residential work?

Present British residential child-care institutions have evolved as a jumbled response to orphaned, lost or abandoned children, those whose parents 'so persistently failed without reasonable cause to discharge the obligation of a parent ... as to be unfit to have care of the child' and 'children guilty of offences punishable in the case of an adult with imprisonment' (Children and Young Persons Act, 1969).

The origins and present practice of such establishments is clearly rooted in ruling class fear of 'the dangerous classes', specifically 'control' of wayward adolescents and/or feckless parents. Joseph Fletcher, arguing for the adoption of 'Cottage Homes' in England in 1851, emphasized these points strenuously (Pinchbeck and Hewitt 1973, 525):

> Labour must be the staple of the poor man's training. To live is the first necessity ... and in all the best continental institutions for these classes, therefore, labour on the land and industry in the workshop is the first desideratum, religious and moral training on example realized in daily life the next.

As a consequence few radical thinkers have been able to conceptualize the possibility of developing progressive practice within these institutions. This reticence has been compounded by radical social work's concentration upon theoretical critiques steeped in labelling theory and varieties of marxist functionalism (Clarke 1979). Although of vital importance, these critiques have been preoccupied with theory rather than with developing usable practical knowledge. Moreover, their theoretical tools have often been very crude, relying too heavily on functionalist assumptions. One concept in particular, social control, has been over-utilized and symbolizes all these defects.

Case Con, the now defunct magazine for radical social workers, devoted one issue to residential care. This, as other issues, was liberally scattered with references to 'control' being exercised through social work services on behalf of the state. One example will suffice: it speaks of 'the integration of children's Homes into the overt deviant control process' (*Case Con* 21, 4). We could find many other examples that similarly accuse all social work practice, particularly in the field of child-care. Yet just what alternative exists — for children who cannot, or should not, live with their parents — that can avoid this accusation: adoption, indenture, slavery, foster-care, abandonment or infanticide? Social control has been given such a wide and vague application as a tool for analysis that it ends up as a useless, blunt instrument.

We should hardly be surprised that bourgeois state legislation will aim at protecting bourgeois institutions, but merely to point to the reactionary consequences of bourgeois social policy, as the use of this concept does, is unenlightening. It produces a mere pessimism of control (Clarke 1979) whereby everything is created by capital, and radical practice becomes impossible. This concept, in short, has absurdly circular consequences, as Gareth Stedman-Jones (1977, 164) points out:

> It is not difficult to demonstrate that a casual usage of 'social control' metaphors leads to non-explanation and incoherence. There is no practical or ideological institution which could not 'in some way' be interpreted as an agency of social control ... no indication of who the agents or instigators of social control may be: no indication of any common mechanism whereby social control is enforced: no constant criterion whereby we may judge whether social control has broken down ... since capitalism is still with us, we can with impunity suppose, if we wish to, that at any time 'in the last three hundred years, the mechanisms ·of social control were operating effectively.'

The supreme, irony, of course, is that radicals direct this elastic concept not only at social work institutions but at the family also (Wilson, 1977):

> ... the state looks to marriage and family life to calm the worker and turn him from a militant into a responsible worker.

Despite their crudeness such analyses do provide a stark recognition of how difficult it is to be a radical social worker. How *do* you advance the interests of the working class while being employed by the bourgeois state? Foremost one has to recognize the contradictory nature of welfare provision in capitalist societies — it must not be reduced, as so often, to policy that always aids and abets the interests of capital. Whilst this is relatively easy to appreciate for welfare provisions such as council housing or the health service, where working-class political action has imposed definite limitations or demands on capitalist development (structural impositions), such analyses are not so easy to apply in the field of child-care policy. So just how are we to avoid being part of the repressive state apparatus?

How do we practise radically? The essential point is to learn to practise 'the art of the seemingly impossible', to recognize that we are capable of struggling for ideological limitations to capitalist hegemony where at present there is no possibility of establishing real structural limitation. Perhaps we can best illustrate what this means for child-care practice by suggesting first what we do not mean by it. Another quotation from *Case Con* on residential work (Goldup 1976):

> Many people would argue that it is perfectly legitimate to remove a child into care for the protection of life and limb. I would agree — if the proper safeguards exist. But the conduct of most juvenile courts is so flabby in regard to the rules of evidence, the burden of proof, and the proper representation of the 'accused', that many children at the moment are being rushed into care aboard the baby-battering bandwagon, not because any properly constituted court would accept it as proven that the child was at risk, but to satisfy the paranoia of a locally eminent medical consultant or the press-phobia of a Director of Social Services. Many solicitors advise parents to accept charges of baby-battering based on the flimsiest evidence, in the hope that a kindly social worker will allow them to keep the child at home under a care order. It is not changes in the law, or its more stringent application, that will eliminate those situations in which people feel so trapped that they can find no better means of expressing or acting on their situation than assaulting their children. It will be changes in our society, in the values that arise from its distinctive way of organizing the production and distribution of wealth.

The assumptions implicit in this passage are quite discernible and superficially seductive to socialists. In the short run, care will be imposed for repressive reasons,[4] therefore it should be opposed.

4 Of course, we would not wish to deny that children are often taken into care for repressive reasons — over-reactions to delinquency by magistrates and social workers (Thorpe *et al.* 1979); paranoia over bad publicity about child-battering; mothers being convicted of prostitution etc. What we are suggesting, though, is that too many radical commentators automatically 'read' such

The article approvingly quotes the NCCL estimate that 70 per cent of children in community homes could be as successfully, or even more successfully, treated in the community.[5] In the long run though just as for Mothers in Action and so many others, there will be no problem and the revolution will magically sweep away unhappy people and unhappy children.

The only practical guidance such ideas can offer would-be radicals in residential care would be to resign, become a field-worker and 'keep families intact'. Romanticizing long-term goals results in a failure to generate anything other than defensive day-to-day objectives and then not in the field of residential work. Being content with such compromised, misplaced aims for the short term which offer the illusion of radicalism (the protection of children, the prevention of discrimination against working-class families etc.) such theory disguises an absence of long-term aims other than the millenium.

It is important to reiterate that if the challenge for the initial ideological limitation is to be successful there has to be constant attention to the long-term consequences of our action. If we seriously wish to see the eventual adoption of collectivist, socialized forms of child-care and the abolition of the nuclear family then our *present* practice must reflect this desire. Only in this way can we attempt to avoid the perennial reform/revolution dilemma — 'the choice between being "defined out" as irrelevant and "defined in" as undangerous' (Mathiesen 1974, 23). We have found Mathieson's concept of 'the unfinished' invaluable in this search, and this article is an attempt to adapt it to residential child care and the family (Mathieson, 16):

> ... the foreign and fully formed message is unfinished in the sense that it is outside the established — empirically tested and tried — system, but it is at the same time finished in the sense that its final consequences are clarified.

It is the lack of this kind of clarification that has proved such a stumbling block to the development of radical thought in the field of child-care.

repression into all situations where children end up in care. Care becomes unambiguously repressive; and this patently need *not* be the case.
5   For an excellent corrective to such community care euphoria, see Scull 1977.

Pursuing this concept of 'the unfinished' we are able to recognize that residential care, whilst being part of a system of repressive control, can also offer potentially fertile grounds for radical intervention. As Abigail Gooden argues in one of the more sensitive contributions to *Case Con* 21, *Residential Work* (p. 7):

> I still think, despite the bad experiences and consequent criticisms we have had, that residential care can be creative and holds the potential at least towards being a liberating force. If honestly and clearly accepted a kids' Home is an experiment in group living. This means among other things that it provides a variety of possible relationships quite outside the scope of the family and ideally it should be free from the backlog of conventional wisdom which states that 'little birds in their nest agree!' Not everyone likes other members of their families but it is easier to be honest about these dislikes once outside of its grip, and kids can learn to gain support from each other in discovering the complexities of relationships which contain good and bad. Furthermore, in living in close contact with a wide variety of adults, kids can gain a further assurance in validating their own feelings and emotions in discovering for instance other men, who are gentle and quiet, or women who are handy with a spanner and screwdriver. To make the group work will, however, mean we need to be absolutely honest in our assessment that a group is not a substitute 'home' in the conventional sense of the word and we drop such words as 'housemother' 'housefather' or worse still 'auntie' and 'uncle' and confront each other in cool honesty as a group of people.

This is our point entirely, and one we wish to develop in the rest of this paper.

One last clarification though. We are not advocating that field and residential workers should actively encourage the tearing of children from their mother's breast so as to develop collectivized mini-soviets. That would be absurd. We do recognize that the decisions which lead to children being removed from their parents often reflect middle-class child rearing standards. Our intentions are more limited. They re-emphasize the truth of most critical analyses of the family, that for many people their families are intolerable, and attempt to advocate residential care as a possible forum for the development of reasonable alternatives which could point the way to new forms of creative, collective living.

Before going on to look at the implications of this analysis for practice, it is vital at this stage to differentiate our approach from an existing one often regarded as so unconventional as to merit the designation 'radical'.

The liberal-therapeutic tradition

Our society has created the myth of the broken home which is the source of so many ills, and yet the unbroken home which ought to have broken is an even greater source of tension as I can attest from bitter experience.

G. Greer (1971)

In a sense residential care has not been without its radicals, strong sometimes charismatic individuals who for various reasons and on differing grounds have worked in ways which seem far removed from the common assumptions about alternative care. They have unquestionably tried to counteract the punitive, controlling and containing functions of residential living and have adopted a basically *therapeutic* approach. People like Wills (1941, 1947, 1965), Lyward (Burns 1956), Lennhoff (1960), Dockar-Drysdale (1968), Shaw (1965), Neil (1962) and more modern representatives like Balbernie (1966) and Wills (1965) are the most notable of this amorphous grouping. All, except at the moment Balbernie, have worked in the private sector: the much more extensive residential provisions provided by the local authorities have not produced comparable personalities. For this reason, and others, they have attained a high degree of independence which has actually threatened their influence. They are easily regarded as detached and isolated personalities with nothing relevant to say to the 'mainstream'. This is sustained by the strong idealistic element in their work and ideas.

David Wills, in our opinion the most important and politically significant of them, is a Quaker. From this he derives the principle that if you treat people with love and respect, share responsibility with them and regard them as intelligent they will become more 'complete' and sensible. There is in all this a basic principle of responsibility towards, and accountability to, the 'living community'. Once this is established it is assumed that it can be transferred to society as a whole because it becomes internalized. Consequently he adopts an approach in which each individual is cherished in his individuality and encouraged in his responsibility to others. This is in marked contrast to the unthinking and debilitating conformism which seems so often to be the tacit objective of much residential care.

Wills realizes that the problems of the young people he has lived with largely result from social misfortune or overt inequality. At the beginning of the honest and touching book *The Hawkspur Experiment* (Wills 1941, 7) he explains that the Q camps, effectively the first unconventional units for young people in this country, were:

> for training in a free environment on sympathetic and individual lines, young people who — mainly through environmental causes — present difficulties in social adjustment or have been in unfortunate circumstances (whether or not they are actual law-breakers).

Despite society being seen as the origin of the problem the individual is expected in the alternative environment to cope with the results. In other words, the problem is seen in the *consequences* rather than the *causes*. The deprived respond to their circumstances in a certain way, they have problems in 'social adjustment'. It is to counteract these effects that compensatory or therapeutic experiences are provided. Thus the deprived are offered in retrospect some of the advantages of everyone else. Adjustment is not however seen as an end in itself but as a necessary precondition for obtaining the key to personal integrity. It seems that one does not have to be enamoured of one's lot in order to derive benefit from it. This evokes the image of industrial workers rushing each day from plant they neither own nor control; they have completed their routine and repetitive tasks in a state of alienation approaching anaesthesia, but once the day is over they are free. They return to some significance, to the home, the family, the pigeon loft, the pub and maybe even a holiday in Majorca. Work makes this possible, it is not pleasant or enjoyable or invigorating but it is necessary. This might explain why the pacifist Wills is able to approve, or at least not explicitly disapprove, of the decision of some of his boys to become soldiers.

The overwhelming concentration upon the individual and his or her problems is a major feature of the work of the liberal therapists, and leads to a number of shortcomings. Firstly, the units they have created are idiosyncratic — which is not to make the usual objection that they are entirely dependent upon the charisma of their founders. That trivial notion has been shown to be false. It remains the case, however, that such establishments are special and their methods only to a very limited extent generalizable. Secondly, there is the problem of effectively detaching the individual from the social. Once the social genesis is described it is then ignored. The development of the individual then becomes a process of differentiation which must culminate either in social absorption or alienation. By attempting to remain neutral about the conditions that exist in the wider society they end up tacitly supporting it. The failure to confront this issue leads to a myopic view of society seeing the individual as necessarily alienated from the social. This imposed antagonism between personal needs and social possibilities is the very essence of the competitive individualism demanded by the capitalist mode of production. It is necessary for the socialist to be constantly reminded of the principle attributed to Hegel by Marcuse (1941) that 'the facts in themselves possess no authority.' In the end the liberal therapists accept not just the reality but also the *truth* of the consequences of a form of society of which they are tacitly critical. For them it is better to survive than be submerged. We feel, however, that residential care has the possibility of going beyond the question of survival of developing potentialities which will be remembered under a non-repressive form of social organization (Jacoby 1977).

The family is expected to produce the individual meek and compliant, repressed and exhausted, realistic and conforming. The transient struggles of the child against parental authority culminate in the required result, reinforced by the subsidiary institutions of child indoctrination, particularly the schools. The liberal therapists have demonstrated, although not conclusively, that it is possible to counter some of the more repressive features of child-rearing under capitalism. Their work has taken place outside the family and thus stands as a possible reproach to it. It is unfortunate that the critique of family life implicit in this work has never been systematized, or even noticed, which has resulted in many of the lessons which might have been drawn remaining obscure. We do not wish to evade the issue by implying that the only way the radical can function is to formulate theory and wait for the revolution. It must always be borne in mind, however, that the reality principle will continue to operate, this being defined as the historically-conditioned form described by Marcuse (1969) as the 'performance principle'. Of course residential establishments should not set themselves up as bases of sanity in a sick society and effectively ignore what is going on beyond their gates. Young people who have lived in alternative environments will still have to join a society based upon crude competition and obsessional individualism. It is not necessary however to compound the error of the liberal-therapists of validating the social system by assuming either its necessity or its inevitability.

The principle of much established residential care has been to enforce strict conformity to the demands, practical and ideological, of the social structure. This is sometimes produced in a confused and confusing manner, but the reactionary implications are very clear. Take this excerpt from a statement about the aims of a community home with education (Programme for the Carlton School Fete, 1978):

> The aim is to help each boy to overcome the deprivation which caused his admission, to develop his full potential and grow in responsibility, so that he can fulfil his own needs in society without depriving others of the ability to fulfil their needs. A positive, caring and friendly atmosphere is basic to the method of developing relationships.

It is incredible to believe that by being placed in residential care the boy is able to overcome the deprivation which brought him there. Such deprivation is socially constructed and perpetuated. If he is helpless in any direction it is that one. The problem of course is that such ideas convert the social reality of deprivation into an inner state. Again cause and effect become ideologically obfuscated. Much the same could be said of the concept of 'need'. We all experience different sorts of needs but their legitimacy is socially determined. It is your position in the class structure which determines the needs you may have, and the authors of this programme are *incapable* of recognizing this. The unconscious double-think implicit in the statement is, to some extent, due to the crude appropriation of some of the ideas provided by the liberal therapists. Care is seen as a method of enforcing conformity, not just to prevailing social conditions, but to the dominant ideology. This is not advocated by the liberal therapists but their interminable formulations do nothing to prevent its occurrence. This is because they are reactive rather than politically conscious radicals: their radicalism is a state of mind, idiosyncratic and individualistic. It has nowhere to go so it ends up firmly rooted in the only reality available — the existing one. Thus is their challenge tamed and their practice made acceptable, if not quite respectable.

By now it should be apparent that we believe residential child care can transcend the limitations we have attributed to the liberal-therapists and be developed as a vital crucible for testing the political possibilities of alternative forms of care.

How is it to be done?

When it's a notion
When it's still vague
It is praised
When it looks big
When plans are in motion
Objections are raised.

Bertolt Brecht

We intend to locate our discussion of how to do radical residential work around a pamphlet by the Socialist Child Care Collective (1975). This document is within the current we have described as socialist feminist. It contains a list of aims for a children's community day-care centre in Camden. With some modifications and developments we think it could be applied most effectively in residential care. Our only disagreement with the document as a whole reflects our earlier critique of the various radical currents and their failure to confront the crucial, determining feature of bourgeois family life, the privatized reproduction of labour power. The Camden collective ignores this question to such an extent that they are able to describe China and Cuba, where admittedly there exists a more advanced development of *day-care* facilities, as two examples of cultures practising socialist child-care (3). This is at best premature and at worst absurdly reactionary.[6] Leaving this aside, however, the aims they outline are to: 1. challenge competition and individualism; 2. to develop group awareness and interdependence; 3. to build up self-confidence and interdependence of each child so that they can take a full part in the group; 4. to break down hierarchies; 5. to challenge the domination of the weak by the strong; 6. to break down stereotyped sex roles; 7. to develop warm emotional relationships not exclusive to the nuclear family; 8. to develop an understanding of political questions.

For some reason they ignore the combating of racism; we would certainly wish to include it. We are of course wary of producing blueprints for the practice of others. All the advice contained here could be rejected simply because some detail cannot be made to apply in particular circumstances. However, we will make some fairly general points about some of the issues which are likely to accompany any attempt to implement these principles.

First an earlier argument must be expanded. One of the major contributions of Freud to psychology was his discovery of the 'reality principle'. This is not fixed or unchangeable, it simply means that the circumstances in which life has to be lived and the context in which choices have to be made is realistically apprehended. As well as understanding the irrational links which bind the individual to the early childhood past, it would be as well to take account also of the equally irrational and capricious world in which people are forced to live.

We do not wish therefore to avoid the pervasive effects of the existing reality principle. Children leaving a children's home, for example, must have some regard for the problem of making a living — namely they will have to join the world of toil or of the dole. It would be wrong to falsify that reality by producing a rarefied environment which does not take this into account (Socialism in one Children's Home). Children have to face the effects of a discriminatory society conditioning many of the

6   There is ample evidence to suggest that the mass expansion of women into the labour force in China, particularly, has as much to do with the primitive accumulation of capital as with concern for sexual equality. (Harris 1978). There is also evidence to the effect that women are used as a reserve labour army (Davin 1976), through sporadic campaigns such as the 'Let's be pretty' campaign (1955) and the new socialist housewife campaign (1957).

problems which face them. It is important that in any discussion with the children the political implications are not avoided (point 8).

It is necessary, in particular, to examine the central problem of authority. Children and staff enter the Home by very different routes and are subject to different structures of control. It is unrealistic to pretend that some sort of absolute democracy is possible. In fact if it is true that reality must always be borne in mind it is necessary for the inequality of the situation not to be falsified. It must be negotiated. In a large children's home it was clear that mealtimes and bedtimes had become a source of irritation and confrontation. When this was discussed the staff argued that if these basics did not exist children would behave irresponsibly and stay up until all hours. The children advanced the view that 'things would sort themselves out' and that a trial period could be allowed to test it. For a few days the place was *chaotic*, but it settled down and alternative ways of having meals and going to bed were developed to the mutual benefit of children and staff. Concessions had to be made on both sides but the creative nature of the experience was stimulating.

That is not to imply that it is always possible for children to do everything they might want to: the group may wish to put limits on behaviour and the adults may wish to protect the interests of a minority by insisting upon a certain course of action. This may be uncomfortable, but at least it does not falsify reality or lead to the subtle manipulation of power which in the end is put beyond challenge. Children should have a comprehensive understanding of the circumstances under which their home is required to function. This can be used to help them appreciate how institutions, of whatever scale, actually function. It might also be pointed out that, as Marcuse (1969) has said, there are some forms of control which are not repressive, which may indeed be the opposite. If a child is taught the reality of crossing the road and instructed in the proper drill that is far from repressive and may even be seen as liberating. All too often this simple and pragmatic approach to reality is replaced by the attempt of adults to impose the conditions of their own guilt and anxiety (of their repression) on the children. Another of the possibilities of residential care should be to release children from artificial restraints upon the spontaneous expression of feeling. Repressed feelings are often accompanied by guilt and anxiety from which may come hostility, defiance and even violence. It is interesting to note that it is often people called 'mentally handicapped' who show a direct concern for and intuitive understanding of the needs of others as well as being able to openly express their own feelings. Possibly that is why the 'normal' and 'reasonable' find them so embarrassing and shocking — their responses go beyond the institutionalized constraints of the public super-ego. Perhaps that is also why crash programmes of highly efficient techniques are applied to them through the anti-psychology of behaviour modification. Even they must be infected with the ethic of toil despite only the most meaningless tasks being available to them. To make a more general point it is often the case that the work ethic is imposed as the whole basis of reality. This is expressed in the slogan 'Play is children's work.' The main casualty here is imagination, a term nearly always used with a pejorative implication in our culture. Nothing threatens the established reality principle as much as this. It is imagination which comes into contact with the instincts, with a dimly-remembered past which might light the hope of a non-repressive future.

So we see residential child-care as providing alternative experiences which challenge the immutability of present social forms but which at the same time do not run away from the reality the children will have to face. What are sometimes known as 'enlightened child-care principles' often pay scant regard to reality. In a small hostel a group of teenage girls lived with a group of staff who subscribed to just such principles. They paid a lot of attention to the girls, listened to them and encouraged them to make allowances for each other. Gradually they established an environment based upon trust and mutual responsibility. Yet most of them were destined to work in the local pie factory, an institution of such primeval nastiness, of ruthless competition, that any but the most aggressive found survival impossible. Often such idealized care is used to validate personal hypotheses or to satisfy staff needs; but it is not helpful to a person who has to add to the unremitting hostility of the outside world the fact of having been brought up in an alternative way.

This is particularly important for the growing number of black children living in Homes. A black child recently came back to the residential nursery where he lived to ask the matron why she had never told him he was black. This sensible woman was genuinely perplexed and pointed out that he saw himself in the mirror every day. She had not taken account of the fact that such a perception is political. Around him all the time he saw differences which did not seem to make any difference. But when other children in the school, no doubt indoctrinated into accepting the discriminatory values of their families, applied their racist principles the child was shocked and confused. In another home a group of black children have formed themselves into a special association. They spend a lot of time together, eat at the same table and are involved in what would be called 'consciousness raising' or 'solidarity' groups. They had not heard of such terms until a politically conscious member of staff explained them. This was not a challenge to equality within the home but a recognition of the special needs of some groups who encounter special problems. Perhaps we will also see similar groups forming amongst girls and homosexuals. It might be said that this example is taken from a fairly conventional children's home, which indicates that the potentialities are considerable.

This last example highlights the importance we attach to the practice of conscientization, or liberating education (Freire 1972, Alfero 1972, Leonard 1975) in residential work. We must resist children in care being led to understand the world through fatalistic experiences; of being persuaded they are always victims of cycles of deprivation and/or feckless parenting. The children must be provided with dialogues and information that can allow them to develop a critical consciousness. A useful example is the type of discussion that should be encouraged around children getting into trouble with the police. Serious attempts should be made to explore with the children why working-class urban areas are 'policed' more regularly and heavily than middle-class areas; why lower-working-class and black children are over-represented in the crime figures (Box 1971); the nature of those figures and why society tends to have periodic moral panics about youthful working-class behaviour (Cohen 1973, Hall *et al.* 1978). Such dialogues could be truly radical by providing the children with critical and alternative information on many issues.

We have not looked in detail at all the aims proposed by the Camden Collective — many of them are self-explanatory — but it is very important for those who wish to implement these principles to think about them very carefully. Nothing is worse than the imposition of half-baked ideas upon children. We have merely tried to give the flavour of what it might be like to do radical residential work.

Implications for policy

Before going on to discuss the implications of our analysis for policy we must enter a caveat. Social services departments and other established agencies are hardly likely to concede genuinely radical demands. Remembering the concept of 'the unfinished', it is however possible to suggest a number of limited changes for which it is essential to agitate. These would include:

The politicization of staff

There are a number of groups working in social services whose work is essentially unprestigious: home-helps, foster-parents and childminders are included amongst these as well as residential workers. In passing it might be noticed that they perform tasks normally undertaken by women in the family — tasks which almost be definition are culturally regarded as not requiring skill, i.e. can be done by anyone. Such groups lack status and kudos, are poorly paid, badly organized and of course exploited. So it is vitally important that residential workers should be unionized (that is, join NALGO) — very few have done so at the moment. We entertain no reformist illusions about trade unions under capitalism (Clarke and Clements 1977) but they do provide the *only* vehicle for the necessary struggle to improve conditions of service, abolish emoluments, provide parity of salary with other social workers and establish a comparable career structure.

The conscientization of staff

The conservative orientation of many residential workers, rooted as we have noted in the punitive legacy of orphanages, prisons and lunatic asylums is reinforced by their isolation. It is necessary to bring workers together so that they can explore and examine their experiences and begin to be less defensive about their practice. When you are isolated and feel yourself beleaguered it is not surprising if you feel compelled to defend what you do. Residential work will never become critical, and thus improve the chances for change, until this has happened.

'Positive discrimination' in training

This will necessitate establishing the right of all residential workers to have priority over field-workers in obtaining admission to CQSW (Certificate of Qualification in Social Work) courses (this is very important because of the discrepancy in the numbers of residential workers who are trained compared to other social workers). At present only about 12 per cent of residential staff hold a residential work qualification.

There must be a total rejection of the duplicity and hypocrisy of CCETSW (Central Council for Education and Training in Social Work) for introducing, against a veritable cacophony of protest, the CSS (Certificate of Social Service) which was ostensibly intended for those occupations 'ancillary to social work' but which has become a second-class training almost exclusively for residential workers. Residential work is social work and the appropriate qualification is CQSW. This may require the setting up of part-time qualifying courses for residential workers who cannot get away from home to attend full-time courses.

Fighting closures

Socialists have been active over this decade of savage cuts in welfare expenditure in defending the 'gains' of the welfare state. Yet those socialists who have been prepared to be active in defending day nurseries, hospitals and libraries have been reluctant to combat the closure of children's homes. This is a mistake, and the recent example of children and staff at the Kingsthorpe Home in Woodford, Essex of refusing to vacate their home and channelling their case through NALGO should be applauded (Turner 1978). As should the children in the care of Birmingham Council who have set up a defence committee, Rights for Children in Care (Blackmore 1979), to resist the selling of homes and fight for wider rights.

Fighting stigmatization

Currently the decision to place a child in residential care implies that for one reason or another he has failed in or been failed by the working-class family. It is in this context that radicals have often argued that the removal of a child into care is dominated by the imposition of middle-class standards. All too often this is the case. But such reactions obscure much of the good work that goes on in residential institutions and begs many of the questions we have attempted to raise in our article.

It is important to remember that the privileged classes pay to send their children to institutions that deliberately design regimes every bit as uniform and rigid as the worst children's home. The Dartington Research Unit (Lambert and Millham 1968, Millham *et al.* 1975 a and b) have drawn our attention to the harsh, repressive style of life prevalent in many preparatory and public schools. Phillips (1977, 493) cites some of the unit's research which indicates that 16 per cent of the children in such schools come from disturbed homes. This research concludes:

> Many ordinary boarding schools face the sorts of problems we associate with disturbed adolescents: exaggerated, attention-seeking behaviour, temper tantrums, absconding, deviant and promiscuous sexual behaviour, failure to achieve, extreme withdrawal and violence.

Families who send their children to such schools, far from being considered suitable cases for social work, are held in high regard. Indeed, it might be argued that the major difference between our children in boarding schools and children's homes is that the latter feel deprived for not having two caring parents, whereas the former are led to feel privileged for being packed off deliberately into institutional care by such parents. The absolutist standard that our culture uses to judge successful socialization — the necessary presence of two loving parents — which so affect the self-development of children in children's homes, appears to be somewhat tergiversating when judged in this way.

Social workers must be more prepared to challenge the stigma that pervades the practice of residential child care, allowing periods spent in residential communities to be seen as a normal part of the experiences helpful to growth.

Standards and supervision

In her article *Homes for children* (1977) Phillips also correctly draws attention to the 9000 children in England and Wales who are cared for in private (as opposed to voluntary) homes. This compares with a total number of 40,800 in residential accommodation (in 1976). Whereas with voluntary homes there is a local authority power of inspection, no such access exists for the private sector which, by definition, operates essentially to make profits. The Department of Health and Social Security does have this right but it is obviously difficult to exercise. As we have said earlier, a great deal of the pioneering work in alternative care has been within the private and voluntary sector and it would be pointless to curtail it in the short run, despite our obvious desire to see all provision eventually publicly owned and democratically controlled.

It is however a matter for concern that an unspecified number of private homes escape inspection. But we must remember that the quality of care provided in many local authority homes is poor, despite compulsory inspection. Overt physical damage is probably minimized by such formal checking — e.g. investigating the diet, fire and punishment books — but little else. An adequate solution to this question therefore involves more than the necessary extension of the existing inspection procedures to the private sector. It requires attention to the general quality of care throughout the services. This is as difficult to define as it is to legislate for, and we must not be unrealistic in thinking that much more than minimum standards can be assured. But it is worth attempting, and difficulty of itself is not a justification for avoidance.

Whilst we would like to see a much more dynamic approach to residential care, the business of imposing minimum standards is important. We realize, however, that some of the most satisfactory developments in child care would not have happened had they been judged by the standards of the time. It is difficult to specify and recognize unacceptable standards and it raises wider issues like training, professional status, salary and conditions of service, staffing levels etc. It should be the job of the local authority social service departments to ensure that minimum standards are applied throughout the service. At the same time, staff should be encouraged and supported in developing new styles of care. This would mean that the common practice of combining the roles of line manager and staff support should cease. It is useful for the care staff and those who support them to engage in the struggle to raise standards and conditions. It is impossible to do this if the person who is supposed to be supporting you is also the one whose other function is to inhibit change.

So, whilst Phillips is correct to raise the issue of the immunity of private homes from inspection and control, wider and more intractable problems are raised by it. In our opinion radical residential workers should not be chary of joining the debate about standards of care, by contributing to Committee on Professional Standards of the Residential Care Association.

Social control revisited?

In the same article Phillips (1977, 493) points to another important issue: the confusion which often besets the declaration of the purposes of a home:

> The trouble is that there are not enough suitable places. As a result children tend to be inappropriately placed, causing the homes' functions to become confused. Are they to punish, contain, control or rehabilitate?

In this she may be accused of being somewhat optimistic. The vast majority of residential establishments today suffer no such confusion. Their clear, if unadmitted, role is to 'punish, contain, control', and that is the end of the matter.

Of course the whole business of posing objectives in this oppositional and mutually exclusive way is that it understates the enormous complexity of the residential task. Elements of control and containment, and even of punishment, will exist as a normal part of any social grouping. But the question is wider than this and involves the overall objective of care. With increased bureaucratic control of residential care the emphasis has moved from a broad definition of the needs of the child to a narrow insistence upon the control of immediate behavioural manifestations. The social and personal history which has created the situation is largely ignored, and for the future all that can be offered is *survival*. Conform now, survive later. This is a most negative and debilitating way of looking at things. But it is easy to see how public pressure and media interference leads to this response. *The Guardian* (Phillips 1979) reports that a county council was found to have exercised insufficient control over a child of 12 who slipped out of the house and did damage to a local church. The council became liable for a sum of £99,000. Mr Justice Forbes is reported to have said:

> The boy must have walked out of the home at a time when all four of the permanent staff were on duty. I am satisfied that closer observation would have prevented him from walking out as he did.

Apart from its total lack of understanding of what such close observation would mean in terms simply of organization, this statement also implies quite unequivocally that supervision must be total. So once more the pressure is in the direction of increased control and a denial of the difficult process under which the child may more clearly understand his/her predicament and make choices about the future. All the signs are in the direction of closing up the system; and this is reflected in the growing number of secure units, often disguised by euphemisms such as 'intensive care units.'

Moral panics and secure accommodation

The last decade has certainly witnessed a steady growth in the demand for secure accommodation in Community Home (CHEs) and Observation and Assessment (O and A) Centres. It is difficult to establish exact numbers, but we can compare divergent figures from alternative sources. The Regional Plans of the DHSS, presumably a reliable source, estimated in 1978 that there were 202 places in O and A Centres and 214 in CHEs (Taylor, forthcoming). Yet in March 1975 the DHSS had established the 'need' for 673 secure places based on local authority bids for a sum of £5 millions made available for such provision in a speech by David Owen, the then Deputy Minister at the DHSS. A recent Howard League pamphlet, *Unruly children in a human context* (1977) estimated that there are plans for nearly 1000 *new* secure accommodation places in the child care system over the next few years.

Whilst the figures may be vague, the general trend of an increasing demand for secure accommodation is well established. Such agitation must be seen in the context of the general right-wing attack by authoritative organizations on the limited advances made by social welfare and social democratic ideology in the post war period (Hall *et al*. 1978, Taylor, forthcoming). For our concerns this attack has been directed at the alleged treatment-oriented excesses of the Children and Young Persons Act of 1969. The police and magistracy, in particular, have mercilessly criticized this piece of legislation and provided countless titbits for the popular press about the so-called rising tide of juvenile crime. Countless headlines such as 'Police have hands tied behind backs' and 'Youths laugh up sleeves at magistrates' have contributed to a growing fear of violent youth. This clamouring was reinforced by events such as the National Association of Schoolmasters' dubious survey in 1972 attempting to demonstrate 'the grim reality of violence in our schools' (*The Sunday Times*, 21 October 1972).

In general, social workers' response to this debate has been ambivalent, often conceding that there has been the growth of a disruptive youthful minority. There is no better illustration of this allegation than the concessions that social and residential workers have made to the arguments for secure units. They have been, at best, accommodative with some distrust and unease but little systematic argument and, at worst, capitulatory.

Hoghughi (1978) argues that there is a pathological minority in the open CHE and School system of about 10-15 per cent which cannot be dealt with in the system. He therefore enters into a general defence of closed units such as the one for which he is responsible for, Aycliffe School, in the following terms (61):

The secure house would not be needed were it not for the 'inadequacies' of our present care system. However, it would betray a particularly unsophisticated view of the workings of a complex society such as ours to suggest that we would *ever* reach a point of adequacy to give ... the kind of specialized help such problematic children need. Almost all of the factors we have isolated as being associated with these children's disturbances are on the increase at a rate and in a manner disproportionate to the increase in our society's resources. [Our emphasis]

This is a particularly negative position to have reached and one that does not even allow for 'liberal' social criticism. If one of the defects of the present system is that the state fails to provide adequate resources in manpower, buildings, money etc., it is surely possible to argue that it must do so. To state that the problem will increase no matter what we do is to accept the continuation, even necessity, of existing social forms. Of course, we would argue that capitalism *is* unlikely to make available the provision which is required. This is a fundamental criticism of that society. We should not, however, sit back behind the traditional, conservative defence of inevitability. For even if the problem is inevitable — which we doubt — the ways available for dealing with it never are. It is intolerable to think that the only thing we can do is lock children up in mini-prisons.

Recently certain DHSS 'design recommendations' for secure units were leaked to *The Guardian* (8 August 1978). These suggest that such units should have sheet steel facings on bedroom doors, observation panels to enable staff to look into bedrooms and exercise yards with walls 13 feet high. Foucault's (1977) 'carceral city' with its thousand small theatres of endless, calculated, rational punishment comes ever closer. Social and residential workers must not make concessions in their practice or theory to arguments that only serve to give credibility to the worst excesses of the periodic, reactionary moral panics about youth; and radical social workers must strive to organize to resist the steady growth of secure accommodation.

Growing out of care?

Perhaps the most tangible issue radicals need to tackle immediately is the appalling lack of provision for children having to leave long-term care at 18. A well-informed guess from the Director of Social Services for Devon estimated that 60 children a week are in this position. Activity should be directed towards demanding that local authorities provide group homes where there would be a gradual reduction of supervision, working towards total independence. The benefits of collective living could continue to be built on, if the children desired.

Again we have been cautious about producing explicit guidelines for practice. Our article will have achieved its purpose if it merely allows practitioners to recognize, and radicals to concede, the possibility of radical residential work whatever the specific implications for practice.

Conclusion

Socialists talk a great deal about alternatives of child rearing, but this often means no more than that they indulge their own children in a slightly different way. What they have failed or are unwilling to notice is that a forum of care amenable to socialist principles is right under their noses. We have tried to argue that residential care is not a 'non-starter' as a potential arena for radical practice: on the contrary, it contains all sorts of hidden and dangerous possibilities for the bourgeois social fabric, but surreptitiously, like the Trojan Horse.

We would like to thank Sarah McCabe and Stuart Bentley for their advice in the preparation of this paper. Neither are, or would probably wish to be, responsible for the content. We should also like to thank Ian Taylor for letting us use his material on secure accommodation.

Postscript

This chapter was completed some twelve months ago and we feel it is important to point out that there have been important additions to the literature since that time. We wish to draw your attention to the contributions made by M. Hoyles (ed.) *Changing Childhood* (Winters and Readers, London 1979) and H. Jones *The Residential Community* (Routledge & Kegan Paul, London 1978). Moreover we feel it important to stress how the socialist feminist current in the Women's Movement has grown and developed since the paper was written.

6

Radical practice in probation
Bruce Hugman

This chapter is written for those who, like me, are struggling to find some practical expression of their political commitment and personal philosophy in their daily work as probation officers. It is an important enterprise because few practical guidelines have emerged from the extensive radical analyses of recent years; but it is also a hazardous one, because it is likely to fall so far short of the apparent promise of radical theory. What I hope it will offer is a starting point for changed practice and for the development of more coherent programmes.

I write from the position of one much persuaded by the insights of marxist analysis, but nevertheless committed to democratic solutions. Consequently, I risk the obloquy of the far left, but hope to make useful sense to the substantial numbers of social democrats who are looking for ways of expressing their political commitment through their work.

I shall take as read radical analyses of society and of the criminal justice system which see the interests of class and wealth as central to existing structures, and the establishment of the rights and interests of the great majority as the principal goal of socialist transformation.

Definitions

I shall talk both of 'radical' and 'socialist' action and must, therefore, distinguish between their commonly confused meanings.

The word 'radical' describes people, policies or action which illuminate, penetrate or activate the roots or fundamentals of individual or social life. While it is certain that definitions of those roots or fundamentals must derive from a political position, 'radical' itself is a politically neutral word. (In the 1979 election campaign the Tories — accurately — described some of their policies as radical.)* 'Radical' as applied to social work is usually an ellipsis for social work analysis and practice informed by a commitment to marxism or social democratic principles. It is an unhelpful abbreviation because it deprives us of the distinctions between radical socialism and its other more or less active or inert forms; and between the *quality* of action, and its purposes.

The left-wing radical is one who strives to understand and act in ways which are not defined by conventional wisdom or practice; who is alert to latent as well as apparent meanings; who sees in individual instances the manifestations of general rules or wider structures; who rejects the deluding comforts of simple schemes or generalized prescriptions; who recognizes the complexities and contradictions of human society yet is not made impotent by them; s/he is creative and original; s/he is not necessarily a revolutionary, though the revolutionary will certainly possess many of the attributes of a radical.

The most truly radical stance may be that of resisting long-term commitment to a view, an analysis, an ideology altogether: it may be remaining faithful to certain fundamental values without rigid prejudice as to the details of the means or ends through which they may be most nearly fulfilled.

A socialist is a person committed to building a society in which the control and administration of all resources are communally exercised in the interests of the community as a whole. Marxists and social democrats share this ideal, though their analyses of present society may, and their means to the achievement of the ideal certainly do, differ.

From this discussion it is possible to see how an individual may adopt a radical stance which, at first, or in the longer term, does not imply a particular political philosophy: a determination to examine fundamental issues does not necessarily lead to socialist conclusions — though I and others might see them as the most suggestive and hopeful that we have. But the adoption of a radical disposition is essential, in the first place, to knowing and under-

*See note at end of chapter.

standing the world more clearly, and in the second to the development of an authentic, responsible personal and political philosophy; radical purposes expressed through action, can emerge only through such a commitment.

One of the problems of words such as these, and the ideals they embody, is the extent to which they encourage an other-worldliness of thought, and suggest 'pure' solutions. Ideological purity can exist only in the mind, and ultimately its pursuit can lead only to withdrawal from society, to say nothing of withdrawal from the probation service.

The existence of the world is essentially dependent on the concurrent and consecutive interaction and balance of opposites, which produce a sense of relative stability within a large and inevitable process of change. It is a world of processes, not absolutes, in which the elements of contradictions engage to produce new arrangements and new contradictions. Every 'solution' brings with it new problems; every 'good' is measured against some concept of 'bad'; every redress of balance brings an imbalance elsewhere. These ideas hold good for the smallest details of one's personal life as well as for international issues and even for the physical reality of the universe.

Engagement

In the pursuit of ideals, one can choose to operate by engaging in the complex interactions of social life, or by exhorting or coercing from outside them. In my view, engagement with them is the only practical, effective and just way forward.

Alinsky — that tough, effective and amusing radical — writes convincingly of the strategies essential to realistic socialist radicalism:

> As an organizer I start from where the world is, as it is, and not as I would like it to be. That we accept the world as it is does not in any sense weaken our desire to change it into what we believe it should be — it is necessary to begin where the world is if we are going to change it to what we think it should be. That means working in the system.
>
> There's another reason for working inside the system. Dostoevski said that taking a new step is what people fear

most. Any revolutionary change must be preceded by a passive, affirmative, non-challenging attitude toward change among the mass of our people. They must feel so frustrated, so defeated, so lost, so futureless in the prevailing system that they are willing to let go of the past and chance the future. This acceptance is the reformation essential to any revolution.

(Alinsky 1972)

There are times when being a left-wing probation officer or social worker feels like being in a position of implacable contradiction: if one's analyses of society and of the statutory services within it are pushed far enough, hope for substantial change seems an idle delusion. My anger, my energy, my impatience cannot tolerate the slow and painstaking and painful path forward. And yet I also know that, short of coercion or tyranny, there is no other way to pursue, in action, the idea of a transformed society. I do not know what kinds of revolutions will be possible (though I know what kinds of revolutions I would like), but I work in the belief that the world can be transformed only when the vast majority of its population come to realize both their strength and their true interest.

To this transformation I suspect that professionals in the welfare and statutory services can make only a small contribution through their work, and are very unlikely ever to spearhead any major change. The utopian promise of community work has long faded, and while much locally useful work has been and is being done, we can no longer expect the new age to arrive if only more projects were begun. Professionals simply do not have the influence or muscle to initiate or precipitate major changes. The briefest glance at the political work of Jack Mundey and the Australian Builders' Labourers' Federation, for example, puts welfare and professional efforts into a profound shadow (see Curno 1978, 199-218).

But this is no cause for despair. Many utopian schemes are based on the notion of sudden changes in consciousness, of a 'new dawn' breaking dramatically on the world; but there is no evidence that such things ever have happened, or will happen. Indeed, the most significant change and learning for most people is a haphazard, gradual process: we can make it less haphazard, but probably cannot alter the processes of assimilation, accommodation, reorientation which must be parts of fundamental personal and social change. If there are enough energetic people talking, working, organizing as far as possible on their socialist principles, then we may hope for a time when such principles become the assured property of our general political and social life. If we initiate, support and encourage activities based on such principles, through conflict or negotiation, and through the forming of widely-based alliances with others who share our hopes, a climate for more radical change may well be brought about.

In relation to community work, Jim Radford makes some remarks which apply equally to the Probation Service:

> ... if we want to think of ourselves as revolutionaries we must accept that ours is a piecemeal revolution that must be built step by step, and that must convert and carry people with it at each stage. (Curno 1978, 111)

The political nature of welfare

The myth that only the left brings the dirt and danger of politics into any sphere of activity dies hard: those who espouse the values of the status quo rarely see their commitment as political, or recognize the inherent militancy of their positions. Nor is it commonly recognized that daily decisions about agency procedures or methods of work derive, not from neutral principles based on objective truth, but on political interpretations of the world and identifiable political purposes. They are, consequently, open for challenge and discussion, and subject to the scrutiny of reason.

It is often implied or argued in the service that helping individuals in need is not a political act. While it is not exclusively so, it is nevertheless based on an implied or explicit commitment to how the world is or should be, and the nature of the act and its consequences have effects which are political: they confirm or challenge the existing distribution of power, the allocation of resources, definitions of human behaviour, and so on. And, further, they take place within a context that is essentially political. It is a delusion to retreat into liberal, humanitarian notions which isolate such encounters from their wider social and political meanings.

That the service is enmeshed in the political reality of the world can hardly be denied:

The Probation and After-Care Service is an arm of the state —
it is given a job to do, and, by and large it does it. Probation
Officers do not like being reminded of this ... but when we try
to ignore this simple fact, we often appear vague and precious,
creating a mystifying wonderland where 'professional' values
and judgements flourish without political constraints. The
Probation Service cannot be viewed in isolation from the
society which it serves and it is surely not a body which could
conceivably possess or operate a discrete philosophy of its
own.   (Beaumont 1976)

Acceptance of this position roots us firmly in the contradictions
of the real world and allows us to make sense and use of what
might otherwise seem to be insuperable difficulties.

Politics and the probation service

This is a particularly fertile time for the energizing and politici-
zing of the service: many of the old certainties have collapsed and
we can no longer speak with any confidence of the 'effectiveness'
of the service's activities, except in symbolic or economic or negative terms (good enough bases for its existence though these may
be). In terms of its function within the criminal justice system, the
question of its credibility, other than as a bureaucratic servicing
organization, is already being raised (see Croft 1978, for
example). Not surprisingly, this has led to considerable demorali-
zation within the service, and it is very possible that we are
approaching a time when officers will feel 'so frustrated, so
defeated, so lost, so futureless in the prevailing system that they
are willing to let go of the past and chance the future.'

There is no doubt that there is much purposelessness and dis-
content in the service, and that there is great hope in the
possibility of collective acknowledgement of this and a collective
determination to develop new thinking and practice within the
work as it is now, and towards the nature of the service as it might
be. Some of the frustration and difficulty arise from the
irresistible contradictions of the job, but many arise from
absurdities remediable through individual and collective action.
The union — lately professional association — is clearly a
potentially powerful body through which to work for both minor

and major change. Its relative ineffectiveness over the years, especially in matters of penal policy and service development, is indicative of the power of its conservative roots expressed in a reactive rather than an initiatory disposition. That can be changed by an active, participating, imaginative membership, and there are signs that such changes are slowly afoot.

It is only recently that any number of members of the service has begun to develop an active political consciousness, and that probation officers have been seriously examining the political potential of their roles. It is only recently that the union has begun to take action on social and penal policy issues, salaries, alliances with other groups, and structure and practice issues in the service with any degree of political purposefulness or commitment.

Current policies, for example, for the pursuit of the '£6000 a year probation officer at 1978 prices', the non-preparation of social inquiry reports in not-guilty pleas and on political offenders; the refusal to supervise paroled political prisoners; resistance to Criminal Trespass legislation; affiliation to trades councils and other socialist organizations, would have been unthinkable a few years ago. It is true that a proposal for a union membership agreement (closed shop) was substantially defeated, and a single-salary scale for all grades was eventually rejected after acceptance at two AGMs: but one should not be surprised that an organization has not progressed from political virginity to a closed shop in seven years or so. Movement has in fact been fast.

The most controversial issue of recent times has been the National Association of Probation Officers London Branch's joining of the Grunwick picket line. They were threatened with suspension by the chairman who declared the action 'ultra vires' — outside the constitutional powers of the Association. This issue and others have, probably quite realistically, been seen by some as attempts by a relatively right-wing HQ to impose unacceptable limits on the freedom of branches to respond to local political issues. Debate about changes in the objects of the Association are now in progress, and the central issue is the legitimacy of a group of workers concerning themselves with issues which are beyond the strictly defined limits of their work roles.

The NAPO Members' Action Group, espousing explicitly marxist analysis and prescription, emerged in the early 1970s in reaction to the political flabbiness of NAPO, and its members have played a considerable part in the substantial politicization of the last few years. Its membership, interestingly enough, covers a broad spectrum of the left, and one might infer that one of its attractions is the opportunity for more vigorous and searching debate than takes place in any other forum.

It is significant that not all probation staff are members of NAPO, that active support for some of the policies referred to earlier is by no means general, and likely that some, at least, see recent changes as dubious, if not regrettable: entering the world of explicit political commitment means the loss of many comforts. The Action Group has been the focus of several 'red-scare' responses both from within and outside the service, but these have absurdly overestimated the autonomous power of such a group *within* the probation service, and have failed to take account of the fact that several socialist proposals from the Action Group and others have gained acceptance at a number of Annual Conferences. As yet, however, the Action Group has had little to say about *practice*, though we can look forward to something before long.

A congruent style of life

Radical practice grows inevitably out of a thorough, coherent, tough-minded radical stance as a person: it is not something which can be adopted by or attached to a personality which is essentially wedded to orthodoxy and the status quo. In or out of the job the radical personality will not be pushed around by officials; will not remain silent or inactive when s/he is aggrieved; will be aware and unafraid of his/her needs, drives, strengths, weaknesses; will not be afraid of change; will be thoroughly conversant with the political nature of most taken-for-granted habits and behaviour.

Socialist practice grows out of a consciousness of what are the unrealized true interests of the great majority of the population; an understanding of the largely structural and institutional sources of much oppression and unhappiness; and a persistent faith in the collective resources and strength of people to find solutions, whether at domestic, local or national level. Such a consciousness affects one's perceptions of and reactions to everyday events: how one approaches local political issues or tackles problems in the office, as well as the larger formulae which one devises for the salvation of the world. Always, as one sits alone facing some apparently insoluble problem or demand, one should see through the walls of one's isolation the dozens or hundreds of others who may, at that very moment, be in a similar position, or, if not at that moment, have faced or will face the same challenge and need and can offer support.

The most creative radicalism or socialism depends, too, on other qualities: 'political consciousness' is not enough, for it can lead to a dry, rhetorical, utilitarian disposition; it leads often to rigid perceptions and explanations which may have little to do with life as it is experienced — even by those who speak and write with apparent confidence and authority. Being human is more than being political: it is also knowing and valuing man's spiritual and aesthetic capacities; it is being compassionate and loving — and much more. These qualities often have political dimensions — we can speak of the fascist sensibility in architecture or music, for example, as much as we can distinguish the same element in individual behaviour or relationships — but they also transcend politics, and without them politics is a dangerous and barren employment. Those seeking a political identity for themselves will be as well to read as many novels and poems as political tracts.

Most of us have a considerable amount of personal work to do before we can launch into radicalism in our jobs. An anecdotal detour will illustrate this point.

I recently met a group of newly-appointed officers who had just finished the first day of an induction course. Some were complaining vigorously about aspects of it, and among them, one self-styled radical and socialist, more bitterly than others. Later I heard the DCPO (Deputy Chief Probation Officer) responsible for training asking this man how the day had gone. 'Fine, fine,' he replied. Somewhat incredulously requesting clarification of this apparently inexplicable inconsistency, I was told that there was clearly no hope for change and therefore no point in voicing complaints. There was, therefore, a double failure: not only did he fail to represent his views clearly as an individual, but also he did not think to test out the views of the whole group in order to discover if there were a collective view to be represented, which could have been significantly influential. Some people mistake general anger and resentment at being alive for political commitment, and ascribe their personal unhappiness and helplessness to some exclusively external ailment. I am not without compassion for their pain, but I am alarmed at their lack of understanding of themselves and the threat they pose to the cause of radical change.

It is difficult to see how help can be offered to the disadvantaged and oppressed by those who do not understand and cannot remedy the oppression in their own lives:

> ... as social workers our experience with authority is reflected in our dealings with clients. Each instance of deference without principle to higher authority, or avoidance of conflict for personal gain, corrupts us and increases the likelihood of our demanding the same from our clients. If we are alienated in our work situation, oppressed by a powerful bureaucrat, can we do other than pass this along? Being controlled, we in turn control our clients on behalf of our bosses   (Garrett 1973)

The danger and the challenge are clear:

> Part-time radicalism was one of the crucial elements in the failure of the old Left. A commitment to radical politics must mean a commitment to a style of life which is congruent.
> (Ehrlich 1970)

There are considerable pressures working against the development of such integrity at work, and it will be instructive to review them.

The pressure of agency norms

New staff are very rapidly socialized to agency norms. This may be simply by association; or by the powerful influence of orthodox practice presented explicitly or implicitly as the only possible way of doing the job; or by explicit management pressure to toe the line under threat of non-confirmation or other harassment.

It has also to do with the often overwhelming demands of a large, individualized workload, which prevents thoughtful consideration of how most rationally to go about the task, or of the collective resources of a team, area, or of the agency as a whole. The traditional autonomy of POs is powerful in encouraging certain kinds of conformity, and the sense of isolation militates against innovation and creativity. There is a tendency for officers to relapse into 'learned helplessness' in a hierarchical authority structure, and through resignation to the supposed immutability of things, to support and consolidate that which is resented or despised. The resistance of many members of the service of all grades to proposals for changes in management structure, to the single-salary scale, to the democratization of the team, reflects, amongst other things, personal *needs* for paternalistic relationships: those who like exercising authority; those who like or need to be controlled; those who hope to control others in the future. Difficulties of this kind lie deep in the service's relationships, and, of course, in the society of which the service is a part. They have serious implications for the work of the service with clients, as we shall see later.

New recruits and established members of the service are demoralized by bureaucratic demands: the keeping of records and statistics, expenses claims, and the immense amount of other paper work. These requirements exercise very powerful controls on an individual's sense of freedom and creativity. They are one of the many sources of repressive guilt, in essence trivial, but in effect powerful.

Another of those sources is that of working hours. There is a pervasive and oppressive commitment to the 9-5 working day even when much work may be done out of those hours. It is extraordinary, for example, how many otherwise civilized, thoughtful people go in for harassment of the 'Had a nice holiday?' type when one turns up at 10.30 am after two or three hours' work the previous evening. Such stuff is insidious in the extreme: it reinforces the 9-5 gremlin lurking in one's head and limits one's ability to determine the pattern of one's work. It has a further effect in its implication that one should be 'working' all the time, and should be seen to be so, and, on the whole, 'working' does not include reading a recent book on, say, research in criminal justice, *at home*.

Linked to the rapid socialization to agency norms is the powerful effect of the apparently rigid boundaries of possible action. This is often exacerbated by the ludicrously inappropriate and disabling physical environments and geographical locations in which people are expected to work. More often than not, the office is the base and centre, and its influence is little short of tyrannical. It is profoundly demoralizing and stultifies creativity and imagination in establishing contact with clients in a variety of more appropriate settings and ways.

These kinds of pressures, assumptions, needs, lead to a range of practices which embody many of the same conservative traits. Generally speaking, clients are put in dependent, disadvantaged roles: the office setting alone establishes those, and the arrangement of chairs, desks and so on often confirms them. As officers work individually, so clients are seen individually, thus imposing on them the same demoralizing isolation experienced by the officers in their work: this is clearly *politically* significant. It confirms, amongst other things, the definitions imposed on the situation by the courts, and those are the individual's responsibility, deviance, wickedness within a good society where the interests of some are seen to be the interests of all. It seems to be rarely realized that such practices result from unacknowledged *choices*, and that other paths are available.

Many officers are aware of these issues, but feel powerless to effect change. And here we return to the point made earlier: the willingness and ability to effect change in one's own life, to adopt radical or relatively radical solutions, has crucial implications for one's work with clients.

The radical left in social work, sociology, criminology, has had little to say about what to do in practice. As I now approach the point at which I am going to attempt that task, I have some sympathy with those who have not quite got round to it: in contrast with the drama of many of the ideas, the practical possibilities seem modest to the point of insignificance. But we must start somewhere, and only by making what will certainly be a modest start shall we have any foundations on which to build. What follows will be modest in contrast to our ultimate hopes, but it will take us a very long way forward from where we have been. Mountains were never climbed by leaps of imagination in the valleys.

The beginnings of radical and socialist practice

What follows will be a review of principles illustrated by examples of the kind of practice they suggest. I shall attempt to make some distinction between radical principles and socialist principles in the belief that a radical stance in itself may open up new possibilities beyond the relatively limited options we have at present. To be fully committed to particular political solutions may close our eyes to the subtle indicators of important alternatives or of the extent to which our analyses are out of accord with reality.

The radical challenge

The radical person will not be afraid to question and challenge: thorough questioning of things as they are reveals the tentative, relative status of all things: what is novel and threatening today will be tomorrow's orthodoxy; what is maintained with passionate conviction in 1979 may be lost forever by 1989. As this is true of large, national and international issues, so even more is it true of the relative trivia of the daily concerns of a tiny state agency. Maintenance of an energetic vigilance is necessary with regard to what one is told to do, expected to do, what one imagines one is supposed to do, and the reality or fantasy of authority which lies behind such things. It relates also to the large questions about what the agency's purposes are.

Why am I expected to write in this way? Is time in this meeting being well spent? Is keeping my records in this way helpful, realistic, economical? What purposes are being served by seeing this endless succession of people for half hours? Why am I stuck in this office? What are the real priorities? What is the meaning of this instruction, this procedure, this method? What are the real limits to my choice and what are imagined? Why am I always tired? What power has X to enforce or demand this?

Questions of this kind lead to startling revelations: things happen because they've always happened; because one way is someone's idiosyncratic preference; because one's never stopped to ask how else they may be done; because alternatives require time, energy, imagination, and there's little enough chance of finding them in the hurly-burly; because the service is chronically amateur and flabby in its conducting of meetings, setting of priorities, asking of questions, accepting of uncertainty. And a whole world of immediate possibilities appear:

1   Rational, selective methods of record-keeping can be

devised. A team can discuss and negotiate its own norms and thus remove many of the fantasies and pressures. Officers may decide, for example, to keep the barest minimum of notes on 50 per cent of their cases; slightly fuller notes on 25 per cent; and thorough, detailed notes on the other 25 per cent. The 50 per cent would involve no more than a note of the date and time of contact and any action or decision arising, supported by three-monthly summaries, and so on. Records hang like millstones about probation officers' necks: it is possible to face the issues, take them apart and master them. Significantly, such an administrative adjustment may lead to a more discriminating perception of clients: who are those for whom there really is no need to write more than the minimum? Why is that? What implications does that have for my allocation of time to them? Are our transactions together actually worth recording? The processes might, more logically, of course, be taken the other way round, but the nature, purpose and usefulness of records is a good issue through which to ask more serious questions.

If records are kept principally for managerial or supervisory purposes, then that issue needs examination. We have to ask how much records can actually reflect what goes on between worker and client beyond the bare facts of contact, and if, consciously or unconsciously, we cannot (do not?) use them to report or withhold what we please. We must know for whom we are writing, to what purposes the writing will be put, and must acknowledge that having neat, full up-to-date records says little more than that we are good at keeping our records neat, full and up-to-date. There are issues of accountability as well as self-assessment in record-keeping which are legitimate, but let them be clearly identified and disentangled from the myth. Those who created and perpetuate that demoralizing myth have much to answer for.

2   Meetings with clients can be arranged elsewhere than in the office. If one is not fortunate enough to be based in a decentralized, local office, then some collective action in pursuit of that must be a priority in the long term. Institutionalized, office-block warrens have nothing to do with *service*: they stifle, cramp, depersonalize, limit and debase human encounters. From time to time, selectively office meetings will be appropriate or, on balance, the most convenient for worker and/or client, but, more

often than not, places where meetings can be arranged on more equal, open and helpful terms need to be used.

Short of that, offices need to be made as congenial and welcoming as possible. Every effort has to be made to counteract the chronic disadvantage in relation to authority, and chronic dependence in relation to officials that working-class people have endured throughout their lives. The wording of notices, the styles of receptionists and clerical staff, the quality of waiting areas, all require careful thought and planning. Every officer is in a position to influence these things.

3   Priorities for offices, team, area or district can be firmly established, and meetings can be streamlined and invigorated. The probation service often seems to have learned little or nothing from half a century of social and industrial psychology and management studies. Meetings are crucial to the morale of an organization: their style, assumptions, effectiveness have wide-ranging effects. If they are merely rubber-stamping decisions, if they are meandering and purposeless, if they deal only with trivia, if they inhibit participation, they will undermine the morale of an organization far beyond the concerns of the meetings themselves. Agendas are customarily constructed so that a mass of trivial business precedes the important items for which there then remains little or no time. Absurd. Priorities have to be established — balloting is one method — and time-limits imposed. Most of us will talk as long as there is time and, as with clients, the significant interchanges often take place only in the last few minutes. We know that, yet it rarely influences how we conduct meetings. There is much more which anyone with a little motivation and energy can discover about the conducting of meetings. (The Video Arts film, 'Meetings, Bloody Meetings', with John Cleese is a good starter.) If we do not have the ability to conduct effective meetings and to make decisions, then we have no means of examining priorities or of gathering ideas for the initiation of change. Such apparently minor matters are of great importance.

The weariness, even despair, which the prospect of a week's meetings inspires in many people is potentially a powerful stimulus for change: with a little initiative, skill, energy and planning it can be harnessed. Further, the issues of the purposes and style of a group's meetings take one inevitably into discussion of the relative power and influence of the group's members, and thence into an examination of the political reality of the group: where does power lie, is that where it should lie, what can be done about it?

4   The question of the exhaustion which many officers frequently display is important. Some of it, certainly, relates to the issues of confusion and uncertainty which are discussed in this chapter. If one is awash in a sea of conflicting demands, uncertain and undifferentiated purposes and priorities, frustrating meetings, endless paperwork, ill-defined relationships with colleagues and clients, pressure to be 'at work' from 9-5, and so on, then one is going to be pretty debilitated and depressed. Occasionally one will be tired because one has worked hard, but it is easy enough to be exhausted after a day at the office in which nothing useful has been achieved, and that is serious. It is something which needs to be tackled and remedied, and I hope this chapter will assist in alleviating the problem, for it can be alleviated.

5   Confirmation can be seen for what it is: a negative process which does not select the good, but weeds out the incompetent. It requires very little skill or sophistication — and very little compromise — to ensure confirmation: avoid making an ass of yourself. In view of the provisions of recent Employment Protection legislation (and for a number of other good reasons), confirmation is in any case technically and practically redundant.* Yet officers still sometimes have an anxious and oppressed first year under what is an empty threat. Work towards its abolition is an obvious and worthwhile commitment.

We should not assume, of course, that all POs are angelic and effective, nor that some measure of quality control is undesirable, nor that sensitive, supportive and challenging supervision is necessarily oppressive. What we should not subscribe to are systems whose operation breeds conformity and anxiety, especially in the crucial first year of the job, and which take no account of the consumer's view.

The collective challenge

The individual fighting a lone battle may be able to stimulate

*See note at end of chapter.

change, but his power is as nothing to the power of a group, area, district or union. There are few issues or problems round which a group of some kind cannot be formed, and many which cry out for the tapping of wide resources. One must never forget that even in the smallest area the immediate collective resources in terms of numbers are considerable: dozens of staff and hundreds of clients; in some areas, hundreds of staff and thousands of clients. Policies need people to implement them: if they are not implemented they do not work; if they are challenged by whole groups of people, there is always the chance of negotiation and change.

Collective action through the union, and with other unions, is a base of real power for local and national change. To deal effectively with local issues probation officers need to make use of their union branch as well as ad hoc groups formed round particular issues. Workplace representation would substantially invigorate discussion and resolution of local issues and it is to be hoped that current discussions will soon produce workable schemes.

For those who feel that branch meetings are dull, or that the union does not represent their interests or preoccupations, there is only one answer: it is not a body with an autonomous life, it is what its members make it: if it is not as one would like it then, like society itself, one must engage with it, invigorate it and change it. Its potential is massive.

One has to ask whether the current divisions of interest within the union are creative or damaging: the withdrawal of ACPOs (Assistant Chief Probation Officers) to their own Assembly; suggestions for a main-grade-only union; and a tendency among some to 'resolve' conflict by splitting off, may well be indicators of destructive political naivety. Divided against ourselves we shall have even less strength for the serious battles to be fought elsewhere. 'Management' have much to answer for in the increasing alienation and conflict within the service, but we may be contributing to the worsening of those processes if we simply confirm the distance and difference by destroying the collectivity of the whole service. Withdrawal from court work, on the grounds of its contaminating and compromising effects would be similarly naive.

I have referred earlier to the probation service's tendency to maintain a reactive rather than an initiatory stance. It is vital that some notion of what is wanted for the future should be developed, that positive proposals and strategies to meet the changing needs of a changing world should be debated and published, and that we should not simply wait for Green Papers to arrive before we address ourselves to major issues of policy. In local and national service matters we must ensure that we are represented in places where major decisions are made (on Probation Committees, for example) so that our energies are not mobilized solely in response to *faits accomplis*. Determined and skilful groups of people with original and coherent proposals can and do bring about change.

Client collectivity

As collective action by professionals must be one of the crucial elements in precipitating radical change, so must it be for clients and society in general.

T.D. Campbell (1978) has pointed out that:

> One fundamental right of the citizen of a liberal democracy is the right not to be treated arbitrarily.

and further:

> It remains to be proved that the welfare and therapeutic benefits of allowing social workers discretionary powers adequately compensate for the very real risk at which this puts the rights of that increasingly large class of persons who fall within the purview of the social worker.

We have only the slightest notions of what it is like to be a client of the statutory services, and no notion at all of what clients say to each other about them. In our common neglect of that perspective we run the constant risk of being, or of seeming to be, arbitrary. Clients, like consumers of commercial goods, have rights to be heard, and rights to pursue remedy against action which they feel to be arbitrary or unsatisfactory. Such rights can be exercised only out of the strength of group solidarity and only if officers actively seek to establish means to encourage the exercise of such rights. We need to build such opportunities into our daily practice.

The model of self-determining, task-centred, democratic groups, even within a statutory framework, as operated for example in the Sheffield Day Training Centre, seems amongst the most fruitful for the development of progressive work with some offenders — that is to say, work which at least does not reinforce orthodox definitions and does not stigmatize, alienate and isolate individuals further and, at best, opens up opportunities for the development of personal and political understanding and strength.

Particular issues suggest various kinds of collective action. Realistic budgeting is clearly a legitimate interim goal with clients, but only if it is in the context of negotiation, pressure and collaboration for higher pay and welfare benefits through collective union and client activity.

If there were some contentious issue in local housing policy, one can envisage bringing together all clients affected by it with a number of officers, and examining ways of bringing the problem to public attention, putting pressure on the local authority, enlisting the support of other groups, and so on. The very act of bringing people together is politically significant and may begin to shed some light on the nature of social problems for the victims of them.

Much of the work we do is compensatory for the failures of other institutions to deal justly with people. The failure of education to provide people with the skills and information to survive in a complex and changing world is the most stark example. Day Training Centres, literacy schemes, social skills training, welfare rights work, as well as more traditional approaches, are all doing things which a realistic, imaginative, twentieth-century education system ought to be doing as second nature. But if we provide the compensatory services without also providing some understanding of why those services are necessary, without relating individual need and 'failure' to the failure of whole systems, and to the functions and purposes of those systems, then the nature of our conservatism is all too clear.

Kids who are bored out of their heads at school accept their pain and frustration as inevitable, feel tightly imprisoned and helpless. It is nothing short of cruel to insist that they put up with it, without offering some idea as to why it is often so awful for so many, and without suggesting that there are some steps that can be taken to investigate paths of remedy. Kids (like probation officers sometimes) don't even consider complaining or, if they do, imagine that it will be an entirely fruitless activity. It is likely that helplessness is learned most completely at school, and that patterns of unexpressed resentment and frustration are established. It is possible for kids not only to complain, but also to suggest positive alternative plans; for them to point out to teachers that they are bored and fed up and would like to spend their time more agreeably; it is possible for probation officers who know a number of pupils from one school to initiate discussions with groups of pupils and sympathetic teachers; it is possible with skill and commitment to initiate change: teachers labour under a sense of great burden — they too are often victims of the system in which they find themselves — and the politically sophisticated will find ways of tuning in to that frustration and beginning to establish a wider collectivity.

Individual action with clients

There will always be situations in which individual need demands an immediate, effective response: the 'first-aid' role; and people for whom a committed, warm, sustaining relationship will be the most humane and realistic resource. Stan Cohen warns us not to 'sell out (our) clients' interests for the sake of ideological purity or theoretical neatness' (Cohen 1975) and that is a salutary warning for radical practice: utopian rhetoric can cloud our perceptions of the present state of human nature and need.

But the way in which we respond to individual needs is determined not only by altruism but also by our political stance. The politics of casework are, by now, thoroughly exposed, and those of us who largely repudiate them must be sure of the values and assumptions underlying our new view of the work.

We should, for example, ensure that relationships are formed on a basis of such equality as the situation permits. A recent paper provides a good starting point. The notion of 'help' is substituted for 'treatment' — which gives rise to the following changes in practice:

Diagnosis	becomes	*Shared assessment*
Client's dependent need	becomes	*Collaboratively-*

as the basic for social work action (Bottoms and McWilliams 1979)	*defined task* as the basis for social work action

The further implication of this model is that recommendations in social inquiry reports can be made only with the consent of the client. Without such consent, no recommendation can be made. Bottoms and McWilliams record other implications of the model:

> ... the modern-day bureaucracies which probation services have become will be subject to 'bottom-up' monitoring from the client's eye-view, to see whether they are so organized as best to deliver the services required by the clients. ... Other implications may follow: the decentralization of agency structures in order to be able to respond more closely to client requests for help, a greater use of voluntary associates, and so on. Above all, there is a need to develop specificity within the agency about exactly what kinds of help are available at the client's request, and to devote considerable care and thought to methods of ensuring that clients are informed of the range of services available.

This requires a radical shift in disposition of the service as a whole and, for each of us, a profound examination of our values and motives for being in the job. One after the other professional prescriptions and analyses have been shown to be inaccurate, irrelevant, ineffective or out of touch with clients' realities. Our capacity for self-deception is dramatically illustrated by our talking for years about 'starting where the client is' (for which read: 'where we think the client is') and 'self-determination (for which read: 'where we think the client ought to go') and imagining that we were acting on those principles.

Commonly there is some confusion between the ritual nature of much of what the service is required to do as a result of the processes of the criminal justice system (to 'supervise' offenders, which, in the light of new understanding of the limitations of rehabilitative possibilities is unlikely to achieve anything as far as reconviction rates are concerned, and is, therefore, a largely symbolic activity) and the opportunities offered by contact with the service for help in matters which may have little or nothing to do with the offence. This is partly the legacy of casework, where the making of a probation order was seen by officers to legitimize powerful interventions in the intrapsychic and family life of offenders, but also by officers' needs to feel they were *doing* something. Many of the expectations others have of the service have no basis in the real world (especially the notion of 'reforming' criminals); and it is difficult for an organization to accept or say that the basis for its existence is at least tentative, and to perform essentially ritual functions (e.g. surveillance) which do not satisfy professionals' occasionally pretentious views of what they ought to be doing.

We have, I think, to make such distinctions for the sake of the sanity of both our clients and ourselves. We may then have a less bewildered clientele, and a less oppressed profession. Clients would be given genuine freedom to say what they needed or wanted, or that they wanted nothing. They would have an equal part in decisions about what was to be done, how it was to be done, and with whom it was to be done.

Let us suppose that we are dealing with a young thief with whom it had been agreed that a probation order was an acceptable recommendation, and on whom the court had subsequently made the order. In the discussions during the preparation of the report, and during the first few meetings, one would be concerned to share and explore some of the following ideas (they sound a little bald and artificial put like this: in reality they would be elaborated, modified, even abandoned if the client's reality showed their inappropriateness or inaccuracy): You chose to steal this article, knowing that there was a risk of being detected and taken to court; that was your decision, and, in truth, there is little or nothing that I can do to prevent you doing it again if you want to. Because you've broken the law, the courts require you to pay some kind of penalty: in this case, that you should report to a probation officer at agreed times, and keep him informed of your address. We'll talk about that in a moment. I'm required to keep in contact with you and to keep a record of our meetings. That is all: you are not under any obligation or pressure to do anything else. Quite separate from that, I am required to offer — and I want to offer — advice, assistance or friendship, if they are any use to you and you want them. This is what I and my team and the local office can offer:

help: in negotiations with DE and DHSS and other local

   agencies;
   in personal and social problem-solving (e.g. employ-
      ment and housing)
   in finding educational or recreational resources;
counselling with personal or marital problems;
informal discussion of things in general from time to time;
group meetings with other probationers to share and explore
      experience;
groups for improving reading and writing skills.

'Or, if you were interested, there are a number of people who themselves need help with several of the things listed, which you might be able to offer.

'There's also a group which meets each week, without any probation officers, to discuss the services being given by probation officers, and to offer suggestions for improvement, which you're welcome to attend.

'There's a group of us who work together and I'd like you to meet them. If there is anything you need, you may prefer to go to one of them rather than me, or if I'm not here sometime, you'll at least know the other faces. They're each introducing themselves to a new client now and we've agreed to meet up.'[1]

   Then follows a meeting with perhaps five officers and five clients, ideally also with established client or clients, in which the general issues can be discussed; each officer can introduce him/herself and talk about his or her particular experience and resources; established clients could talk about their experience and changing expectations and perceptions and new clients could ask questions or talk about themselves.

   Now, this is merely a possibility among many: there would be many clients for whom such a process would be too elaborate and/or threatening; a client's attitude to his or her offence would affect the drift of discussion and other arrangements; one's priority might be to undo the effects of a court experience (e.g. with a marginal unlawful sexual intercourse case) and quite different tactics would be appropriate.

---

1 A more detailed and coherent account of this kind of approach can be found in Bryant *et al.*, 'Sentenced to social work?' in *Probation Journal* 25 (4), Dec. 1978; and a challenge to the approach in James, 'Sentenced to surveillance?' in the March 1979 edition.

It has to be made clear that the acceptance or refusal of more than the basic contact is an entirely voluntary, non-prejudicial decision, and that refusal, especially, can in no way influence the formal aspects and decisions of the order.

My personal preference is, with agreement, to set up four or five weekly meetings at the beginning and then to negotiate mutually acceptable frequency thereafter, with quite explicit discussion of what should reasonably constitute a breach, so that the responsibillty vis-à-vis the courts is a joint one.

This approach does raise the ethical question of the possible exercise of pressure on a client to sample resources about which s/he is then expected to make voluntary decisions. The fairest way, though it does not answer completely, seems to be to ensure that such issues are clearly discussed and agreed as part of the package of accepting probation.

Approaching the job from anything like this position — as opposed to sliding into a comfortable — or awkward — series of aimless meetings — requires considerable strength, energy and clarity on the part of the worker. It is not at all easy to discuss such issues in a clear, non-mystifying, helpful way; but it actually is far less easy — and responsible — in the long term to leave things in a state of ambiguity and muddle. Crucially, such lack of clarity leaves clients confused and doubly alienated in a society which cares little enough to share decision-making or to work through accessible processes.

The team and the clients

Choice about with whom agreed work is to be done implies freedom to choose officer or officers or other clients or resources through which the help is to be obtained. The specifying of available resources to clients requires the prior discovery by a team of what they collectively have to offer. This requires a positive move from being a mere group of people who happen to work in the same office, to the openness, flexibility and collaboration of a true team. This implies moving out of individual offices, dispensing with individual filing cabinets and caseloads, and creating environments for contact which at least allow for the meeting of clients half-way towards their own worlds.

Differences, conflicts, doubts among team members are in the open, shared with clients and, of course, at the same time, common needs and issues which arise from the client group and the worker group can be tackled by collective strength. 'Teamwork' does not imply consensus, sameness, unanimity — except in a shared commitment to knowing each other more openly and honestly, and sharing resources and power in the group more openly and imaginatively.

Team boundaries may be as wasteful of resources within areas as individualized work is within teams. A more flexible structure in an area, based on functions, may be much more realistic and effective.[2] This is not to suggest necessarily exclusive specialisms, though they may be appropriate in some circumstances, but rather a structure which permits those with common interests, skills and commitments to work together from time to time to service the needs of a whole area. One officer might well belong to two or three such function-based groups.

The traditional one-to-one relationship pressurizes the PO into feeling that he/she is the major — if not the only — resource through which help is to be given. This has several damaging effects: it leaves the isolated officer with the burden of feeling that he/she must be capable of tackling every kind of task — clearly an impossibility; it sets up a situation in which failure to bring about significant change (e.g. in local housing policy) reinforces his/her own and the client's sense of isolation and helplessness; and this last process may suggest that it is the officer's personal failure, and not the result of the bad administration or discriminatory policies of bureaucrats or politicians, and hence divert anger from its proper objects, and disguise the essentially political nature of the problem and of possible remedies.

In almost any situation the power, imagination and creativity of two people are more than the sum of the two sets of individual qualities: in relationship with others, creation takes place and new doors are opened. Community of interest rather than conflict of interest, or sheer indifference, becomes the operational norm.

We must find ways of permitting the main grade in any district both to feel that they have the possibility of influencing local policy and practice, and creating local structures through which that influence may be exercised in action. A hierarchical struc-

2 I owe my first thoughts about this matter to Mike Mulvany.

ture, conventionally represented as a pyramid, has effects upon those within the structure which are independent of personalities. One of the most noticeable is the sense of oppression in those who find themselves near the bottom of the structure, i.e. the main grade, residential and ancillary staff, to say nothing of clients who, though beyond the structure itself, are in receipt of its effects daily. The sense of oppression is often partly fantasy, having something to do with the assumptions about life commonly held in our culture, which when tested often dissolve; but it is also based in the reality of insensitive, thoughtless, non-consulting management practices, and a determination to keep a monopoly of power.

The resources of the main grade, in terms of energy, commitment, ideas, and morale are crucial to the healthy life of the probation service, and they are ignored through intent or indifference at peril of the service's health and credibility. Staff meetings are customarily rather empty, ritual affairs, poorly attended and much moaned about: why cannot they be the basis for local democracy, and a determining voice in local policy? The main grade, after all, do know about the service's principal reason for existing: service to clients.

Resistance to change is not the exclusive preserve of management, however. There are times when specific or general opportunities for change are offered by management and they are ignored or discredited by the main grade. This creates a demoralizing, vicious circle of cynicism. We have to work to create a climate in which positive and responsive change is valued at all levels, and, while we have our current organizational structure, we must try to ensure that people of radical and challenging views are promoted, and that they are supported in holding on to and developing their radicalism.

The meaning of criminal behaviour

Few people working in the statutory services would be foolish enough to suggest that they could offer credible general explanations of criminal behaviour. Society in general, however, seems to have fairly rigid views about crime and what should be done about it. The probation service — within the criminal justice system as a whole — is expected to control and prevent criminal behaviour and to reform (as well as punish) criminals.

We know that many of these assumptions and expectations are absurd, and that only by looking at the nature and operation of society and its institutions as a whole can one begin to offer tentative suggestions: suggestions which point to major structural deficiencies, to blatantly discriminatory policies and to fundamental illogicalities and inconsistencies of judgment.

At the basic level of spreading information, of educating public, judicial and governmental opinion, the probation service has a major role to play. If, for example, it were objected that the kinds of collective action described earlier were not a proper activity for probation officers, our unapologetic reply must be that there is always likely to be criminal behaviour in a society which neglects the right of hundreds of thousands of people to decent, secure housing. If, when we insist on the futility of custodial sentences for most criminals, we are reminded of the threat they pose to the stability of society, our unapologetic reply must be to describe the nature of the prison population; to elucidate the negative effects of custody; to pinpoint those who bear some of the greatest costs (a prisoner's family, society as well as the prisoner himself); to speak of the 'dark figure' of crime and its implications; to point out the class-based nature of the operation of the criminal justice system; to ask questions about white-collar crime, tax evasion, and so on. We have an obligation to be uniquely well-informed on such matters.

We have to demonstrate that the people selected for prosecution are selected on demonstrable criteria which make nonsense of any notion of justice. We have to demonstrate that the 'failure' of criminal justice processes to halt or reduce criminal behaviour, is in fact the failure of society to halt or reduce fundamental inequities and injustices. We have to expose the impossibility of the task we are given and to lay the foundations of a truer consciousness. The probation service is in a uniquely authoritative position to do this.

> ... the role of the social worker is generally to raise socialist political consciousness ... but a crucial part of this process is to undermine the acceptance of, and often support for, the legitimating institutions of society. The social worker thus uses his professional role to expose the very system of which his pro-

fession is, at present, a part: a dangerous but not altogether ignoble role!

Alternatively,

> ... and perhaps for the socialist more optimistically, if the existing structure has within it already extant considerable areas of working-class power whose values are increasingly put into operation, then, despite the stultifying effects of the agencies of legitimation, it is possible to push forward *through existing channels* to a socialist transformation. (Pritchard and Taylor 1978)

Defensive action on behalf of clients

Even within the constraints of current roles and definitions the probation officer has considerable power to protect clients from the least and worst excesses of punitive or discriminatory action, or to reduce or neutralize the damage they cause. Much of the previous discussion has had this principle at its heart, but it is of sufficient importance to examine on its own.

The amount of discretion which probation officers have in their work offers considerable scope for defensive action. In recent years the use of probation orders has declined considerably[3] and while precise reasons are unclear, it is likely that it may be partly explained by fewer recommendations for probation as a result of the service's loss of confidence: supervision no longer holds out utopian hopes. While we must ensure that we do not encourage the imposition of sentences which might be, or might be felt by clients to be, more severe than might otherwise be imposed, there may be many individuals for whom a negotiated recommendation of probation order and its subsequent imposition would be the most progressive course of action, granted even that little or no *work* flowed from it. Officers have discretion to interpret an order more or less as they wish. There are circumstances in which an order could offer the lowest level of stigmatizing or damaging intervention, and that alone would more than justify it. The interpretation of this view to courts would be an important task.

3 See, for example, the NAPO newsletter for November 1978 for a partial discussion of this.

Diversion from custody must be a priority aim, not only for the welfare of individuals and their families, but also as a major step towards abolition. (En passant, one must note that it is impossible to imagine a situation which would justify a probation officer recommending a custodial sentence.) In the pursuit of that important aim it is vital that credible alternatives are vigorously developed. That can be achieved only if we bring rational planning and priority setting into the rest of our work to release time and energy.

The probation officer's role in court is one which needs careful examination. It is my impression that there is a tendency for court work to be undervalued. There is some debate, for example, as to whether a morning spent waiting for a case for which one has prepared a report to be heard is a justifiable use of time. The implication is that there are no pressing reasons for staying with an offender through the process, nor for being in court when the report is presented.

The reasons for such a view are not entirely clear: is it because the contradictions of the role are most painfully and intensely apparent in court? Is it because the challenge to the integrity of one's position is most acute and public, and therefore the risk of unacceptable compromise or failure most real?

It seems to me to be both of these things but, for those very reasons, a challenge which must be met head on. A probation officer may be the only person in court who can articulate significant, alternative explanations of human behaviour, or speak with any insight or authority about the wide context of an offender's personal and social reality. He or she may be the only person willing or able to expose some of the underlying assumptions or unintended effects of some decisions (demanding sureties of those who clearly cannot provide them[4] or imposing suspended committals on those who clearly cannot pay fines), or placing possible decisions in the context of the knowledge we have about them (the differential effects of sentences on first offenders, for example). If the role is not seen as passive and subservient, but as potentially abrasive, it will become one through which real influence can be exercised on events and decisions crucial to an offender's life.

4   I am indebted to Mike Lloyd for this example and some of the ideas in this passage.

We should not undervalue the offender's view of what he or she wants of us: support, information, rehearsal, staying with them, 'getting them off' may be high priorities in offenders' minds, and such things may be amongst the most practical and important help we can offer, however insignificant they appear in the grand socialist perspective. Humbug is an important source of lubrication and energy in institutional life: exposing it is a skilled and significant activity.

A further issue relating to Social Inquiry Reports deserves more attention than it has been given. An element of explaining away criminal behaviour, especially by psychological or circumstantial mitigation, has long been an uncritically accepted activity. Are there not aspects of this which are an affront to an individual's dignity, autonomy, responsibility? Is this not, sometimes at least, a way of shirking the truth of an individual's freely and responsibly chosen action, a way of demeaning his integrity? And worse, of course, a way of shirking the political meaning of the behaviour? These remarks apply most obviously to such areas as unemployment, drugtaking, prostitution and some other sex offences as well as some acts of theft and others. None of these can be explained solely by individualized, psychological theories, nor solely by generalized structuralist theories: given a whole range of constraining factors, people also choose. To deny that is to subscribe to a view of people which makes them less than fully human.

Professionalism

One of the profession's major tasks is to undo the corrupting effects of professionalization over the last few years. We must cease to mystify ourselves and others with pseudoscientific jargon; put behind us the absurd delusion of 'objectivity'; reject positivism and embrace uncertainty; open our practices and procedures to scrutiny; resist bureaucratization and the intrusion of illegitimate notions of management and control, and see the 'profession' as a means, not an end, and a means which may, one day, or in some circumstances, be redundant. The true interests of probation officers, as relatively low-grade state employees, rest not in foisting upon society notions of their esoteric skills and superior professionalism, but rather in the common struggle for a fair living wage for all, a just and equitable society, and the effective redistribution of wealth and power.

A note on style and tactics or, On with the motley

Alinsky writes that if he were working in a Jewish quarter he would not arrive eating ham sandwiches. Sound advice, I think, and advice which has great significance for anyone who hopes to change the world by changing personal and political consciousness. There will be times for confrontation and conflict, but there will also be times for negotiation and persuasion, for tackling issues, even, which cannot be won. The effective radical socialist will have at his command a whole range of tactics and styles: he will use serious, rational argument as well as humour; he will search out common interests as the basis for collective action and he will also canvass and persuade individuals; he will not become enmeshed in jargon and procedures; he will not be boring; he will interest and intrigue people; he will learn from the opposition and use its strengths for his purposes; he will be skilful, subtle, persistent, adaptable; he will not see compromise only as betrayal, but as sometimes a means to real change; he will keep his options open to avoid both the dismissive label of 'extremist' and the dangers of absorption into the system by rejecting radicalism. Ham sandwiches in Jewish quarters: jeans in court — what's the difference? All the world's a stage.

Conclusion

This chapter has not offered much detailed prescription for the daily work of probation officers: that is an impossibility, but adoption of the principles and ideas I have suggested would inevitably affect almost every transaction and decision of every day whether with clients, colleagues, management, the courts or other agencies. To those who say, 'You can't tell a radical or socialist officer from what they *do*', I suggest that they may not be observing radical or socialist officers, other than the part-time variety referred to earlier. Some aspects of radical or socialist practice may appear superficially indistinguishable from orthodox practice, but their subjective reality — experienced by workers and clients — will be very different. And much of such practice will be clearly distinguishable.

The material of this chapter is limited: many of the changes suggested are of form rather than of substance. This results from my intention to concentrate on daily practice within a state agency, and the inevitable limitations imposed on anyone who chooses to accept a pay-cheque from the state. Within the grand sweep of political possibilities in general we may not be able to do much, but there is still much to be done. Cohen points out, 'This might mean living with the uncomfortable ambiguity that [our] most radical work will be outside [our] day-to-day job.' The radical possibilities within the job now, and certainly within the service as it might become through our efforts, need to be grasped and pursued: if they are not, others — managers, politicians, bureaucrats — will soon enough impose their ideas and plans. We must engage ourselves energetically in the complexity of it all, and relish the challenge.

* During the year since this was written we have, of course, seen a thoroughly radical Tory government in action. Amongst the many other atrocities perpetrated, the period of unprotected employment has been extended to twelve, from six, months. That technical objection to confirmation no longer stands, therefore.

Note: I wish to thank Bill Beaumont for his fraternally honest comments on the first draft of this chapter, and a number of friends and colleagues in South Yorkshire who have offered comments and suggestions.

7

The sub-office; a team approach to local authority fieldwork practice

Bill Bennett

Introduction

This is an account of the work done by a community-based sub-office team from a social services department over a period of four years, drawing out the implications for implementing a 'team approach' to neighbourhood fieldwork practice. It begins with an outline of how the office came about and with a description of the administrative arrangements. A chronological survey of the team's developments then takes up the main body of the account. Finally, a summary draws together the beliefs which have underlined the team's approach and identifies the constraints encountered.

Moving out to a small office based within its own catchment area presented the team with a unique opportunity to pioneer new ways of working. How the challenge was accepted was influenced by many factors, of which the needs of the area, the nature of the staff group, and the willingness within the department to support and encourage innovation were paramount. It was the intention from the outset to be a resource for the area; and in seeking and developing the skills and methods required, the team has steadily incorporated intervention at local, inter-agency and organizational levels as essential means of covering the full range of area team duties. This style of work grew in conjunction with the development of a team philosophy which helped promote high morale and a low turnover of staff. As a result, team members became well known in the vicinity; a factor which increased the opportunities for them to encourage and enable genuine participation by residents in local matters. Practical examples are used to illustrate these developments.

Throughout, references are made to the potential for fieldworkers to make better assessments, promote neighbourhood resources and contribute to the planning and formulation of departmental policy. To this end, the account highlights the significant changes in attitudes and perceptions that are imperative to the adoption of wider roles and the development of a 'community perspective'.

The proposal for a sub-office

Area 3 in the London Borough of Hammersmith and Fulham is one of the Borough's four area offices and serves North Fulham and West Kensington. In 1971 it had been decentralized from offices in the town hall to a separate building based within its geographical boundary.[1] By the summer of 1972 office accommodation was already becoming overcrowded, and following area staff discussions it was proposed that a sub-office should be set up and based in West Kensington. This proposal was agreed in principle by the social services committee.

There were a number of reasons for choosing West Kensington. It was believed that throughout, there was a lack of community feeling, few local resources, a lack of play space or meeting places, an inadequate level of day-care provision and a high incidence of multi-occupied housing bringing with it loneliness and alienation. In addition, the main office was relatively inaccessible and it was known that the health visitors based in the area dealt with many of the problems which might normally come to a social worker.

As a general trend, area office staff were keen to see a movement of fieldwork provision toward a more neighbourhood-oriented service and with this in mind they included a recommendation for the appointment of a community worker in their proposal.

1   This followed the reorganization of social services under the Local Authority Social Services Act (1970), based on the Report of the Committee on Local Authority and Allied Personal Social Services (1968 — 'the Seebohm Report').

Planning the sub-office

The preparation for setting up the sub-office took place during the 18 months between February 1973 and its opening in August 1974. The first task was to find premises: after much fruitless searching, it was decided to purchase two portakabins[2] and site them on an open piece of land in close proximity to a new council housing estate. At the same time discussions were taking place about choice of catchment area boundaries. In terms of community identity, it would have made most sense to cover all of West Kensington (population approx. 18,000); but the small size of the staff group made this impossible, and an area of population approximately 12,000 was chosen. This decision meant that a section of the population near the sub-office was not within our boundary; a factor which was naturally obscure to some of the agencies which had not been party to the decision.

The area itself is densely populated and about one mile long by half a mile wide. It has only one park which lies well to the south. For such a small area, it has many diverse neighbourhoods and comprises council and trust housing estates, older terraced property, blocks of mansion flats, the Queens Tennis Club and quite a large sector of multi-occupied housing. Due to the wide availability of private rented property, a relatively high proportion of overseas students and visitors are attracted to it and residence is taken up by immigrants of many nationalities. In common with most of Inner London there is a considerable delinquency problem as well as a high number of elderly residents. One of the major features of this predominantly residential but transient area is that it has few amenities except for various shops, cafes and public houses; and many residents have to travel for employment, secondary schooling and entertainment. As can be seen there is little to encourage the formation of community networks, though a number of people, including the ministers of two churches, work hard to do so. To add to the difficulties, the area is dissected by two major roads into four 'islands'. In partic-

2 'Portakabin' is a trade name for a temporary, mobile building often used as office accommodation.
3 In September 1976, however, following a reorganization of teams and boundaries within Area 3 as a whole, the sub-office catchment area was expanded to cover all of West Kensington. At the same time a corresponding increase in staffing took place.

ular, a six-lane arterial road into central London presents a formidable barrier, especially for the elderly and handicapped and families with small children. To the south of this road is the post office and the tube station, whilst to the north there is the bank and library. This splitting effectively prevents the formation of a natural shopping centre.

The problems of the area had added considerable weight to the proposal for a sub-office, and it was hoped that for similar reasons a community-work post would be added to the team's staffing quota. However, because of cost, lack of precedent and considerable political fear, the request was turned down. But the team believed the post was essential to achieving their aims, and after examining the issue thoroughly, agreement was obtained to appoint a community worker instead of a social worker to one of the social-work posts. Agreement for an additional clerical officer was much more straightforward, as it was fully recognized that a second office brought with it increased administrative and reception duties. Here it should be noted that the recruitment of clerical staff required particular attention, as in addition to working within a small team, they both were to act as receptionists in an office based on an exposed and vulnerable site.

For the Area 3 sub-office, it had always been assumed that the managerial, supervisory and accountability aspects would be kept within the departmental norms so that uniformity could be maintained across the borough. Day-to-day management of the office was therefore to be undertaken by the team leader, who in turn was to maintain close links with the area officer. However, there remained considerable discretion in how the team would undertake its practice. In this respect, the arrangements made for 'intake'[4] and caseloads were of utmost significance to the future development of a more open relationship with the neighbourhood.

4   'Intake' in a general sense is the process by which an area office receives and assesses requests. It implies the establishment of a team of workers to cover a duty rota, deal with emergencies and assess referrals. Cases could then be passed to a long-term team as necessary. The purpose was to release other social workers from the everyday bombardment whilst refining the assessment procedure. It has the added advantage of developing and concentrating information and knowledge of resources in one team. There is a wide variation in practice.

Following the confirmation of a sub-office team in July 1973, the team members restricted their allocation of new cases to those arising from within the probable catchment area. Thus by August 1974, through a process of staff changes, selective reallocation and natural wastage, very few allocated cases within the sub-office team came from outside the then established sub-office boundary. There had been an earlier suggestion that the sub-office team might only serve as an annexe and, as such, only be accessible to those people on existing caseloads. In this case, daily referrals were to continue to be taken by the main office intake team.[5] However, the sub-office team was adamant that it be open to the general public and gave the following reasons:

(a) it would make a fieldwork service more accessible to people of West Kensington;
(b) it would offer an understandable point of reference to local agencies;
(c) it would enable the team to broaden its community perspective so that a more balanced picture of needs and resources in the area could be established;
(d) the community knowledge gained would be of benefit to requests for advice from the public.

As the sub-office team was numerically too small to cover a full duty rota, this proposal required the backing of staff who were to remain in the main office. The degree of willingness varied from worker to worker, but it was finally decided that the sub-office would open for referrals in the mornings, with the main office intake team covering any emergencies which occurred in the afternoons.[6] In order to develop some continuity in the monitoring of referrals, I was to act as sub-office 'duty-senior' each morning.

Within a small team, a duty rota is quickly affected by sickness, leave and staff shortage. However, despite these difficulties our resolve has remained strong enough to ensure that the cover has been fully maintained. There had been some fears that the

5   At this time the remaining three teams in the area office were made up of an intake team, which covered the bulk of the short-term referrals, and two long-term teams.
6   It was not until May 1976, following an increase in staff, that we took full responsibility for our own duty system.

advantages of increased accessibility would be offset by the reduction in opening hours. Our experience has proved these fears groundless. From the outset, the referral rate more than doubled and it has remained at that level since. It is our belief that as the curiosity of local residents began to wane a potential drop in the referral rate was prevented by the public and the local agencies becoming more aware of our function in the area and more eager to make use of it.

These planning decisions were all interrelated and together they determined the sub-office's eventual structure and character. Although the need for coordination had been recognized, a number of these decisions were inevitably made incrementally and, from the point of view of coordination, were ill timed. However, the later changes in catchment area, staffing and intake demonstrate the value of grasping opportunities and building up from there.

A new group in a new office

Area 3 sub-office opened as a referral point in September 1974. It was staffed by a relatively new but fully qualified team which had recently undergone a change of team leader. At the time of opening the staff group comprised two clerical officers, a community worker, three social workers, a social work assistant, a trainee social worker and a team leader — myself.

We soon recognized that here was an opportunity to tackle some of the dissatisfactions and frustrations of the past. These included pressure of work, low morale, high turnover of staff and often poor conditions of service. In addition, we had experienced a feeling of being suffocated by procedures and legislation, and there was little understanding of how to do anything about it. All these factors had had a cumulative effect and could lead to diminishing returns on extra effort. In the light of this awareness, we recognized the need to create a team ethos which would enable a combination of experience, potential and motivation to flourish for the ultimate benefit of the neighbourhood. For us this meant a move away from a position where qualifications and place in the hierarchy defined status and speaking rights. We also felt it was important that workers should not feel hampered by false modesty but should feel comfortable in expressing what they had to offer as well as their own developmental needs.

The early mood can be characterized by the questions being asked of each other: questions about who could use the office, who should be our clients, and the differences between community work and social work. Though loosely defined, these questions were used in team discussions as catalysts to broaden thinking and free minds from the norms which previously we had seldom challenged (Hammersmith Sub-office 1976a).

For example, we were used to throwing out phrases like 'statutory work' or 'too many forms' as the reasons for our own poor performance and for our shortfall in preventive work. Now we became concerned to determine a mode of social work practice, as opposed to responding predominantly to demands in a piecemeal fashion.

From the outset, a number of factors played an important part in the development of team cohesion. First, we were responsible for all the work arising from within the catchment area; and deliberately so. This meant that the performance of each individual team member had implications for the team as a whole. Secondly, there was some pressure from all sections of the community to account for ourselves and to explain our actions. This called for a high degree of integrity in our contacts outside the office and for a more consistent and honest approach to our work. Thirdly, we all experienced some feelings of vulnerability from working on such an exposed site (often used as an unofficial tip, and covered with missiles), and we were not accustomed to there being so little distance between the sanctuary of the office and the general public. As a response, good communications became a team goal. In terms of our daily work, we were a small enough group to be able to tackle the question of priorities as a collective. As colleagues, we had to learn to be more open with each other; to air disagreements, endeavour to resolve conflicts, and offer care and support at times of stress. This led us to accept each other as people; not an easy task, particularly as different workers carried different levels of accountability. For example, take my position as team leader — deprived of a peer group of 'seniors', I still had both an executive function[7] and a need for colleague support. We managed to

---

7 This executive function included ultimate responsibility for allocation of work, for references, leave and authorization of expenditure.

achieve a balance within the team by identifying task-oriented objectives and by exercising what our community worker called 'good manners'; a mixture of integrity and respect which, as we grew in confidence, we were able to extend to all areas of work.

These considerations formed the backdrop to the team settling in and to our determination to break new ground. For the future we had established a pattern of mutual education; a crucial factor to many later developments.

The pioneer days: August 1974 — December 1975

A major achievement of our first eighteen months was the development of a strong team identity. Of crucial importance to this was the weekly team meeting. This had traditionally been the 'seniors' meeting, concerned with disseminating information allocating cases and discussing specific areas of policy.[8] By determining an agenda which reflected *our* priorities it also became the place to coordinate our work, share feelings and ideas, make decisions about future courses of action and to monitor our collective beliefs. In effect it became a true team meeting, committed to the widening of perceptions. One invaluable and practical aid to communication was the team book in which agenda items, minutes, messages and feelings were noted.

Of further benefit was the services of a consultant (Jo Klein). Principally engaged for the first six months to help integrate a community work element into our predominantly social work oriented team, she also played a valuable part in enabling the team to 'gel', work out objectives and examine differential roles.

On an informal level, the pioneering spirit brought with it an air of generosity and the strong wish to learn to work together. A 'family' atmosphere developed, and lunch became a daily landmark for all team members.

As the team increasingly learned to share its responsibilities, task allocation became part of the day-to-day functioning of the office. In this respect, allocation meetings were disbanded. In their place, team members took on work either in supervision sessions or through personal initiative. Alternatively, and

8   This usually followed requests from management for fieldwork comment about issues such as the use of supervision orders or provision of telephones for the elderly. These topics might also at times fall within our priorities.

especially at times of crisis, we would naturally meet both to share out tasks and to discuss particular cases. This shared responsibility led members to examine the management aspects of their job. As a result I was increasingly called upon to coordinate different levels of work — a task supplemented by 'being around' on duty, vetting referrals, making contact with local agencies, attending interdepartmental meetings and supervising staff.

The pioneer days were also a time for getting to know the area, promoting new ventures and establishing the office as part of the locality. From the outset our community worker, together with team members, undertook a land-use survey of the area providing detailed knowledge of each street. This was displayed on a map in the office. Information gained in our daily work was shared both informally and at team meetings. It should be noted that to have an area small enough to walk round was crucial to the quality of this knowledge. One major revelation was to find out how little we knew about West Kensington, and it was a salutary experience to discover a number of valuable local resources, including a community centre hitherto unknown to us.

Our involvement in community work projects added to the impetus of the move. These projects included:

The Wedgwood Club (Hammersmith Sub-office 1976b). This was a weekly self-help club for elderly ladies held in a local school. Activities included dancing, singing, discussions about welfare services and occasional outings. A major achievement of this club was to establish a mutually supportive network of contacts between the residents of a sheltered housing estate.

The bed and breakfast project (Hammersmith Sub-office 1977a). An attempt to provide daytime facilities for homeless families placed in nearby bed and breakfast hotels. Although the day centre was not a success, later spin-offs included a babysitting club and an action group which, by lobbying councillors and local newspaper reporters, succeeded in improving the conditions in the hotels.

The Crescent Youth Club. This followed a request by the management committee of a community centre for help to make this resource more relevant to the immediate neighbourhood. By our enabling the participation of residents, the centre's facilities were extended and one positive result was the formation of weekly senior and junior youth clubs, both organized by local people.

An attempt to promote a group for unsupported mothers hardly got off the ground. This was mainly due to our fundamental error of making the decision that a 'group' would be the most appropriate method of intervention, without consulting the mothers themselves.

Through the forum of our team meetings we developed a critical ability to evaluate performance and learn from mistakes.

We invested time and effort in establishing working relationships with local agencies, and early contacts were made with general practitioners in the locality, with the leaders of the nearby adventure playground and with the staff at the local health clinic. In the latter case, a weekly social work surgery (Hammersmith Sub-office 1976-7) was set up with the purpose of improving our availability to residents, health visitors and the district nurses.

Alongside these developments, work with individuals and families continued and statutory obligations were fulfilled. As the team grew in confidence both within itself and in terms of its relationship with the locality, the pre-occupation of coping with the bombardment of referrals and with caseloads became less the norm. Emphasis was increasingly given to working out priorities within a context of time, skills and resources available. This entailed developing as comprehensive a pool of information as possible, and also acknowledging the demands of the department. In addition we began fully to realize the time it takes to develop trust and build working relationships.

Steadily, the team adopted a 'village mentality' — an intuitive understanding between each other of our habits, humour, potential, and of the stages we had reached in our professional development. 'Consciousness raising' (a term borrowed in our case from the women's movement) became part of the team's ethos and with it came a corresponding growth in personal confidence and awareness.

The halcyon days: January 1976 — July 1977:

Team developments

During the pioneer days, we developed a sound base for our

work. This groundwork was deliberately undertaken, not with any specific project in mind, but with the purpose of developing an awareness of the area in which we were based. In order to do this, it would not have been sufficient just to gain knowledge of the *existence* of relevant agencies and local organizations: we needed to know their strengths, characteristics, peculiarities and susceptibilities. In addition, by coming into contact with an increasing number of local people, we had built up a feel for what it was like to live in West Kensington and for the ordinary day-to-day problems faced by the residents. This has led to the development of a more realistic appreciation of needs and a recognition of the time it takes to build up trust. In the team we called this awareness a 'community perspective'. This could only have been developed *in conjunction* with the people and agencies in the neighbourhood. We therefore had worked, and have continued to work, simultaneously on team, community and organizational levels.

By working on this wide front, we became aware of the many potential 'projects' in which we could be appropriately involved. We responded by not going overboard on exciting new projects, and by setting ourselves the task of evaluating how best to use our time and resources. But despite developing selectivity in what we did, this continual process of evaluating our priorities and then working to them stretched our capacities to the full. At the same time the intensive work with individuals and families was extremely tiring. As part of this process, it was important that as a team we acknowledged each other's individual needs for job satisfaction, development of professional interest and for the room to grow, and that we balanced these against the major task of fulfilling our responsibilities to the distressed and disadvantaged in the neighbourhood. This entailed developing team communications; and in order to maximize our potential it became necessary to recognize each member's contribution to the corporate work effort as the team's, and of equal value. In this way, we were led to identifying the possibility of developing a collective approach within the team, and in response a measure of answerability grew between workers. The team developed a sense of self-determination, and there grew up a level of uniformity and consistency amongst us which became most noticeable in our responses to requests from outside agencies. Based on a common understanding of office capacities and priorities, we called this consistency of response the 'sub-office line'.

Interdepartmental work

With these team developments came an increase in confidence, and we began to take active steps to extend our contacts to many departments of the council. This was particularly the case with the housing and leisure and recreation departments. We had already been involved with the housing department over two of our community projects. In addition there had been conflict over the housing position of a number of individual families. After a joint meeting, a contact was established with one particular housing-aid worker. This greatly improved communications and often prevented situations reaching deadlock. In addition, we were able to offer the public a more informed service when housing advice was requested.

Contact with the leisure and recreation department had already been made through the playleaders on the adventure playground situated next door to our office. We had shared mutual concerns, particularly about the lack of provision for teenagers in the area. They had also been the ones to brighten up the external appearance of our portakabins. But we became fully involved with their director when we attended interdepartmental meetings, called to plan the provision of additional amenities on our site. By acting as a 'catalyst', our community worker was successful in bringing the local tenants' association together with the council officers for this meeting, injecting a degree of participation into the project.

A further development which added a wider perspective to the work of the office was my attendance at an interdepartmental meeting dealing with community care and community development.[9] This added a policy-making dimension to the relationship already developed between the team, and the Community Devel-

9 The community care and development group was an interdepartmental meeting designed to pool the information required for corporate planning. It also acted as a support group for the community development unit. The meeting therefore made policy proposals to council committees about developments in care provision and community resources. It would be concerned with making recommendations about the allocation of grants and funds and was very relevant to our community worker's contact with local groups and organizations.

opment Unit[10] situated in the chief executive's department. For fieldworkers, this style of working represented a departure from normal practice, and was not without political overtones. There were no hard-and-fast rules and we quickly had to develop skills in negotiation, taking opportunities and planning for change. Throughout it was imperative that we demonstrated our viability to our management. This was achieved in three main ways: by circulating written reports on projects we were undertaking, by fostering good working relationships, and by making a team decision to pay particular attention to covering our statutory responsibilities. This last requirement was seen to be necessary for our survival, as we believed ourselves to be vulnerable to accusations of sacrificing traditional responsibilities to allow room to try out alternative methods of work.

Here it should be stressed that we received considerable support from our directorate, particularly at times of conflict, and well-researched proposals (for example, for an urban-aid funded project) always received a sympathetic hearing. In turn, as our fieldwork contribution to policy became increasingly valued, we received a number of requests to send a sub-office representative to attend working parties. Topics have included child abuse procedures, use of day-care provision, developments in the field of mental health, sheltered housing and stand-by duty.

Contact with our main office remained mixed and some natural rivalry continued. Even so, in September 1976, and following full staff discussions about sub-office developments, Area 3 was fully re-organized into a 'patch' system. Here the bridging role played by the area officer and area administrative officer were all important.

Community work

We were aware of the need to maintain and develop the projects and contacts already begun. However, there was still the resource and motivation within the team to take on new initiatives. One of the features of the pioneer days had been the reluctance of the

10 The Community Development Unit (CDU) comprises a community development officer, four community workers and three policy analysts. It is situated in the chief executive's department. One of its tasks is to manage a community resource centre based in the centre of the borough.

sub-office social workers to become directly involved in community work projects. As they grew in confidence this reluctance gradually diminished. For example, one social worker began attending a group for local mothers and children with the purpose of sharing information about child-minding and fostering, and to explain the criteria involved in allocating social service provisions such as day-nursery places. Her role gradually changed to one of helping this group accept new members and facilitating their discussions about the role of women in society.

As we became known in the area, we built up many local and informal contacts for the purpose of exchanging advice and information and to offer mutual support. This had the benefit of rendering it easier for the people concerned in particular issues to come together and plan appropriate courses of action. For example, the beat policeman, a tenant association secretary, the adventure playground leader, our community worker and myself met to arrange a meeting between the tenants and ourselves to discuss the dangers of glue-sniffing for children. The meeting itself broadened into other issues, and concluded with our social work assistant sharing with tenants the difficulties caused by the lack of adequate provision for psychogeriatrics. As an extension of this, we have been concerned to identify opportunities for residents to participate in discussions about issues which directly affected them. For example, the leaders of two self-help groups attended a joint social services department/voluntary associations meeting to add a consumer's point of view to discussions about the care of the elderly. We believed this process to be preferable to our acting as advocates or spokesmen.

It should be noted that our approach has been toward the people of West Kensington and that we do not regard our 'clientele' as a fixed group. Here, the value of recognizing 'consumers' as 'resources' should be stressed. Amongst the many examples, we have seen local mothers organize and run youth clubs, young people subject to statutory orders develop their own provision and elderly people, though in need of services themselves, visit the housebound, organize activities for all ages and manage their own clubs. Residents have developed craft groups for children and a number of self-help groups for mothers and young children are now in existence. Many activities have been facilitated by two local ministers who have contributed funds, rooms and pastoral care, and our involvement has ranged from very slight to fully participative.

Developments in social work practice including work with local agencies

We have felt that the detailed knowledge gained from the earlier described groundwork, combined with our wider understanding of the strengths and weaknesses within the neighbourhood, has enabled us to make better and more open assessments, and to offer a more realistic service to the daily requests as well as to the individuals and families on our workloads. This has been helped by our gradually meeting our aim of adding a range of informal community resources to those already available within the council. In this way we have been able to view our individual contributions to the work effort within a balanced perception of the needs of the area. This was particularly the case for the social-work assistant, whose work with the elderly and physically handicapped was greatly enhanced when she established a 'safety net' for those at risk. This was done by creating a network of contacts between herself and the local clubs, groups, neighbours, porters and shopkeepers, in addition to establishing working relationships with both general practitioners and the consultant psychiatrist.

For all of us a clear professional identity, combined with an appreciation of our positions as social service department employees, produced more confident and honest relationships with our clients. In addition our responses to outside bodies became less reactive than in the past. By being party to the 'sub-office line', and by determining a level of responsibility appropriate to our priorities, we were able to combat the false expectations of outside agencies and to avoid falling prey to a previous tendency to feel responsible for everything. On many occasions we have been asked to ensure that particular families conform to certain, and often unrealistic, patterns of prescribed behaviour. The alternative was for the family to suffer some unpleasant consequences (e.g. an appearance in court). This has been tantamount to blackmail. We have resisted making such promises, leaving the requesting agency with the task of working out its own policy and attitude towards families as opposed to using social workers as convenient intermediaries. As a result, we have felt less subject to a 'trade in guilt' and subsequently have not been demoralized by a continued failure to do the impossible. We believe that this stance avoids misleading families into thinking that we have ultimate powers of protection, which is patently not the case. Instead, we have concentrated on our task of working with people to help improve their situations.

In addition to the health service links that had previously been established, great strides were made in developing the psychiatric provision for the area. This was done in partnership with the consultant psychiatrist and his medical social worker[11] and resulted in a demonstrable improvement in the domiciliary and after-care services for the mentally ill. This had the effect of altering the balance of workloads within the team. We developed further links with a local day nursery, a child guidance clinic and the residential homes in the locality. It was our impression that, as team members grew more confident in their roles, our mutual contacts in this field became increasingly honest and supportive. As a result social workers began taking on a greater proportion of cases involving interpersonal, marital and family problems. We believe this came about as the result of receiving more appropriate referrals, which in itself was a response to the team offering a more intimate knowledge of resources and a wider range of skills. This led to a demand from team members for further skill development. As a response, we held our own workshops on casework and in addition actively began to seek out courses, initially in community work and then in working with children, marital therapy, family therapy and advanced casework.

In general, we became less frustrated by the forms and procedural aspects of the department, and began using them for the benefit of the service we were offering. In addition the statutory responsibilities began to take their rightful place as part of the office workload. In the past we had blamed these aspects for our not being able to do the 'real' work; but under close examination we realized that in terms of distress we would in any case see many

11 Fortnightly meetings were held with the consultant psychiatrist. These were not seen as 'interest groups' but as an essential *team* activity. The medical social worker also visited the office, and would spend one morning a fortnight working alongside the sub-office team. (The catchment area hospital was 13 miles away.)

of these cases as priorities irrespective of their statutory connotations.

Training

From the outset the office has played its part in receiving students on placement. During the first year, students were placed in the usual manner, that is, allocated by the college. For subsequent placements, students have only come to us following a visit to the office and agreement by all three parties involved. In all cases, and in addition to the formal supervision arrangements, the whole team has taken an active interest in the students' progress. In turn the students have been expected to participate as team members.

A further contribution to formal social-work training began late in 1975, when we began to receive requests to give lectures and seminars. The topics were usually on the work of the sub-office or the integration of community work into an area team. These requests were undertaken by different members of the team, sometimes in twos or threes. By way of reciprocal benefit we have had useful discussions with a number of college lecturers in the office over a working lunch.[12]

Comment

As the office became an established part of the community, many callers would stop by. These included the beat policeman, general practitioners, education welfare officers, tenants' association secretaries, adventure playground workers, ministers, kids looking for comics, sheltered-housing wardens, porters and leaders of self-help groups. These informal contacts all helped to cement the formal links we had developed. The benefits inherent in improved communications were quickly accepted as natural spin-offs from

12 Discussions with workers from outside the office often took place over a working lunch. This created the opportunity to share ideas and perceptions and seek out common ground. People who have been to lunch include health visitors, officers from juvenile bureaus, leaders of self-help clubs for the elderly, local general practitioners, the director of social services, the assistant director for fieldwork, advisers from the town hall, visiting college lecturers, colleagues from other area teams and our main office, and our area officer.

working in a community-based office. We began to broaden our allegiance to include a number of local residents, and many workers from different settings. We became less naive about possibilities for initiatives in the community, and well aware of the hard work required to create opportunities for new ways of working and of the consequent role strain. We believe it is a social-work task to work alongside residents to promote better use of social-services resources. There is therefore an important role for fieldworkers in enabling real participation by residents so that there is a genuine influence on planning rather than the pseudo-participation exercises which tend to prevail. However, to achieve this, social workers have first to recognize the need for a change of attitude:

> if they are going to fulfil their statutory obligations and remove people and children from their homes, then in addition to 'preventive casework', they have to be involved on a wider scale and encourage the development of community networks, local resources and more humane procedures;
> they do not have a monopoly on caring;
> they need to be willing to get involved in the procedural aspects of their authorities or agencies.

For the sub-office, we learned to work as a team and to incorporate a range of methods of intervention in our approach. It should be noted that this was instrumental in affecting these changes in attitudes.

Maintenance days: July 1977 to date

By the summer of 1977, the pioneering spirit was no longer in evidence, and that period of rapid growth in development and consciousness which usually takes place during initial stages of new learning experiences was over. The excitement of the earlier foraging days had given way to the less inspiring work of maintaining established links and keeping in touch with existing projects. At the same time there was a comforting feeling of being 'older' and more used to each other, which in turn helped promote a high degree of confidence in holding the 'sub-office line'. We discovered how tired we all were, and we became concerned with maintaining the consistency and standard of our service in the face of fluctuating demands. In effect we felt we had reached a plateau.

With these changes in mood and pace the team settled back. As a result, some discrepancies from the team philosophy began to show, together with disparities between workers. For example, attempts were made by some team members to give status to specific areas of work and it became unacceptable to show pleasure in team performance or talk in terms of beliefs. This overall tendency to become too inward-looking challenged our collective ideology, and in particular the extent to which we were able to refer to shared responsibilities. Despite this a high standard of work was maintained. This was because the team almost automatically adhered to its first principles, and for all team members identification with the sub-office remained a strong motivating element.

For the groups in the community, in contrast to the mood of the office, this period proved to be one of maximum development in self-determination. An example of this change in trends was the increase in self-sufficiency shown by some of the local groups. This was highlighted by the change in the use of departmental community-work 'seeding' money. This fund was initially obtained through our community worker's efforts in 1974 and allowed up to £30 to be given as a grant to enable community groups to start new projects. During 1978 seven such grants were made to groups within the sub-office area. All were requested by the groups themselves, in contrast to the former practice of workers making the application for funds for a group they were initiating or leading. This change of emphasis showed we were achieving the aims of our team philosophy. It was therefore heartening for the team, and for our community worker in particular, as it underlined his belief in the concept of mutual education.

Our approach to community group work gradually became more flexible and we began to look outside the office for skilled involvement. For example a group of depressed women, initially led by a student in the office, was successfully transferred, when the student left, to the group worker based in our main office. There were further lights on the horizon. I had been chairman of the management committee of the West Kensington Detached Youth Work Project; a project sponsored by Bishop Creighton

House Settlement. After running it for 18 months, the youth worker left the project and a review took place which resulted in a recommendation for the provision of a youth house in West Kensington. This idea coincided with those being put forward by a group of girls who, with the help of our community worker, were attempting to form their own youth provision. Following good across-team communications, proposals were combined and an application to the Inner City Urban Programme for funding was successful. This project is currently in progress.

It should be remembered that basic to all the work done was the effort put into the administration, referrals and allocated cases in the 'engine room' of the office. This was a phrase we used to give dignity and purpose to those workers who predominantly dealt with the more routine work. It was acknowledged that this work was important in its own right as well as essential for our survival as a unit and for our credibility within the department.

We continued to search for ways of improving contacts with agencies, which we knew had the benefit of improving the quality of referrals in both directions. We had already established good working relationships with a local general practice. After discussions, a pilot project was proposed in which one of our social workers would attend the surgery for one session a week to pick up referrals and discuss areas of work. Similar to the social work surgery at the health clinic, it was hoped that this project would have mutually educative benefits and further our accessibility (This attachment began in January 1979.)

One of the major difficulties faced by the team was the feeling of becoming something of a showpiece. We had always seen ourselves as a permanent social services office, attempting from a community base to widen perspectives and develop the skills to offer a range of methods of intervention. We therefore found it hard to hear that we were being quoted as a practice example for other people's pet theories or ideals. We were cited as examples of (a) abolishing casework, (b) having no allocated cases, (c) having only group supervision or (d) having a totally collective approach to management — none of which was the case. We were also at times being seen as a potential subject for research. In these circumstances it became necessary to assert that we were not trying out the latest fad, and that it was totally against team philosophy to consider ourselves as experimental in a laboratory sense. To us these suggestions seemed to deny the task-oriented nature of social services fieldwork and the functional basis on which we had developed. Jo Klein said in December 1974[13] that the team had a 'clear sense of priorities and direction and felt secure enough to withstand random pressures to change.' Fortunately, we believe this statement has remained true throughout.

Although the team will probably never again build up such a head of steam as in the halcyon days, a high standard of assessment and decision making, sound judgment in planning on all levels and a good community and inter-agency network has remained. All of this has required continual feeding and a lot of effort has gone into maintaining contacts and developing skills. Earlier we had believed that we had reached a plateau. But now we can see that future changes will go through a cyclic pattern, based on a 'framework for practice' which has evolved from the outset:

> knowledge of the area and its resources, including the informal community resources we have helped promote;
> a good team understanding of its position in the department and of departmental procedures and resources;
> a developing knowledge of the skills required to work within a wide spectrum and range of methods of intervention;
> an acceptance of contributions and information based on people's experiences, irrespective of their status;
> a team responsibility for its involvement in the area and in consequence for deciding how work should be allocated;
> an understandable support network, both from within the team and outside, which has aided the adoption of wider roles amongst workers.

Here it should be noted that throughout it has been an essential task to evaluate team strengths and work to them.

Summary

The overall development of the sub-office has been based upon a belief system whose roots lie in a collective ideology. Beginning

13 In her report for the department, *Aspects of community work in locally-based teams* (December 1974).

with the team, this means that in addition to being responsible for our own performance and contribution to the work effort, we each have had a responsibility to facilitate growth in skills and confidence in each other. Team members have been encouraged to think through new ideas, and those contributions made with honest intent have been valued. This has made room for creativity within the team's basic orientation to the task of meeting need in West Kensington.

The ideology has had a dual effect for team members. On the one hand previous patterns of working in an isolated and individual manner have been modified, and the feelings of dependency which occur on stressful occasions have become shared on a mutual basis. On the other hand, our individual potential for personal and professional development has grown. This is best described by saying that the office has created an atmosphere for continued learning.

It has been our aim to enable people in the locality to widen their choices and to increase their decision-making abilities in matters affecting their lives. Fundamental to this aim has been the recognition that people have the potential for change, personal resources and some right to determine their own actions. Within the team there is a strong dislike of paternalism, of presuming needs or wishes without asking — or, having asked, of believing that replies can be understood without an appreciation of the context in which they were made. These beliefs form our *collective* radical and political awareness.

On the practical side, these beliefs have led us to consider our resource in a wider context and to perceive all activities as part of the team's total effort to meet our collective aims. In this light we have redefined the term 'referral' to include all requests for use of office resource.

Most referrals formed part of the day-to-day work of the office, where our response was well known to us and governed by the factors which make up the 'sub-office line'. However, at times when we felt we were losing direction or when we received requests to be involved in major projects, we invoked an evaluative process of collective priority-testing which we called the 'one step back'. This has usually taken place during team meetings, though the following questions have also formed the basis of more informal gatherings:

How essential is the task or referral?

Is it an appropriate one for us?

Have all the relevant people been consulted and is outside help available?

If we were to establish a contract, have we the time, the resources, skills and knowledge (known in the office as 'space') to make a worthwhile contribution — in other words, can we keep our side of the bargain?

Do we need to seek further information or training and if so who will do it, how and where?

How agreed are we as a team? Do we first need to evaluate team perspectives and consciousness?

Decisions based on this framework not only provided an initial response to a referral but in themselves were creative, acting as a springboard to the development of new methods of work. Over the years and by considering a wide range of items in this way, we have established a team awareness which has contributed a strong philosophical element to the more practical side of the 'sub-office line'. In this way we have determined a team philosophy:

the office is a resource for the area;

people have skills and, given opportunity, can establish and administer resources for themselves;

people have a right to field workers who know what they are doing and why;

an appropriate level of collective responsibility should be maintained with the team;

fieldworkers have a responsibility for the management aspects of their role.

To varying degrees, we have found our perceptions substantially different from those of our fieldwork colleagues in social services. In our opinion, this change has been due to two major factors: to our development of a community perspective, which has brought with it a much better appreciation of the reality of the area in which we work, and to our attempt to develop methods of intervention that are in tune with an assessment of need, rather than categorizing people into particular client groups which in turn dictates the deployment of a limited range of methods and resources. This has entailed offering people a range of alternative sources of action or help as *appropriate* rather than, for example, a worker making a decision to run a group primarily because it is interesting or useful for professional development.

By carrying the team philosophy with us in all aspects of our work, we have been able to influence policy decisions. For example, during inter-departmental meetings which were in the main concerned with making recommendations for additional services, we have indicated possibilities for public participation. In this area of work, our aim has been to facilitate communications between residents and council departments so that people become increasingly involved in the setting up and running of local amenities, such as community halls. The educative work done by the team in the neighbourhood has been essential in bringing this about.

At times we have come into conflict with colleagues from outside the office, both over cases in common and over policy matters. This has happened when, for example, due to lack of community knowledge, outside workers have shown a tendency to err on the side of safety when making crucial decisions. These actions are often governed by the worker's own anxieties and personal values. It is also important to make an informed and critical contribution to the formulation of policy and procedures, otherwise these might end up designed for administrative ease or political ends and work against the disadvantaged in the community. If fieldworkers are to act in advocacy roles (as well as educative ones), then we believe it should be in these areas, which for the public are generally inaccessible and obscure.

Because the team has been able to hold firm to the sub-office line, and develop self-respect, outside agencies have received well-thought-out responses to their demands. This has influenced their attitudes, if not toward all social workers, at least toward this team.

> But let a person stop performing within the range of organizational acceptability, and there will immediately become visible the membership of his role set and the expectations which they hold for him.   (Katz and Kahn (1966), 176)

In effect, we reversed our tendency to take on board their anxieties and responsibilities and we have refused to be treated as handmaidens. Our beliefs were fundamental to achieving these changes for, as Hinton says: 'First and foremost, was the decision to struggle, to dare to fight, to dare to win' (Hinton 1966, 122).

This method of standing firm to bring about change was not applied as a technique but followed naturally from the original approach we adopted. This was because the approach itself was based on an understanding of the everyday realities of West Kensington. As a team, we have placed emphasis on the planning and preparatory stages of our work so as to avoid continually having to make the best of decisions made retrospectively. This has given us self-determination as professionals and the confidence to respond to change. In essence we have become task-oriented and have refused to meet expectations randomly. People have told us we are either loved or hated, and perhaps this is why.

There are many historical precedents within the department, and longstanding perceptions and procedures are difficult to change. However, the level of delegation to the sub-office has been sufficient for us to exercise a fair degree of professional discretion, including involvement in recruitment; and within limits it has been possible to make mistakes and cross hierarchical boundaries. At times we have unintentionally upset the established rules and bypassed levels of management. However, relationships have remained supportive and it would not have been possible for sub-office developments to have taken place without some backing from within the department. Extending our knowledge of constraints and procedures to include those which apply within the local authority committee structure has proved beneficial, both to applications for funding and to the quality of the information which we have passed on to local groups.

The constraints on implementing the team approach which we have experienced within the local authority have been both practical and attitudinal. We have experienced an unwillingness, particularly among middle managers, to accept contributions from certain workers despite their relevant experience, because of their low hierarchical status. On a wider scale there has been a tendency by management to accept our developments and use them to develop practice, but at the same time demand that we conform to procedural rules which were intended for large area offices. This has reduced our flexibility in implementing a neighbourhood-related service. For example, insistence that we cover intake all day (including lunch times) has meant that there is no time the team can 'peacefully' be together, and even working lunches are subject to interruption. Whilst we have enjoyed a fair degree of autonomy, to some extent this has been carved out by the team itself exhibiting a high level of responsibility.

Additional practical difficulties have occurred due to the critical level of staffing margins in the area office. This becomes even more acute for the sub-office because, for example, maternity leave or delays in recruitment quickly have a significant impact on manpower. In addition, there has been the local authority view of each individual worker fulfilling a list of duties detailed in a job description. This has laid the day-to-day accountability for workers' performance with the team leader. As a result, I have had to learn to combine management accountability with my contribution to the collective approach. This has required a high level of integrity by all team members.

As an office, we have gained the respect of the people who live in West Kensington and of the departments and agencies with which we have had contact. This respect has had the result of increasing our power base. In consequence, we have had to be careful not to be pressurized by outside agencies and misuse the respect we have earned or to use our statutory authority to detrimental effect. In particular we have learned to become more accountable for the limitations of our service, and as a result we have had to cope with stressful exchanges.

We have recognized the importance to our developments of being a small team in a community-based office with collective responsibility for a defined catchment area. In addition, the administrative and intake arrangements have played an integral part in our adopting a wider approach. Our accessibility has increased the likelihood of us being called upon to answer to the neighbourhood for our actions. This meant that we have had to sharpen up our social work identity and lose some innocence. It was also important for us to retain our right to exercise confidentiality. We have also developed an understanding of the levels and skills involved in community work which we have been able to integrate into our day-to-day thinking.

It should be stressed that a wider perspective enhances assessments, providing that the skills in synthesizing information have been developed. We first learned to do this as a team, and later developed individual abilities by learning from the team experience. This has led to a demand from team members for skill development, particularly in the planning and intervention stages of casework as well as in the broader roles of community work, group work, inter-agency liaison and planning. This has not been without role strain for all of us, and we have recognized the need to tolerate openness within the office, and the exposure of work to colleagues. In conclusion, there is room for honesty, anger, humour, banter and caring in a team where all workers feel they have a chance to do the work for which they were actually trained. This is a condition of our being able to form a balanced, consistent and yet flexible approach to the community.

8

Beyond CDP: reaction and community action

Marjorie Mayo

'Axe falls on urban projects — bang goes another community plan'
'Grant cut closes deprivation unit — poverty reports "gagged"'
(NCDP 1977b)

Despite their apparent topicality, these headlines refer, in fact, to the mid-1970s. Without in any way belittling the significance of the policy changes initiated by the present government, even these shifts have to be set within a longer historical perspective. The last Community Development Projects were being buried in a wider atmosphere of gloom which predated the present period of cuts in the social services; high levels of unemployment and increasing demands for the very services which were being restricted. Yet this was the same period that the last government embarked upon yet another initiative to combat urban deprivation and urban decay. Although the focus was clearly different, the White Paper on the inner cities still included references to the value of community development: 'Every effort will need to be made to establish and maintain good relationships with local communities who have a vital part to play' (HMSO 1977). Despite all the real and significant policy shifts since the change of government in May 1979, the Inner Cities initiative still, at the time of writing, remains, even if the bottom has been knocked out of it, through the latest round of public expenditure cuts. Meanwhile, the European Economic Community has launched one anti-poverty programme and is considering a further programme for 1982.

This chapter attempts to examine these apparent contemporary contradictions and to set them in the context of the policy dilemmas of the seventies. The first section summarizes some of the pressures which led central and local governments to reproduce a series of 'community' initiatives — small area projects with some built-in citizen participation. This section also looks at some of the lessons which the State learnt, however imperfectly, from these experiences, and focuses upon the increasing pressures for more effective control. Although the public expenditure cuts have exacerbated these pressures, they stem from political as well as from economic factors.

The second section concentrates upon the lessons which community workers and their client community groups learned in the seventies. Despite all the present setbacks, the chapter concludes that the CDP phase led to both experimentation and consolidation. Community work survived the decade with developments of great potential, whether or not this potential can now be realized. Finally, the conclusion raises some of the current dilemmas for policy both in Britain and beyond, in the EEC.

Continuing pressures for 'community' solutions

The reasons for the government's formal entry into priority areas projects such as the Educational Priority Areas, and into community work with the launching of the CDP initiative, have already been amply debated elsewhere (e.g. NCDP 1977b, Higgins 1978, Mayo 1975). In summary, these explanations have centred around two major themes: governments' attempts to devise more effective and sensitive means of social control in areas with a high incidence of social pathology; and governments' attempts to rationalize social welfare provision, and maximize cost effectiveness, to curb the increase in public expenditure on the personal social services, whilst if possible improving their efficiency and flexibility in meeting the increasingly vocal demands of their clients. This is not to imply that CDP was particularly effective in this respect, rather that it was one of the original government hopes for the project. The current implications of this second theme are particularly relevant when extended to the wider rationalization policies of central government — in its directly economic as opposed to political and ideological functions — the strategy for the rationalization of British industry to restore its profitability. In one sense, CDP represented the first applications of this strategy to the social services — rationalization to obtain better value for the same resources, thereby forestalling the need to expand the level of expenditure. Additional resources would then be freed from the sphere of social reproduction for more directly productive investments.

In another sense, as *Gilding the ghetto* (NCDP 1977b) points out, CDP fits into the general concern of the Wilson government with social consequences of industrial reorganization, since redundancies and closures amongst industry's 'lame ducks' would inevitably hit older working-class communities disproportionately hard. Beneath the obvious differences, similar pressures can also be traced behind the launching of the inner cities/ partnerships proposal. The inner city areas chosen for the partnership schemes[1] and the 28 districts designated for less extensive assistance under the Inner Urban Areas Act 1978 were also chosen in part[2] at least because they contained concentrations of high unemployment, social problems and environmental decay. These blighted central city areas, then, were symptomatic of the social consequences of the Labour government's industrial strategy, to encourage private enterprise to expel living labour as part of the rationalization process to restore falling rates of profit, and to invest in new capital-intensive rather than labour-intensive machinery.

In addition to the partnership programme's concern to isolate and thus cope with the social consequences of these broader processes within confined geographical areas, there would also appear to have been a concern to deal with some of the more directly economic contradictions. In particular, the rationalization and centralization of British industry has entailed the rapid decline of the small firms sector — proportionately smaller than any of its western competitors. There was some evidence of government concern that this process had gone too far. Small firms can after all be extremely useful if only in supplying large firms. Thus the Inner Urban Areas Act concentrated upon providing assistance (mainly in the form of loans and grants for

1 These are in Birmingham, London's five dockland boroughs, Hackney/ Islington, Lambeth, Liverpool, Manchester/Salford, Newcastle-upon-Tyne/ Gateshead.
2 There were also evidently direct political reasons for these choices.

acquiring or improving land or buildings) to the small firm to stem this decline.

Yet, as Nick Sharman (1979) concluded, 'any employment contribution to the Inner Cities from the small firm will be small at best.' Meanwhile, the industrial decline of areas like Docklands continues — together with its social consequences. As the operational programme for the area pointed out, 'There is now a very wide gap between the assessed employment needs of the area and the fulfilment of those needs.'

It is not altogether surprising, then, that the previous government reincarnated elements of previous community/small area intervention programmes before these had been finally, let alone decently, disposed of. Neither the problems of deprived communities nor the demands of their inhabitants had decreased since CDP was launched — rather the reverse. Yet fundamentally more effective and politically plausible alternative strategies were not immediately obvious, within the existing framework of constraints.

Despite the most obvious political differences between the present government and its Labour predecessor, the formal framework of inner city policies remains so far intact. Whilst the combination of public expenditure cuts and the restructuring of the welfare state have been undermining the last vestiges of these policies, the Tory ideology of anti-Statism and self-help nevertheless remain potentially contradictory pressures. Meanwhile, as it has already been suggested, the EEC has taken up the mantle — devising one anti-poverty programme and considering a second programme for 1982 to lend the community a human, caring face.

So what, if anything, has been learned?

The continuity behind the pressures to launch CDP and the partnership schemes was not of course the only aspect — there were also significant changes. On the negative side government had clearly learned some lessons about the management and control of such initiatives.

The parallels with the USA are obvious — the shift from the relatively more open 'maximum feasible participation' of the War on Poverty to the tighter city hall control of Model Cities. As Marris and Rein (1975) summarized: 'The Model Cities

programme seemed deliberately designed to restore the initiative
in reform to established authority in reaction against the radical
tendencies of community action.'

Control of the inner areas studies projects and the partnership
schemes was defined more clearly than in the original CDP briefs.
Despite the token recognition which citizen participation received
in the White Paper, the partnership committees were to represent
the interests of government departments and local government.
Local people were not among the partners, and initial calls for the
inclusion of community representatives were met with firm
refusals. Meetings were not even held in public, nor were agendas
and minutes publicly available.

Some progress was certainly made, in terms of lobbying from
representatives of groups and individuals who had experienced
having a foot in the participation door and who had no intention
of finding this door slammed in their faces. For example, the
National Council of Social Services coordinated the organization
of a lobby of the Secretary of State for the Environment in April
1978, which included a range of voluntary groups from the
relevant areas. Nevertheless the new organizational framework
for Docklands, for example, the Urban Development Corpora-
tion, announced in the autumn of 1979, was potentially even
more exclusive, of resident participation.

The structure of research was also far more carefully managed.
Instead of giving relatively open briefs to a range of different
university departments to interpret as they chose, the Department
of the Environment used private consultants for the inner area
studies. The first phase of research for the partnership schemes
was carried out on a similar basis, in response to bids from
academic and private consultants.

It seems fairly clear that the Department of the Environment
intended to sponsor research leading to a range of specific policy
recommendations, rather than to the type of marxist analysis of
the sources of contradictions within the welfare state — which
were considered in some quarters to be characteristic of the work
of the CDP central intelligence unit. (*Cutting the welfare
state — who profits?* was evidently one of the least popular of
these publications in the Home Office, and the attempted closure
of the unit so soon after the release of this paper might appear to
be more than merely coincidental.)

The inner city area — and employment policies

To come to the content, as opposed to the structure, of policies and programmes — governments of both political persuasions shifted their definitions of the causes of and the solutions to social deprivation. Most important, although least consistent, of these shifts was the recognition of the limitations of the small-area approach, and of the significance of broader economic rather than personal pathological explanations of social deprivation (see National CDP 1975-6, 1 for a summary of the shift in focus). Undoubtedly these lessons have not just been learned through the CDP experience and research. Some of the conclusions of the Inner Area Studies have also been widely quoted, for example in the White Paper *Policy for the inner cities* (HMSO 1977).

'Studies have shown that there is a collective deprivation in some inner areas which affects all residents' (HMSO 1977, 4). Such lessons might have been expected to become increasingly obvious anyway in a period of recession characterized by rapidly rising unemployment. (Unemployment had risen at least threefold in the period in question.) But CDP made a valuable contribution to this process. Such contribution as CDP did make has, however, typically received scant official recognition, coming as it did from (in political terms) a less than totally reputable source.

Having recognized the significance of broader economic factors in theory, governments have, of course, continued to promote limited small-area approaches in their practical attempts to contain definitions and hence solutions and ultimately expenditure. This ambivalence was particularly clear in the White Paper *Policy for the Inner Cities* (HMSO 1977). The decline in the economic fortunes of the inner areas was admitted to be at the heart of the problem rather than personal or even community pathologies. The need to retain existing jobs and to create new ones was clearly on the agenda.

Yet the range of policies to do this was modest to say the least, concentrating, as it has already been suggested, upon grants and loans to small firms in selected areas. Given the dangers inherent in supporting the small firms sector, including, as it does, sweat shops, this very modesty however may have been one of the programme's greatest advantages from the viewpoint of the labour movement.

Meanwhile, as in the case of CDP before it, the programme was quite uncoordinated at central government level. The Department of Industry was at that time busily engaged, via the promotion of industrial restructuring, in creating the job losses which the Partnership programme was supposed to offset. Nor were the investment programmes of the nationalized industries bent to relate to the Partnership areas' needs, rather than to the requirements of the Department of Industry's industrial strategy.

Nevertheless, the partnership programme's recognition of the significance of employment issues did have another potential importance. Employers and trade unions were clearly both to be affected by partnership schemes as well as local government, and they have therefore been accorded some role in these initiatives, (if only, for example, as participants in local employment conferences).

This recognition of the role of trade unions, in particular, has been defined in some areas in such a way as to legitimize their further involvement and to justify the case for supporting this involvement with partnership funds. The development of community involvement schemes which have included trade union as well as community representatives has been a factor of great potential significance, as the second section of this chapter will argue. It has, not surprisingly been correspondingly under scrutiny, however.

Community work and local government

The discussion has centred so far upon the actions and reactions of central government. Yet CDP was actually located within local government structures and, from the first, adverse reactions to the projects came most obviously from the relevant local authorities. Despite the greater overt conflicts between projects and local government, there have nevertheless also been contradictions and conflicting pressures and tendencies. Local government authorities of varying political complexions did still have some incentives for joining in central government community schemes, such as the partnership ventures, if only for the hope of extra resources and powers — however limited — to cope with the decline of their industrial base. The greater controls on 'citizen participation', as compared with the more open CDP briefs, were added inducements. Clearly not all local authorities see it this way, however. Clearly, too, there are frequently key differences in the reactions of officers and councillors.

Local government is in any case generally not immune from the broader pressures affecting central government, particularly the need to devise more effective yet less expensive means of intervening in areas with high social deprivation/pathology. A further parallel exists in the increasing pressures on local authorities, as on central government, to intervene more directly to sustain the profitability of their economic/rate base.

Thus community work/community intervention programmes continued to be sponsored directly by local government. Despite the climate of cuts, the sense of local government reaction against community work in general, and the attempts to devise more effective control systems, community workers were still being employed in local social service departments, although they remained a tiny minority.

The Department of Health and Social Security's figures for England in 1975 and 1976 gave a breakdown of social service staff which included a separate category for community workers. Despite the public expenditure cuts. In 1975 there were 268 (or 257 full-time equivalents).[3] In 1976 there were 381 (or 366 full-time equivalents).

These figures fit in with the trend for social work staff in general. The total figure for 1973 was 151,162; for 1974, 236,024; for 1975, 253,678; and for 1976, 259,821. The earlier rate of increase in staffing was not maintained throughout the seventies period of the cuts,[4] but overall there was a much smaller increase in staffing, rather than a net decrease.

3 The Joint Action Docklands Group, *Rebuilding Docklands* (1977a) demonstrated for example that the expanded programme did not make up even half of the capital cuts which had taken place over the previous two years.

4 These figures apply to community workers in social service departments. They do *not* therefore include community workers in other departments, e.g. housing/ planning, or those directly responsible to chief executives. Nor do they include those formally categorized as social workers whose work includes a substantial community work element. They would therefore considerably underestimate the number of community workers employed in local government. On the other hand, they do not of course distinguish between community workers in reality from those in name whose job content is in practice closer to a more traditional social work brief.

Staffing in the voluntary sector was of course also affected by the cuts, as grants from local authorities and other sources became tighter. Nevertheless, law centres,[5] for example, despite a series of attempts to cut back or close some of them,[6] not only generally survived but expanded from one centre in 1972 to 30 in 1978.

The current situation is of course more problematic. Typically the cuts in the second half of the seventies were capital cuts; revenue spending and hence staffing levels suffered far less seriously. By contrast the 1979-80 cuts were quite explicitly intended to have an impact on revenue and staffing. Local authorities are therefore bound to subject all spending to scrutiny to see where they are getting what they define as value for money and to cut where they are not.

Meanwhile, as it has already been suggested, community work had been increasingly coming under scrutiny in any case, the disbanding of the Wandsworth CD Unit in 1978 being one of the better known and more politically motivated examples of this period of local government attempts at rationalization.

The aftermath of CDP and community work practice

In summary, CDP demonstrated both that working-class communities can be organized around local issues, and that such organization, in isolation from the mainstream of political struggles, has an inherent tendency to be self-defeating. The early CDP papers (e.g. Home Office 1969) has assumed that 'the poor' were disorganized and apathetic, too alienated to act collectively upon their own behalf; yet none of the CDP teams seem to have found this to be the case. The problem was rather how to prevent such organizations from being either submerged in or totally isolated from the broader political struggles of the area.

The North Shields Project summarized this shifting perspective (Home Office 1978): 'Until the end of 1974 the project worked with groups very much in terms of making a gain — speeding up the clearance process, getting modernization, obtaining recreational facilities etc.'; whereas the emphasis from the end of 1974

5   The number of trainees actually fell from 1706 in 1975 to 1607 in 1975 and 1424 in 1976.
6   Law centres are not, of course, community work agencies *per se*, but many of them do include a 'community' function.

onwards became much more openly political in nature — dealing with 'political problems in a political way'.

Contrary to the belief of some of its critics (Salmon 1978), the redefinition of CDP as 'class politics' did not involve the total rejection of community work and community action, but a clearer recognition of its limitations. The conflicts of interest, inherent in the welfare state, were seen to represent issues of genuine significance for the working class as a whole. Typically these issues are experienced in the 'community' setting, and this is in turn the local initial focus for collective action. Thus the strength of working-class campaigns on housing, for example, has generally developed from the local associations into broader campaigns, rather than from national organizations downwards. The community can remain, then, the starting point for organizing in the arena of social reproduction and collective consumption even when the limitations of this approach are clearly recognized. 'Community' issues such as housing have to be confronted *per se* and (initially at least) with a local as well as a national focus, despite the fact that neither the ultimate causes nor the solutions lie within that locality. As the Benwell CDP concluded, then, the shift away from the original assumptions of CDP did not conflict with the retention of 'the original CDP emphasis on working with local people to develop stronger understanding of and involvement in issues affecting the area' (NCDP 1975-6).

The community work implications of these changing perspectives have already been amply discussed elsewhere, both inside and outside CDP (e.g. Krausher 1976). In summary, community issues were to be 'political' not only in the sense that they were to be analysed in a directly political context but that they were to be tackled within, rather than apart from, the broader political process. This in turn has to involve the community worker both in dealings with political parties and organizations and in building alliances with the rest of the labour movement. As part of these developments, the resource/research and development role of the community worker was highlighted — a reflection, to some extent, of the demands of an increasingly organized and experienced clientele. The establishment of trade union research in the Coventry Workshop and the North East Trade Union Studies and Information Unit, for example, were specialized attempts to provide this function.

In summary, then, one of the reasons for the current review of community participation mechanisms has been their potential relevance in the politicization of 'community' issues which in turn has facilitated the development of links between community action and the broader political and economic struggles of the labour movement. These struggles have been filtering through, and there is considerable evidence of growing understanding and interest — for example at the Association of Community Workers Conference on Jobs and Community Action in 1978.

Organizing in London's Docklands: an example of trends in community since CDP

Accounts of the process of participation in drawing up the strategic plan for the redevelopment of Docklands exist already; so do accounts of the first phase of the united trade union and community campaigns to resist further dock closures and consequent job losses in east London (Joint Docklands Action Group 1977b).

A key theme (and one which follows on from the CDP experience) has been the significance of building alliances between community groups and the trade union movement and, when appropriate, beyond. For example, a march demonstrating against proposed closures of the West India Docks in 1976 included not only trade union and community organizations but also members of relevant local authorities and of the local clergy. In one sense, of course, such alliances have been an established pattern in east London for at least a century — characteristic of traditional working-class communities which lived, worked and organized together. On the other hand, this unity was not automatic (see Fishman 1975, Piratin 1978), but the product of conscious and concerted effort.

The alliance of trade unionists and community groups which resisted the attempted dock closures of 1976 had to be sustained to combat renewed and more far-reaching attempts at closing all the remaining upstream docks in 1978. There have been constant pressures to pare down such alliances by redefining the issue along more confined, traditional lines (one of the principal justifications of the broader approach being, in contrast, to extend the definition of the issues and to follow up the wider implications). For example, in any campaign to resist closures and preserve jobs there are inbuilt pressures to confine the issues and hence the bargaining process within strictly trade union lines — pay and conditions, and the level of redundancy payments; whereas any broader campaign demands that the issue is defined in terms of its wider implications — the ripple effects of the closure upon the surrounding community in terms of jobs, incomes, community services and environment.

Such an approach not only emphasizes the legitimacy of the community involvement in job issues and vice versa (the trade unions' involvement in community/planning issues such as the Docklands strategy). The directly political content is also implicitly emphasized — the underlying conflicts of interest which are the objects of political struggle, rather than of administrative or technical resolution. The dock closures, for example, could no longer be confined to technical questions arising from the container revolution and the impact of new technology (see Joint Docklands Action Group 1978). These rationalizations were set in the national context of the government's strategy to promote the profitability of British industry, and of the costs of industrial change not only to the immediate employees but to the surrounding workforce and community.

The experience both of participation in planning process and of the campaign against dock closures also emphasized the value of both the community and trade union partners, if the broader political struggle were to be effective. The strength of the alliance has depended upon the organizational strength of all the allies, so that there could be no question of overvaluing one to the detriment of the other. By promoting such strategies, community workers are not then putting themselves out of business or even assigning their client community groups merely a subservient role, playing second fiddle to the trade union organizations, as some of the critics have implied (e.g. Smith 1978).

The development of alliances has also facilitated shifts in the research process in Docklands. Research of industrial trends in a small area, and their impact upon the local community, had been underdeveloped and fraught with practical difficulties. For example, Department of Employment data has not been collected within boundaries comparable with local authority areas, although this is to change in the partnership areas such as Docklands. This type of background research has been one of the resource inputs which has acquired increasing significance both for community work in Docklands, and more widely elsewhere. Clearly, rational arguments were not the key factor in persuading the Port of London Authority not to close the upstream docks so far, (1976-78)[7], any more than the National CDP's (1975) analysis of an industrial giant like Tate & Lyle has, by itself, affected the company's operations. The provision of research and intelligence has had its place, however, not only as a propaganda exercise in presenting the case to the relevant structures such as the PLA, local authorities and central government, but also as part of the development of the community and trade union organizations' own definitions and understanding of the issues and the solutions.

Conclusion

This chapter has argued that despite the growing pressures for economic stringency and more effective political control mechanisms, during the seventies, government community intervention programmes still retained some, albeit more limited, room for manoeuvre. In the wake of the CDP experience, in particular, there developed a series of initiatives which demonstrated real progressive potential, the most significant of which centred around the broad alliance between community organizations and the labour movement.

To suggest that some progressive potential managed to survive increasing scrutiny and the first round of public expenditure cuts in the mid and late seventies, however, is in no way to predict that this will necessarily survive the next decade. The community workers and activists involved may be far more experienced now, and better equipped to make maximum use of the more limited space for manoeuvre. Similarly, the organization of public service sector workers may be enabling them (via their trade unions) to intervene more effectively in social policy issues. But these factors have to be set against the current decreases in public expenditure being made available to support this type of community initiative. Nor is there any particular reason to

7   The example of these joint campaigns in Docklands has been quoted not for its uniqueness or originality, but rather for its potential typicality. It does not take into account the changes in the situation arising from more recent events.

suppose that community intervention programmes of this type will survive the present process of restructuring the welfare state, which has already demonstrated the vulnerability of far more 'sacred cows' of the post-1945 welfare state settlement. On the other hand, the present government does not appear to have a clearly-thought-out policy towards community work, or to the voluntary sector more generally, in the same way that it has a policy for the restructuring of public housing, education or the NHS.

There are also some contradictory pressures, arising, for example, from Tory commitment to an ideology of voluntary effort and self-help. Nor is this solely an extreme right-wing ideology, since more liberal and anti-bureaucratic versions of its implied anti-statism have also been proposed (for example, by Lynda Chalker, Sheila Moore and Andrew Rowe, in their paper 'We are richer than we think: how to mobilize community resources to meet community needs'.) At least until the government responds to the debate on the Wolfenden Committee's report on the future of voluntary organizations, there may still be some space in which to press the case for a definition with some relatively progressive implications for funding policies. Clearly the scrutiny process and the tightening of control mechanisms can be expected to continue nevertheless, although not necessarily at their present intensity, if once government policy is more clearly defined.

The other and perhaps immediately more promising potential source of support for community intervention programmes is the EEC. For example, since 1975 the EEC has been sponsoring a range of pilot projects as part of its anti-poverty programme. In Britain these have included 50 per cent funding of three community resource centres in Govan, Glasgow, London and South Wales. Although funds for these projects run out over the coming year, the possibilities for developing further EEC programmes are being explored.

The history of these negotiations may ultimately demonstrate certain themes in common with the history of CDP — the pressures, for example, for the Commission to be seen to be concerned with social issues in the face of rising unemployment, to give the EEC a human caring face, whilst confining expenditure to certain geographical areas, and avoiding overstepping the jurisdiction of member states. In the case of the EEC, the anti-poverty programme's history may also need to be understood in the context of the power struggles between its constituent parts, the Commission, the European Council of Ministers and the newer elected; European Parliament. Despite the differences, there are parallels, both with the British programmes, and with the way in which they in turn learned and failed to learn from the US War on Poverty of the sixties.

More immediately, however, the issues for British community projects and activists relate to whether or not there is a further European programme (or programmes), and, if so, whether or not they can find both funds and sufficient room for manoeuvre within the European programme(s). Finally, even if these developments do occur, will the British government be prepared to meet 50 per cent of the bill, or can any alternative sources of funds be found? Although the prospects are not unremittingly bleak, time is not necessarily on the projects' side.

9

The problem with Authority
Myra Garrett

This article begins with a personal statement because authority is something personal as well as political. My politics have developed from personal experiences, which only lately have begun to be informed by reading and discussing history and theory. The more I learn about socialism and marxism, the more sense I can make of my experience, past and present. This back and forth process between theory and practice is for me an important and essential one. It is by engaging in it that we can make our experiences useful to one another.

I also want to look at some specific social work situations and their underlying authority issues. The assumptions of the welfare state, of professionalism and of our culture in general rest on a set of mystifications meant to prevent too much questioning and thinking. Getting them out in the open and linking them to experience can be both enlightening and liberating. I would like my struggle against the ignorance and liberalism carefully taught me in my family, school and social work jobs to have some meaning for you. The path I've taken, and would openly ask you to take, doesn't at this point have a clear destination. Travelling along together in the same general direction may in the process of the journey make that destination more clear and increase our chances of getting there.

I was hesitant to write an article for a book such as this, and imagine that the others who do so are better able to make clear and precise what they want to say. They are better academics, theoreticians, historians, etc, etc. I am a practitioner and campaigner. But the sort of split which I am imposing on myself is the essence of what I am politically and personally pledged to overcome. The trouble is that writing is an isolated activity, one which is susceptible to ego trips, exaggerations and arrogance. On the other hand, one must take responsibility for what one writes for others to read, and respect the sensibilities of those readers able to see through that which is of no use to them.

Authority is to me ...

My great leap forward in understanding and exposing authority happened at the first Case Con conference in April 1971. A bloke at the back was making a contribution to the debate on the statement of aims, which began, 'We stand in opposition to capitalism ... '. That was pretty heady stuff for an American liberal only just arrived in the UK and only just beginning to think about the politics of social work. Anyway, he told us that six months earlier he'd begun a probation course after years as a skilled worker and trade unionist. He found himself unexpectedly referred to a psychiatrist by his tutor because of his 'authority problems'. This was a development, he said, that was perplexing. 'I've always known that authority had problems with me, but for the first time I'm being told that I have problems with authority.'

Without thinking much about it, I've always been involved in conflicts around authority. My typical pattern of reaction to adolescent anxiety about my self-image, etc, was to become 'teacher's pet', something I found much easier than competing with my peers socially. Beginning my social work practice as a probation officer, I was told and accepted that I would be offering my youthful probationers 'a constructive experience with authority'. At the same time I had trouble getting on with a new supervisor who said, in a probationary report which recommended against my internal promotion to senior practitioner, 'she won't take no for an answer.' On several occasions, I've been described as over-identifying with clients, or students in a teaching situation, which must mean the misplacement of allegiances or respecting the wrong authority.

And, as a woman in relation to men, I adopted either a neuter and thus equal and allowably competitive style in non-intimate relationships, or a passive supportive style in more complex emotional sexual encounters. In looking back, I seem to have alternated between my teacher's-pet syndrome and the more challenging career-woman-with-brains model. This seems to amount to a choice between being, or acting like, an authority, or getting close to one. Maybe this is the way most of us behave and is therefore quite 'normal'. But, once the layers of liberal mystification began to peel away (to which Case Con contributed significantly), I became more and more dissatisfied with my approach, not only as a social worker, but more fundamentally as a woman.

As I became more committed to a socialist perspective on social work and life, I found myself, like the bloke at the Case Con conference, more often than not in open conflict with the authority figures around me. I was becoming more outspoken and questioning, but not in the same competitive way somehow. Important ideas were involved — principles even. And there were so many things which made so much more sense to me. I was at the same time becoming much clearer about what the problems — with me, my clients, social work, the system — really are.

Authority problems

In a direct challenge to the authority of a social services management to dismiss me as a probationary social worker, I found myself in the midst of a storm that was to confirm and expand my newly-found socialist consciousness. I was 'charged' with mishandling 3 cases, and after a number of trade union meetings, demonstrations, threats, etc. it was agreed that my 4 months work should be examined by a panel of inquiry. While I was unanimously supported by the basic-grade members of the team, the senior staff offered in evidence against me the following: the setting up of a group about groups as a bid to obtain the allegiance of the team and a play for leadership; sabotaging a mental health group set up by the senior social worker, allowing a client to sit round my desk and thus have access to confidential material, inflexibility due to a coherent philosophical approach, and lack of warmth and sensitivity caused by strong personal convictions.

Concluding that the case against me was not proven, the inquiry reported: 'On this evidence, we feel it would be a grave and irresponsible step for Myra's appointment to be confirmed.

On the other hand there is no satisfactory evidence to terminate Myra's appointment. We therefore recommend that the Director extends the terms of Myra's probation and seeks ways of testing out the issues raised by Myra's performance in this assessment.' One further quote is particularly apt: 'We would only say that we have been struck by the degree to which Myra with her experience and very clearly worked out philosophy denies her power in the Team, and particularly in relation to the Senior staff.'

I doubt whether any other probationary social worker's work has ever been examined in such minute detail, and I hope it never happens again. There was (and still is in many places) no established procedure for appeal against dismissal during the probationary period. It is considered an area of management pre-rogative for which no hard criteria exist for assessing 'suitability'. The whole procedure thus becomes very subjective. The list of 'charges' and the 'evidence' were mostly things against which there was no 'defence' and which were seen as negative only in that particular situation. Things like being clear thinking and widely experienced were somehow not desirable characteristics. My 'young and inexperienced' team mates, most of whom did in fact have considerable social service experience, were described as 'easily led' by my bid for 'alternative leadership within the team'.

It was a difficult and frightening experience, but one from which I have learned a great deal. I tried at the time to write something about it for *Case Con*, and although that article ('By whose authority') now seems quite idealistic, it does contain the nub of something I've been thinking about ever since. This is the first time I've tried to put down on paper where I've got to since, and is an attempt to clarify in the process of sharing.

There was one other major educational experience for me, again with the same social service management. After three years, I foolishly resigned and went back to the States. After a few months in the land of opportunity, I knew I had made a mistake, and asked if I could come back to work with the team. My old team mates and the trade union were solid in support and took some very effective local action. But I had made several fundamental mistakes. Firstly, I had failed to see myself as a 'dangerous person' to management. Secondly, I put myself outside the protection of the trade union when I handed in my resignation. There were no questions about attitude or suitability this time. Despite the fact that we had been through all that before and that my co-workers were solid in support, it mattered not. The arbitrary authority of the management could not be challenged this time. I had made myself vulnerable to that authority by individualizing my relationship to it. After subsequent rejections by three other Local Authorities it seemed clear I was on some sort of 'blacklist'. A lesson not to be forgotten.

Good social work for whom?

When we take up social work there's probably some sort of idealism involved — we like other people, are committed to a more just and caring society, or some such. But frustration and then cynicism soon set in when we begin to realize there's so little we can do about the problems we are supposed to be dealing with. We have to satisfy ourselves with forming relationships with and maybe even being liked by our clients. 'The relationship is the primary tool of social work' is what my training taught me. We have only such tools to solve structural problems which we all know are not of the individual's making, or within his or our control. If we try to raise these questions and issues in the work setting, soon someone is telling us that our attitude is wrong, or — even more serious — that we have problems with authority. We will never know how many people leave jobs and training courses at this point — 'counselled out' is the usual term — being told and perhaps believing that they are 'unsuitable'. But by whose criteria and unsuitable for what?

What then is a good social worker? It obviously depends on who is making the judgement, but from management's point of view, it's pretty clear. A well-organized, disciplined, caring person who wants to get on in the world and therefore wants to please everyone, including those above. Most of us are taught that ambition and success are good things. Getting ahead — ahead of other people — and doing better in someone's eyes gets us increased status and authority. We must accept authority from above if we want to get some for ourselves, and surely we should tell our clients that this is the way the system works. Why should they or we fight it? Why not get what we can out of it? Adjust, adapt, mature, be reasonable, try harder and be patient?

What about democracy? It's supposed to be about participation, people making collective decisions about important things that affect their lives. But ambition and success require private competitiveness. This individual striving for success, along with the belief that anyone who really tries can make it, flies in the face of the 'caring' rationale — except for those who aren't much good at competition like the old, sick and poor. We don't get together to do things because we might lose the advantage we might have over at least someone, somewhere. We are encouraged to be deferential and passive to authority but ambitious and successful enough to get up far enough to make decisions which affect others. We can afford to care about our clients as long as doing so doesn't interfere with the efficient peaceful running of the department and the smooth relations between management, workers and clients.

The message come through ever clearer. Individual competitiveness and collective passivity induce mistrust in ourselves and others and feed the 'human nature' arguments against collective responsibility. The welfare state, which is meant to be caring, turns out to be mean, divisive and oppressive, like the rest of our society, to both its consumers and workers. Well disciplined 'suitable' workers involve themselves in the enforcement of the social order and its deeply divisive ideologies — the soft cops. Soon they (we) no longer notice that the idealism has vanished or has been transformed into ambition. Perhaps it is better after all to over-identify with the organization or with management than with the client. Social security workers develop the idea that it's *their* money and overlook telling claimants of their entitlements. Social workers accept the job of upholding the moral values of the system and urge their clients to grow up and adapt. The welfare state successfully encourages these tendencies in us and supports the 'soft cop' mentality.

Ambition, individualism, professionalism, respect for authority, even caring seem to depend on deference and passivity. I've grown to mistrust and oppose these things which I once accepted as good and/or necessary. I've come more and more to respect the anger, fighting spirit and collective traditions usually buried deep in us and our clients. Based on this response has come an understanding of apathy — a concept widely used in social work as an explanation for why all sorts of things like democracy won't work. Apathy is probably disillusionment with the democratic myth about success and a justifiable lack of confidence based on the way power is distributed. Maybe it is also about not having much collective experience as a basis for taking action. You stick your neck out a few times, get the chop and you don't do it again. The system runs on apathy, encourages it and then condemns it as a social problem. Apathy is one example of the kinds of tricks of thinking my education and conditioning have carefully taught me.

Practicing or performing?

Beginning to see the world and the welfare state in particular in this sort of perspective is important. Every bit as important if you happen to be a social worker is finding a way to practise social work with the same view. The cost of doing so in terms of the dominant values of our culture can be high. Once convinced of the correctness of the argument, one's sanity demands living by its principles. The congruence between theory and practice has its own rewards, but with such a theory even these go against the cultural grain. If ambition, individualism and competition are antithetical to collective action for collective solutions, then we need to develop a sort of 'egolessness' in our responses and actions. We have to be prepared to question arbitrary, ascribed authority wherever encountered and to be questioned in turn when we slip into the cultural traps ourselves.

'Egolessness' is inadequate and awkward as a description of the concept I'm after. It is an attempt to express the conviction that ideas and principles can be promoted and espoused without promoting the ego of the espouser. Self-confidence comes from being sure where you stand and being willing to say so without concern for being liked, successful or pleasing others. It means, I think, being guided by a set of principles that have to do with collective power rather than individual power. It means being rather odd in the eyes of the various establishments — educational, occupational, familial and even political. It means going against what most of us have been carefully taught about success, and being suspicious of anyone who preaches ideas s/he doesn't practise, or is personally ambitious.

I recently found a rhyme which, despite its sexism, says it all. I don't know its origins — maybe one of the many songs of the 'Wobblies' (International Workers of the World):

A Union man you cannot be,
No matter how you try,
Unless you think in terms of WE
And not in terms of I.

Egolessness in social work inevitably leads to 'unprofessional' relationships with clients, workmates, seniors, management etc. Being a good social worker in the eyes of your clients and work-mates isn't enough to protect you from criticism and hostility. Even being well qualified doesn't help. Such a social worker is almost bound to be viewed with suspicion by management. All sorts of negative motivations are ascribed by others — a bid for leadership, opposition to *any* rules or structure, authority problems, sabotage, disruption for disruption sake, etc. It's just not possible to survive on your own — doing your own thing. The need for a collective approach becomes obvious.

If you define the social work task as the building or facilitating of networks between people so that they can organize to get what they need — and that would include clients as well as co-workers — you can only implement the definition in an egoless way. To the question 'What's in it for you?' you have to say something like change or self-organization. If you have any notion of leading these networks of people anywhere, then you have betrayed the definition. However, the opposition will try to make it appear that this sort of practice is an ego trip in itself and only a means for some sort of self-aggrandizement. Sometimes people working in this way can be thrust into a leadership role, and must make the effort not to believe the label or be sucked in by the cultural values of being in the limelight. I think the reward is taking part in the transformation of ourselves and others, even in little tiny steps, as confidence grows, apathy recedes and cultural myths are smashed.

Is there a proper theory?

Is there any sort of theory on which to base this egoless-network-building social work practice? How does it fit into the 'big picture' of the fundamental alteration of our society? Clearly for me it must be a class theory — one that recognizes the deep divisions between those who own/manage and those who produce/service and confronts the structural and ideological supports for those divisions. Arguments about state capitalism vs. the degenerate workers' state, the permanent arms economy, or vanguard party building, important as they are, aren't really very informative to the sort of social work practice I'm talking about.

We need a theory of a lower (or maybe higher?) order on which we can draw, and which we can continuously test in the context of our own ordinary experience. This process is both intensely personal and collective. It requires the application of class consciousness to everyday issues, situations and relationships. Taking part in practising the process, we experience the enormous power of the status quo (the state, ruling class, military-economic system), the traps of liberalism and reformism and the basic myths of the welfare state. Egoless-network-building social work contributes to the accumulation of experience — consciousness-raising, confidence-building — necessary as a base for collective power. Political ideas like these are usually subsumed under a theory of popular power and often associated with anarchism.

History helps us with the concept of popular power. There have been some extraordinary moments in history which illustrate what can happen when the constraints of our education and conditioning are suddenly loosened significantly and there is optimism about the potential for real change. At these moments, the day-to-day practice of ordinary people often forges ahead of political theories and theorists and even political parties. These moments — the Paris Commune 1871, the Bolshevik Revolution 1917, the General Strike in Britain 1926, Chile 1973, Portugal 1976 — inform my commitment to the sort of social work (and political) practice I'm trying to describe. Historical analysis of these moments, and the swift and brutal repression which followed each, informs my developing understanding of the reaction of authority to such practice, working as it does towards the consciousness of the power of the collective. It seems essential to me that we enter into the experience of this history through our daily lives, and obviously therefore in our social work practice.

I would not agree with the anarchism label, although I think the 'anarchist consciousness' is essential for socialism. I am totally committed to organizing and to collective solutions, but opposed to hierarchies and elites, whether they occur in social services, political parties or trade unions. I don't know yet if there is a 'proper theory', but the more I read, practise and campaign, the more I'm convinced authority and our reaction to it is a key and should be the foundation of our theory.

On the job

If you accept these ideas and definitions, certain sorts of practice follow. Clients begin to look different — more real and multi-dimensional. If every client is a potential link in a network, your behaviour towards them changes. It doesn't really matter whether what you do is called community work or group work or even casework. The basic way of operating remains the same. If you like, this is in political terms the 'integrated method' of social work. What you are working toward is collective strength. A common criticism of social workers who insist on looking at clients in this way is that they are not sensitive to individual needs and expect too much of people in crisis. That can happen, but sensitivity is very much a part of such an approach and there must be an element of judgement, of course.

Some clients don't like the approach, especially if they've been trained by another sort of social work practice to expect something else. I remember a very bright woman, having a lot of legal troubles with an estranged husband, taking me to task because I wouldn't ring her solicitor on her behalf to lodge the latest complaint. I invited her to use the office phone to ring so that she could relay the information first hand. Her comment was that I wasn't good for much of anything, and wasn't I supposed to be helping her? On the other hand, forcing yourself to seek out the positive, the strengths in each person and then thinking of ways these fit into the community and its needs does make things look quite different. Like the agoraphobic on a run-down estate who had a telephone and was the neighbourhood gossip: with a bit of encouragement he became the secretary of the tenants' association and developed a system for recording, transmitting and following up on tenants' repair problems. Lots more repairs got done more quickly and the agoraphobia didn't seem so dominant in his life.

There are lots of examples, but maybe a few in some detail are worth citing. When the method works the results are almost bound to cause trouble within the department, relying as it does on apathy and passivity. People getting together to demand what they need is not what the management has in mind either for its clients or its workers.

Most local authority social service teams probably do very little in the way of services for the blind. The trend is to have a specialist team with borough-wide responsibility, thus encouraging the team social worker to take less and less interest in the visually handicapped. My first blind client was a miserable old bloke who complained that what he wanted was his home teacher back. Things were much better when all the registered blind had home teachers rather than social workers who didn't know much about the blind and didn't seem to care. I agreed that he and his mates were getting very little out of the Seebohm 'generic factory' (the arrangements for generic social work which came out of the Seebohm Report). I didn't know much about blind people, what sorts of special needs they might have, the techniques of mobility training etc. But it was clear to me that this bloke wanted things different and *he* knew about all these things.

To begin with, he said, there should be a social club, but not one of those where they sit you around the room with a cup of tea in one hand and a sandwich in the other. He thought it would be a good idea for folks to get out a bit and that his local pub had a room that he would speak to the landlord about using. What did he want from me? Transport. Did I think I could manage that? It was a bigger problem than I had imagined, but we got people there in all sorts of ways. The idea caught on and lots of blind people were having a really good time singing and even doing a bit of a knees-up when we could get music. Then it turned out that some of *them* were musicians and they made their own music. Even the pub regulars enjoyed Thursday nights. There was an occasional complaint, mainly from the professionals, that some people wouldn't come because they couldn't afford the price of a drink and that it wasn't appropriate to force people to drink anyway. We managed to get a 'refreshments' vote for the club which assured everyone at least one drink, but had to agree that not *everyone* in the patch fancies a night out in the pub.

Fairly soon, there were discussions about what to do about the poor level of service for the blind in the borough. Didn't social services have a statutory responsibility they asked? Couldn't they be taken to court for failing to meet it? Then they heard about a series of meetings around the proposed community use of a recently closed hospital in the area. They wanted some of it for a self-help centre for the blind, and demanded transport to the meetings so that they could make themselves heard. They didn't get any of the hospital, but their careers as protesters and fighters were launched. Eventually they did get short-life property off the council, plus a grant to run a telephone referral service, and all sorts of classes and social evenings etc. It's not exactly revolutionary, you might rightly say, but it's a start. It's a network of people doing for themselves, taking some control over their own lives. It was also an experience for me and co-workers in realizing just how patronizing and condescending we had been in the past toward handicapped people. We learned to trust them to know what they wanted from us and to listen to what they said.

Foster parents are very valuable to social services — as are childminders, volunteers and good neighbours. Often they are badly treated and exploited financially. If they are well enough off not to mind, they are usually very different from the kids they take in. Often they are a long way from where the kids live as well. Some local foster parents wondered why there weren't more of them in the area and decided to try to recruit. They rightly felt that it was better to keep the kids in their own neighbourhoods and schools if it was necessary to take them into care. They were fairly successful in bringing in new foster parents, but were disappointed and disturbed that the vetting took so long and that their recruits were put off at the procedure they had to go through.

The foster parents formed themselves into a group and became quite knowledgeable about the legal as well as the subjective issues. A nearby team decided on an emergency reception into care and placed three kids with a foster family 15 miles away from their neighbourhood. The local foster parents wanted to know why they hadn't been consulted. One of them could have taken the kids. The social worker said it was confidential, a professional decision, and refused to discuss the matter with them. They threatened to boycott the team and any needs it might have in the future for places. They were furious at being told that they were only there to be used when the social worker said so and were not expected to have any say in anything. They eventually got a meeting with the team and began discussion about professional judgement and the involvement of local people in the affairs of their own community. You can't have it both ways, they said. You can't involve us and use us only when it suits you. They are still making life difficult for those who think otherwise, but providing a far better service for lots of local kids.

Management has never been happy with the sort of group that developed, and have since centralized the fostering service. New foster homes tend to be in the suburbs and a tea party is organized for them once a year. The fostering group was not planned with the idea that its members would take on the department and challenge the authority of professional decisions. It was almost inevitable, however, that it would come to that, given the sort of encouragement they deserved. If the door is open to community involvement, then it's open. Otherwise it's just plain exploitation and you could hardly expect anything other than 'apathy' from the community.

In either of these examples, if you felt it was necessary or desirable to defend and/or excuse the department or to deal with each 'problem' individually, the opportunity to assist the growth of a network would have been missed. Furthermore you might well have actively participated in preventing natural linkages between people from happening. An important part of this sort of practice is keeping out of the way, not needing to know, but taking seriously what people have to offer and the things they have to say. It's far better to err on the side of trusting people to know what they need than to assume some superior knowledge as an outsider. Practising social work like this takes a certain amount of confidence in oneself, but more importantly it requires confidence in others. It is not appropriate to demand that sort of trust in return from those labelled clients. My advice would be never trust a social worker, just as I have learned that as a social worker I must never trust or come to rely on management. The reasons are the same for both sorts of relationships.

A union wo/man

Aside from client groups — and there are many many more which could be discussed — tenants' associations, adolescents, battered women etc. — we must concern ourselves I think with our co-workers in the same sort of way. Management isn't keen for clients or workers to get together, to get too confident and well organized. We may feel that we as workers are free of many of the constraints faced by our clients, but the same processes are at work despite our relatively more favourable social position. We also have at hand a ready-made mechanism — the trade union. But do we use it to its fullest advantage or are we also apathetic, deferential and individualistic? My guess is that the social workers most committed to network building are the rank-and-file trade unionists in the work place. The trade union can however be another ladder to success where competition, ambition and individual achievement may get you somewhere. So beware the ego-involved brother/sister almost as much as the ambitious senior on the way to the top. The same sort of can-you-make-it-to-the-top games can be played within the trade union as well as the management.

Troublesome networks of clients out there in the community may need defending within the department from time to time. They may require resources such as transport, money etc. which could be interfered with by management. It is a good idea to have some machinery, usually the trade union, to defend them and your right to work with them in the way that suits them best. Because of the arbitrary authority vested in social service management in relation to the community, such groups will have little power themselves, especially in the early stages of their development — thus the importance of such an alliance. Doing 'innovative' or 'radical' work with groups in the community without some form of defence network for both them and you is just plain foolhardy. As an individual it is easy to get picked off should you or the clients displease those in authority. The trade union and its members may need some encouragement to think about its functions in such terms, but there are plenty of examples of such links being made between the interests of people in the community and at work inside the social services department.

I'm particularly interested in the similarities between encouraging networks in the community and in the workplace. I think I would go so far as to define the role and functon of a shop steward in a social services department (or elsewhere, for that matter) very much as I have defined that of social worker. The aims are the same — collective consciousness and strength. In this case, if charged with trying to build an alternative network to that of management, the plea would have to be guilty. Think about how well management is organized, how much information it has available and the kind of access it has to the top policymakers. It is not correct to assume that *all* policy makers and *all* management make decisions contrary to the best interests of clients and workers, but it is a good idea to be alert for that possibility. Remember that efficient management relies on collective passivity and individualism in order that they can carry on with *their* programmes without disruption. Social service management has to be concerned with keeping the lid on the powder keg of potential grievances, unhappinesses and injustices experienced by both workers and clients. The statutory obligations have to get seen to at least minimally. If not then there must be no attention called to their shortcomings and certainly no adverse publicity. How often is a tragedy such as a battered child blamed on an unqualified social worker? How often on an incompetent or unconcerned management?

My experience over two years as a shop steward sitting across the negotiating table is that management's attitudes are exposed when it gets down to what it is they really do care about. I've heard the most extraordinary excuses for neglecting one group of workers, for creating yet another layer of management, for centralizing a service without consultation. Probably the most classic one was in negotiations over regrading for residential workers. A manager actually said that we didn't want to get the pay too high because we might then be attracting people to the work for the wrong reasons! They see themselves somehow immune from the comeback most of us would expect for making mistakes.

If we do our homework — get our facts straight and take real heed of what our co-workers say to us — we as shop stewards are often in the position of exposing management for its lack of caring and its upside-down priorities. It takes a lot of work and energy. Management gets paid two or three times the basic-grade social work wage to do what we try to do in our spare (that is non-work) time. We get time off for meetings, but there's still the case-load and the uncomfortable silences at allocation meetings which put pressure on to hold up your end of the team workload. Is it worth the investment to make the trade union work for us and our clients?

Management has a way of overlooking the needs and problems

of a weak group of unorganized workers, despite the fact that they may be carrying a heavy responsibility of caring for a particularly needy group of clients. There are plenty of such workers — administrators, home helps, meals on wheels, day and residential staff. In fact, aside from some fieldworkers and most managers, very few are organized at all, though almost all will be nominal members of the trade union. My experience of network building through the trade union with one group of workers — nursery nurses — was particularly educational for me. It convinced me that the potential is there and is definitely worth the investment of time and energy.

Nursery nurses are almost exclusively young working-class women doing women's work for shamefully low wages in conditions most of us wouldn't tolerate. Coloured overalls to indicate your status, no trousers allowed, can't leave the nursery at lunchtime without matron's permission, working a 40-hour week, not allowed to talk to parents or visiting social workers, no staff meetings, no way of questioning what you're told to do and the trade union shop dominated by your immediate boss, the matron. My first contact with a council day-nursery came because I had pushed hard to get a child 'at risk' into one. Initially, I didn't think much about the women who worked in the nursery, but was relieved that the kid would at least be okay during the day. I did feel uncomfortable with the rather formal atmosphere and it was obvious they were not accustomed to social workers taking an interest. Then a couple of nursery nurses approached the shop stewards' committee about their plan to refuse to clean the toilets anymore. They thought it would be better for the kids if they could spend more time with them and less on cooking and scrubbing. They wanted to know if we would support them, and take their case to management. We agreed.

We then discovered serious staff shortages, lots of agency nurses, long unfilled vacancies and a serious morale problem. Management wasn't advertising or showing much concern at all. They seemed to expect the nursery to be full to capacity even though one young nursery nurse could find herself in a situation on her own with up to eight under-fives for most of the day. We negotiated. Management agreed to advertise and to get in domestic staff to do the cleaning. When no adverts appeared there were a series of meetings with nursery staff, which finally agreed after lots of soul-searching to take action. No new children would be admitted after the nearly-fives 'graduated' to school, thus bringing the staff/child ratio down nearer to what it should be according to departmental policy. Management was duly informed. They accused us of irresponsibly exposing children at risk to danger and said we were uncaring, provocative and unreasonable.

However, advertisements appeared rather quickly and as the vacancies were filled, new children were admitted. Soon the nurseries were reasonably staffed with permanent workers. With improved morale, questions of a pay rise and better conditions were taken up. A local settlement for regrading was negotiated, along with a 36-hour week. One of the matrons who had orginally been entirely hostile to the idea of involving the trade union in the nurseries' problems commented that it did seem as though the shop stewards were taking up issues which management should be dealing with. What, she asked, was wrong with management if the trade union had to sort out these things? Despite her tendency to align herself with management, she was at least for the time being critical, and was impressed by what unity with her co-workers had achieved.

During this time links were made between the nursery workers and local campaigners for more provision for the under-fives. Then there was a successful struggle against the proposed closure of a nursery. A number of those women have continued to be active in various child-care campaigns, including raising the demand for improved training for under-fives workers. The fundamental issues raised by an all-female workforce doing low-status women's work were so obvious, once we got into it. But these issues had been easily overlooked because of the lack of organizational muscle of those workers. The relationship between women at work and at home, doing women's work for pay or not — it was all there, as was the potential of women to organize themselves around basic elements of their lives. They understood the link between women's work and low status and pay, but had understood in silence. Through the network of the trade union that silence was broken.

The trade union can provide a mechanism for taking up a very wide range of issues. There is tremendous potential in that mechanism for people getting together to assume a bit more control over their own lives. But a trade union has a bureaucracy and can suffer from the same problems as any other hierarchy — its activities become primarily concerned with the perpetuation of the organization itself rather than the needs of its members. The men (mostly) at the top seem to resent being subjected to the democratic processes built into the trade union structure. But it is these very processes which can make a difference, which can enhance the potential of the organization to work for the collective good of its members. They are there for us to use and improve should we be willing to take the time and trouble to find out about how they work and to get involved. We will never know the limitations of the trade union until we test possibilities. My experience tells me that the further you push the boundaries, the wider they become. With this process goes our own ever widening consciousness of the potential of our collective strength.

Authority is a central issue in my life — as a socialist, as a feminist and as a social worker. It is, I think, the same sort of important issue for all of us. Passivity, deference and apathy are born of disillusionment and/or conditioned ignorance, and allow arbitrary authority to go unchallenged. Competition, possessiveness and individualism are cultural props for the way in which power is distributed and social control maintained. Myths of participation, democracy and caring condition us to accept this arrangement over which we come to believe we have no control. Those of us who try hard enough can even climb up on the backs of our clients/co-workers/comrades to a higher status, with more authority, thus bewildering ourselves into thinking authority is okay, useful, necessary.

If these ideas interest you or make some sense to you in terms of social work, I urge you to read *The politics of social services* by Jeff Galper (Prentice-Hall, 1975) where they are more fully and systematically developed. But also look hard at your own situations — work, campaigns, trade unions, relationships, political party, social work course — and try to tease out the authority-deference-passivity patterns. Try it in *every* situation. It's the way I stay sane in a world I believe can be very different but which at the moment is pretty resistant to fundamental change.

10

Social workers: pawns, police or agitators?

Ron Bailey

It started to rain and get cold as we sat in the waiting room — and that was bad news, as it meant that people's feelings of human sympathy for their friends or relatives would increase. We had been in that waiting room for hours and, frankly, I had been hoping that all the friends and relatives of the family that I was with would turn out to be heartless bastards, and answer 'no' when asked, 'Well, if your friends/relatives and their three children turned up here tonight with nowhere to go would you let them stay if only for tonight?' Many people would rally round and help their friends or relatives in such a situation, and, of course, they would be even more prepared to help if it was cold and raining. So they would answer 'yes' to that all-important question.

And the system would have won another round and claimed another victim.

No! This is not the beginning of a dramatic short story or TV play. It is a real-life situation that I have been involved in, in one way or another, about 2000 times, in locations all over England. So I will explain the setting.

The family are a homeless family who have just lost their home for one reason or another — eviction from unprotected accommodation or from 'tied' accommodation; unlawful subtenants who have had to move on; a fire in their previous home; breakdown of relationships with the family that let them use a spare room because they had nowhere else to go; rent arrears; need to move because of work ... . For the moment it does not

215

216 Radical social work and practice

matter — they are a homeless family. The waiting room is the local Social Services Department where the family have applied for homeless family accommodation. The wait is caused by the fact that the social worker is checking up 'to see if the family is genuinely homeless, because only then have we got a duty to help.' And I am there because the family has already been turned away at least once and left, quite literally, to walk the streets.

Up until December 1977, when the Housing (Homeless Persons) Act came into force (and I will deal later with possible claims that what I am saying is out of date), when families became homeless they were required to go to their local social services department and apply for temporary homeless family accommodation; and in most cases the department was under a duty (pursuant to the National Assistance Act 1948 Part 3 Sections 21 and 35, as amended by the Local Authority Social Services Act 1970 Section 7 (1)) to provide temporary accommodation. In the cases where there was no absolute duty there was certainly a discretionary power to provide accommodation — and ministerial exhortations to use that discretion widely.

However, during the ten years when I dealt with homeless families, between 1965 and 1975, there were usually more families than units of accommodation in most areas. The result of this, therefore, was that the council officers — the social workers — who dealt with the excess families simply turned them away and left them to walk the streets. The official figures for those years show that for every six families applying for homeless family accommodation only one would actually end up obtaining it. The rest were simply turned away.

The official explanations of this discrepancy between the applications and admissions were, nearly always, wholly satisfactory. Those families refused accommodation 'made their own arrangements or were assisted through the various voluntary agencies' (Barking) or the application was 'resolved by advice or other means' (Kingston-upon-Thames) or 'our social workers [found] other ways of dealing with the problem' (Cornwall) or 'the problem [was] solved by alternative assistance from this Department' (Carlisle) or 'when the ''crunch of homelessness'' arises they make arrangements to move in with relatives or friends' (West Sussex).[1]

1 See Ron Bailey and Joan Ruddock, *The grief report* (London, Shelter, 1972), 28-9.

The truth, however, was rather different. In fact what happened in very many cases was that the families were tricked or bullied out of the office, or merely shown the door (in a very polite and caring way of course), and left, as I have said, to walk the streets. But not all walked the streets: some walked along to the offices of myself and other voluntary workers who were determined to ensure that homeless families were treated both legally and humanely.

I would then telephone the social worker who had turned the family away: the reply would usually be polite and concerned — initially at any rate. 'Yes, I'm very sorry, but we just don't have anywhere, I know it's awful, but what can we do if there just isn't anywhere available?' I would then politely explain that this was totally unsatisfactory and that, apart from anything else, the local authority had a legal obligation to provide temporary accommodation. There would then be further explanations as to the difficulty they (the local authority) were in and even perhaps how s/he (the social worker) sympathized with and supported my efforts on behalf of the family, but ... 'Well, I'm sorry, we just don't have anywhere — literally — but perhaps if you speak to my senior s/he can explain better.' And I would speak to the senior and perhaps his/her senior, who would also be sympathetic, but would explain the 'difficulties' which they were in regarding the shortage of emergency accommodation.

This would all be quite amicable and all the social workers would be polite, (perhaps) sympathetic and (probably genuinely) concerned — until! Until they realized that we were just not going to take 'no' for an answer. This was the crucial point. (I will discuss the implications of it later; here I will simply continue the narrative.)

From this point on they would try and get out of what they said earlier, or at least of what their attitude had been. The use of words like 'concerned', 'very sorry', 'understand', and 'sympathetic' would cease: statements like 'well, we don't really have any duty towards that particular family, you know, as our actual *duty* only arises in fire and flood cases' would emerge. A discussion on the law would then ensue, with me quoting the ministerial circulars and the local authority's duty to follow them under Section 35 of the 1948 National Assistance Act.

The social workers, not being lawyers, would find this difficult to counter, and so perhaps a team leader or assistant director of social services would be brought in and the whole process would start again with them, and end up at the same place with 'concern' and 'sympathy' giving way to 'policy' and 'well, we don't have a duty as far as we interpret the law' at the more senior levels.

Meanwhile the family with their three children would be sitting across my desk listening and still having nowhere to go after all the hours that this would take.

Realizing that I was just not going to take any notice of their polite attempts to make me close both the dialogue and the case, and go away, the social workers would sometimes try one last tactic before allowing their ever-increasing irritation to take over and develop into hostility. They would try the 'divide and rule' tactic by taking me into their confidence: 'look we do understand that you've got this family in your office but, well you know, they have lied to us in the past; they're a pretty persistent rent arrears case; been married before; possibly neglect of the children; s/he has affairs; unhappy home' and the like.

I would reply that all this was quite interesting but totally irrelevant to the issue at stake: this family were homeless and wished to apply for temporary accommodation, and were the local authority going to carry out their duty or see the family on the streets tonight? I would then say that we were coming to the office to sort this out.

So we would arrive. The first battle would often be whether I could remain while the interview was taking place. 'We can discuss your problems better in private; a concerned social worker would say to the family who, having had a bellyful of concern, would tell him/her what to do with that.

I would therefore attend the interview, at the completion of which the social worker would say 'The first thing is that we have to see if you are genuinely homeless', and we would be left waiting while this was checked out. But in addition to the reasonable visits to the family's last accommodation the social workers would then visit the family's relatives, friends — indeed anybody — and ask if they had room for the family, and if one of them felt compassionate and said, 'I suppose they could stay for a couple of nights as one of my kids is away until the weekend so they can have his/her room', the homeless family would no longer be 'technically homeless' and so have no claims to temporary accommodation: and they would be dumped on the friends or relatives and forgotten about. Case solved.

Often, however, none of the friends and relatives would have room so the social worker would try again. And we would wait in the waiting room dreading the rain that was starting and the sudden drop in temperature — because this second visit would be very different from the first low-key affair.

This time the social worker would ask, 'Surely you can find somewhere; we are very stretched at the moment; if they arrived here at 8 o'clock tonight and it was still raining and getting colder surely then you wouldn't turn them away.' Faced with this the friends or relatives, being human, kind and decent would find it very difficult to deny that they would let the family stay in such circumstances.

However, the game would not end there. Sometimes the friends or relatives were not very 'kind' — or rather they were too ill-housed themselves to be able to put up with additional strain and overcrowding — and they said so, despite feeling guilty and heartless. At this 'blatently uncooperative attitude' the social worker used his/her final card: 'That's unfortunate, you see we're very hard-pressed just now and all we can do is help the children; we'll do that but, much as we hate it, we can't help the parents, so we'll have to "offer" care for the children.' Then, as the friends or relatives replied merely with stunned looks, the social worker would continue 'surely you wouldn't stand by and see your friends family/own flesh and blood/daughter's or son's children go into care — can't you squeeze them in somewhere?'

If, despite all this, the social worker could not resolve the case by such 'alternative assistance from this department' s/he would arrive back at the office and, at last, tell us what we had known all day — the family were homeless. The family would then receive the same treatment: 'offers' of care were made for the children. (The social workers were always careful to use the word 'offer' because, of course, being professional people they knew that they could not actually take the children into care, and it would be unprofessional to threaten things.)

Many of the families who arrived at my office had already been frightened away by such 'offers'; others had accepted them already, with the result that the parents were sleeping rough while the children were in care. By the time we went back, however, we were in no mood to accept this treatment, and we made it plain that we wanted emergency accommodation for the whole family and would settle for nothing else.

By now the earlier concern of the social workers would have given way to irritation, which would in turn have given way to outright hostility. They were just fed up: they had been sympathetic initially but now we were taking things too far. At this stage, therefore, they would try to ignore us by leaving us in the waiting room until they all went home. To avoid this we would go and sit in the team leader's office, to the absolute fury now of the social workers. The assistant director would be called in to sort out this impertinence — and then the director who, as had the social workers earlier, would go through the stages of sympathy, irritation and hostility.

The whole affair was, by this time, a no-holds-barred battle, with us phoning elected councillors, the press, the Department of Health and Social Security, and them phoning the police to come and remove us. Many times have I and a homeless family been dumped on the pavement outside the Social Services office at 7 pm or later, and I have had to put the family up myself. All the soical workers had gone home, of course!

Battle would then recommence next day — until we won. Usually they would back down around 6 pm on the first day and a unit of accommodation which, for all the day had not existed, would suddenly appear. Despite the social workers' continual insistence that 'we just don't have anywhere, it's a matter of bricks and mortar', it was amazing how persistence could produce not only irritation and hostility but, in the final analysis, bricks and mortar. Sometimes, however, it took two, three or even four days to obtain accommodation for the homeless family: but in the end we would win — after a protracted battle against what can only be described as the enemy — the staff of the local authority social services department.

A day or a week or so later I would go to a meeting called, perhaps, to complain about inadequate social service facilities, or to protest about the disgraceful housing policies of the XYZ Council, and how these affected the homeless. I would hear words like 'disgraceful'; I would hear condemnation of 'capitalism' and 'cut-backs' and 'inadequate policies' and I would witness resolutions being passed calling for any number of improvements and changes. And I would look round the room and I would see in the audience the very same people I had done battle with a few days earlier. The local radical social workers!

Later I will describe my subsequent conversations with them and how they explained their actions — but first I will discuss the implications and the points arising out of the battle over the homeless family.

The story I have told is, I hope it will be accepted, a horror story. It is no isolated case. I have personal knowledge and experience of some 2000 such cases, and colleagues of mine have similar experience.

The cases were not all, of course, identical: some, for instance, would escalate more quickly, but my example is fairly typical. It also, I believe, shows the social workers as reasonable people, initially anyway, and not as unpleasant and officious bureaucrats. Yet still these reasonable people who, I have no doubt, became social workers because they felt compassionate towards their fellow human beings and wanted to do a worthwhile job (and I emphasize here that I am *not* being sarcastic) became bitter enemies of that homeless family and the thousands of others that I and other people dealt with. Enemies to be overruled, exposed and defeated at all costs.

A look at the train of events shows how this situation occurred. The social workers' sympathy for the family and even for my efforts to help them first started to wane when we refused to go away like a puff of smoke — in other words, as soon as we made it clear that we were not going to accept treatment that was inhuman (for can leaving a homeless family to walk the streets be described as anything else?) and unlawful (very many of the cases with which I dealt clearly came within the categories to which the local authority owed a duty). At that point, and indeed earlier, the social worker had a personal choice to make: did his/her duty lie with the policy and practice of the local authority as carried out *then and there* — or with the interests of the client?

They chose — and words like 'sympathetic' turned into attempts to wheedle a way out of any responsibility for the family. At every level this happened and at every level they chose. And their choice made them the enemy of the family — for the only way the family could keep their sympathy was to walk out of the waiting room, into the street, with nowhere to go.

And when the sympathy had turned to irritation and still the family were being a nuisance, the irritation turned to hostility and opposition. The social workers' actions all involved choice — and they chose to enforce the rules *at the expense of the family*. Until this point the social workers were mere pawns simply adhering to practices and policies with which, of course, they did not agree. After this, however, when they started putting the pressure on friends and relatives or putting the frighteners on the families (for that is what those 'offers' of care for the children were, and the social workers knew it) the social workers were no longer mere pawns: they had, in effect, decided to conspire with the system to oppose that family with which they were dealing. And they were the enemy of that family as much as bailiffs, workhouse masters and hard-nosed administrators. In fact they were more effective enemies for their 'concerned' approach would — at first anyway — be much more effective in persuading the families to go away.

But, as I have said, these social workers were not heartless people; so how could they do this? Two things probably enabled them to make the mental adjustments necessary — the family's unreasonable behaviour, and my presence. The unreasonable behaviour was the refusal by the family again (for it will be remembered that they had already done this before coming to see me) to walk out of the office with nowhere to go. As for my presence — I have no doubt that the social workers felt that I was egging the family on. They were right, of course: I was. After all, they had been turned away once already and it was due to me that they had come back. I did indeed urge the family that they did not have to accept being turned away; I did indeed encourage them to fight for their legal rights; and I did indeed offer my support come what may. So because they were egged on by me the families refused to accept being left to walk the streets, refused to accept being split up, refused to let their children be taken into care. I was thus labelled a troublemaker, and many social workers used this as their personal excuse to make the switch they needed to make.

I have no doubt that my attitude was 'unprofessional'. I certainly became very personally involved and I was certainly absolutely determined to support the families until we won. I asked myself what would happen if I did not do this and I knew the answer and so I took sides — but no more than the social worker who, in turning the family away before they (the family) had ever contacted me, had certainly taken sides — 'professionally' of course, as presumably they had not become personally involved. (Although they certainly did later when they would not — personally could not? — back down.)

The point, I suggest, is that not just social workers but everybody, especially those in positions of authority who wield power and resources, has to make choices, and accept responsibility for those choices. I and others like me made a choice — to help our clients. That was our only consideration. And the social workers made a choice: they chose, by their actions, when the chips were down, to support the system. The system which carried out unlawful acts, as many of the families had a right to accommodation and the local authority had a duty to provide it; the system which *required them to carry out unprofessional acts* — for surely it cannot be seriously claimed that the moral blackmail of friends and relatives and the 'offers' to take children into care were professional ways in which to behave. Even — indeed especially — the attempts to categorize families as not being in the groups to which the council owed a duty, (even if such categorization was correct) cannot seriously be considered professional behaviour for *social workers*. Professional[2] behaviour is behaviour motivated solely by the principles of whatever discipline one works to. And the categorization of families as described with the effects as described can never be professional behaviour for social workers. It may be highly professional behaviour for, say, administrators, whose professional discipline requires them to enforce the rules properly and strictly, but not for social workers, whose professional discipline requires them — so they themselves claim — to consider the social needs and strains and problems of their clients.

It may be argued that resources are scarce and that demand exceeds supply and that not every applicant can be helped. True as that may be, it is an irrelevant professional consideration for social workers; and every time a social worker lets such factors influence his/her judgement then that social worker is not acting

---

2 The word 'professional' has two meanings. It can merely describe a worker who is paid rather than voluntary, or it can be used to describe 'a profession' and a code of ethics and behaviour surrounding that. It is in this latter sense that I use the word. This is, of course, the sense in which social workers themselves use it to describe their job.

professionally as a social worker but professionally as an administrator.

If social workers' professional discipline is, as they claim, to consider the needs, strains and problems of their clients, then their actions and recommendations should be motivated solely by those considerations. Thus when a social worker, knowing that resources are scarce, puts the pressure down wards onto the clients then s/he is not only acting as, at best, the pawn of the system, and, at worst, the bailiff or policeman/woman of the system, but also unprofessionally.

This again raises the question of choice: every day every social worker has to make the decision many times. Will the pressure go down or will it go up? Will s/he obey the rules or the needs of the client? Obeying the rules is easier, safer and more respectable, but those who do so should have no illusions — by putting the pressure downwards they are the policemen/women of the system and they are the enemies of their clients.

In other words, I am saying that agitators are the real social work professionals: and social workers need to be agitators to be social workers.

What of the point that social workers are no longer responsible for homelessness since the new law? I hope it is, by now, apparent that this is a specious argument. Indeed in many areas it is social workers that staff the new homeless family sections of the housing departments. But that is a minor point: my argument has concerned roles and attitudes, and roles and attitudes do not end with the repealing of laws and the passing of new ones. The same roles and attitudes are present in very many other functions of social workers: the provision of facilities for the handicapped, the elderly, the disabled and children. All these are scarce resources, and the scarcity factor is a major factor in the allocation of them by people purporting to act as social workers.

Many surveys have shown, for example, that large numbers of elderly and disabled people are not getting their rights under the Chronically Sick and Disabled Persons Act, despite the fact that they receive regular visits from social workers who are quite aware of the provisions of the Act. The reason? Lack of resources. So in effect these people were being 'turned away' like the homeless families I have described, but as it is very difficult to take elderly and disabled people to 'sit in' at the local Social

Services office, the social workers succeed in being the pawns and the policemen/women of the system. But they do not succeed in being professional social workers.

On this subject one story in particular reminds me of the homeless family situation. A district nurse that I know visited a house with an elderly and ill patient who clearly urgently needed an emergency telephone to enable her to remain in contact with the outside world (especially with her doctor should an emergency arise), but the social workers had turned down her application as there were 'none available'. The nurse took up the case with the area team leader; and after an altercation and some off-hand treatment and a refusal by the nurse to accept all attempts to fob her off, a phone was produced in a matter of days — just as I have seen nonexistent accommodation appear for homeless families!

In that case the social workers played the role of professional administrators of the system, not of social workers. To be social workers they should have done what the nurse did and 'sat in' on behalf of their client, thus putting the pressure upwards. Instead they chose to put the pressure downwards; but in doing so they were neither social workers nor the allies of that elderly woman.

At all levels, therefore, social workers should be — *must be* — agitators. The social worker should take things up with the senior and they should both go to the principal who should, etc ... right up to the director of social services. And if s/he wants to be a genuine director of social services and not a director of administration, then they should all go to the chairperson of the social services committee if necessary. And the chairperson should be told in no uncertain terms that s/he may carry out whatever policy s/he likes, but that if that policy is in contravention of our professional opinions of our clients' needs, then, social workers cannot execute it. Social workers do not do this, however: they carry out policies which are detrimental, in social work terms, to their clients, and so they are the pawns and police of the system and not professionals.

But what of the radical social workers? As I have already said, they attend protest meetings and I have, as I indicated, argued with them about their role. The best explanation of it that I have heard goes something like this:

Yes, I agree I did oppose you at the office, and you were right to insist, but I had no choice. You recall that I kept you waiting — that was because I was arguing with my senior/principal/team leader [etc.] but s/he was adamant. I really stuck my neck out and actually phoned the Director, but to no avail: they all said there really was no accommodation [cash/telephones/aids etc.] available, so I had to carry out the decision. And what if I'd refused? Someone else would have come out and done it and I'd have lost my job — I already stick my neck out enough and I'm unpopular because of it. And losing my job would have done no good. I get on well with my clients and I get everything I can for them. If I'd lost my job over that one case my other clients would get another social worker; probably one of the reactionary old guard and they'd all have suffered. So reluctantly I did what I was told, thus enabling me to stay in the system until I become a senior when I'll be in a more powerful position to be able to help.

It all sounds very convincing, but there are three basic flaws in it. Firstly, the seniors said the same thing — only they were waiting to become principals, who in turn said the same thing, and so on right up the ladder. Thus none of them have any power to disobey in the *system's terms*: however high they get they all still find that the system remains in control — and always will do providing it can get its basic food — people (well-intentioned or otherwise; although perhaps it prefers well-intentioned people as they give it a better image!) to carry out its orders at all levels.

The second flaw in the explanation outlined above is that they all — or at least many of them — use it. They all claim to have to make these 'compromises' so that their clients will not get 'one of the others' in future. They are all 'unpopular' with their colleagues because they stick their necks out on their clients' behalf. So if all these claims are genuine then they are all unpopular with each other for doing exactly the same things; there is no need to worry about 'one of the others'; and anyway, if there are so many of them, why do they not choose to organize together in their clients' interests rather than conspiring together to frustrate their demands and needs?

The final flaw in the 'I'll toe the line until I'm a senior/principal/team leader' argument is that the very people who said that to me six years ago or more are the very people who have now reached those positions and are acting in the very same way towards their clients and are saying exactly the same things to the person below them in the hierarchy that was said *to them* all those years ago.

And so the system is perpetuated by the very people who claim to oppose it. And these people are still going to meetings and passing their resolutions of protest, and going on militant demonstrations and complaining about 'the cuts' and 'the Tories' and 'capitalism' and the like. It is all so very easy: what is much harder for them to realize and act on is that, as far as their clients (the victims) are concerned revolution, as well as radical social work, begins much closer to home. In fact it starts — or fails to start — when they first enter their office tomorrow morning or see their first client and when they answer, by their actions with the client, the question, 'Which way will I put the pressure — up or down?'

Notes on contributors

Ron Bailey is a writer, agitator and anarchist who has been involved in struggles against local authorities and in efforts to stimulate self-help and independent initiatives in housing since 1965. Currently he is associated with the Housing Emergency Office, an organization which works to bring empty property back into use. He is also compiling a dossier on high-handed actions, lack of consultation and suppression and distortion of information by local authorities in relation to all aspects of their functions and he would be interested to hear from anyone who has any information on such matters. He can be contacted at the Housing Emergency Office, 157 Waterloo Road, London SE1 (01-633 9377).

Roy Bailey graduated from the University of Leicester in 1963. He has taught in both polytechnics and universities. He is currently Head of the Department of Applied Social Studies and Dean of the Faculty of Social Studies at Sheffield City Polytechnic.

His publications include 'The family and the social management of intolerable dilemmas' in *Contemporary social problems in Britain* (Saxon House, 1973) edited with Jock Young, and *Radical social work* (Edward Arnold, 1975) edited with Mike Brake. He is currently a member of the Professional Studies and Qualifications Committee of CCETSW.

Bill Bennett graduated in mathematics at Edinburgh University

228

(1968) and in social work (Exeter University 1970). He is a team leader for the London borough of Hammersmith, where he is responsible for the sub-office. He is a member of the Labour Party and previously of the Socialist Workers' Party. He is at present writing a book on the work of the sub-office and the adoption of a team approach to social services fieldwork practice.

Mike Brake was in the theatre, and then worked for several years, as an unskilled worker, a social worker and an occupational therapist before going to university. He is a graduate of Leeds University and the London School of Economics and Political Science, and has taught at the universities of Bradford and Kent. He has published *The sociology of youth culture: sex and drugs and rock'n'roll?* (Routledge & Kegan Paul 1979), as well as his co-edited work on radical social work with Roy Bailey. He is currently at Carleton University, Ottawa, Canada in the School of Social Work, and is working on a new reader on sexuality.

Myra Garrett has been a social worker for twenty-four years, the last eight of which have been enlightened by a growing socialist feminist consciousness. She was launched as a militant trade unionist when a London local authority management tried but failed to sack her during a probationary period. As a shop steward and member of the editorial collective of Case Con, she developed a rank-and-file perspective and commitment to organizing at work and in the community. She is at present working with the London Tenants Organization.

John Hart left school at 15 hoping to join the police force. He worked for five years, first for British Rail and then in a psychiatric hospital, before going to the London School of Economics and Political Science, and Bristol and Bradford Universities. His social work experience was in probation, psychiatric and medical social work, student counselling and local authority social service departments.

His publications include *Social work and sexual conduct* Routledge & Kegan Paul 1979). He is Principal Lecturer in Social Work at Sheffield City Polytechnic.

Bruce Hugman has a joint appointment as Senior Probation

Officer in South Yorkshire and Lecturer in Social Work at Sheffield City Polytechnic. He is a graduate in English and a trained teacher; he has taught in a boys' public school, a secondary modern school, a college of technology and in adult education. He started the Detached Probation Project in Sheffield in 1971 and returned to the City in 1978 after four years on a communal agricultural smallholding in Kent.

He has published a critical study of *Tess of the d'Urbervilles* and *Act natural*, an account of the Detached Project. He is currently working on the biography of a young drugtaker and artist.

Charles Husband spent six years in research at the Centre for Mass Communication Research at the University of Leicester, where his major research interest was in the area of race relations. For four years he then lectured in social psychology and race relations at the School of Social Work at Leicester University. He was actively involved in the formation of the recently established Association for Multi-Racial Social Work. He is at present Senior Lecturer in Social Psychology in the School of Social Analysis at the University of Bradford.

Phil Lee was educated at the Universities of Bradford, Kent and London. His present post is Senior Lecturer in Applied Social Studies and Sociology at Sheffield City Polytechnic.

He is currently preparing a textbook on sociology for social workers and jointly editing a book with Roy Bailey, *Theory and practice in social work*, (Basil Blackwell).

Marjorie Mayo was a research/community worker of the Joint Docklands Action Group, concerned with participation in the redevelopment of London's docklands. She is now at the Polytechnic of Central London working on the evaluation of Area Resource Centres. She was previously a lecturer, teaching community and social work students, at the University of Surrey, and has taught at the London School of Economics and Political Science. She has also spent a year's Voluntary Service Overseas in northern Nigeria, engaged in community development, and has worked on the Home Office Community Development Project. She is co-editor, with David Jones, of *Community work: One* and

Community work: Two and editor of *Women in community* (Routledge and Kegan Paul).

David Pithers is Principal Tutor at the Social Work Education Centre in Bedford. He graduated from Oxford and Cambridge Universities. He is a qualified residential social worker who has worked in a variety of residential settings, mainly with adolescents, and has contributed articles to numerous professional journals.

Currently he is engaged in writing a book on radical residential child care with Phil Lee.

Elizabeth Wilson has taught social work in the Department of Applied Social Studies at the Polytechnic of North London for the past five years, and before that was a psychiatric social worker. She has been active in the Women's Liberation Movement since 1971, particularly in Women's Aid and the National Abortion Campaign. She was on the editorial collective of *Red Rag* for three years, and is now on the editorial collective of the *Feminist Review*. Her book, *Women and the Welfare State*, appeared in 1977, and *Only halfway to paradise: Women in Britain 1945 to 1968* is due for publication in 1980.

References

Abbot, E. and **Bompass, K.** 1943: *The woman citizen and social security: a criticism of the proposals in the Beveridge Report as they affect women.* Woman's Freedom League pamphlet.

Alfero, L.A. 1972: 'Conscientization'. In *New trends in social work education* (Proceedings of the 16th International Congress of Schools of Social Work, The Hague). New York: International Association of Schools of Social Work.

Alinsky, S. 1946: *Reveille for Radicals.* New York: Random House.
— 1971: *Rules for Radicals.* New York: Random House. (Reprinted 1972, New York: Vintage Books.)

Allen, S. 1971: *New minorities, old conflicts.* New York: Random House.

Althusser, L. 1977: 'Ideology and ideological state apparatuses'. In *Lenin and philosophy.* London: New Left Books, 121-73.

Bagley, C. 1971: 'The social aetiology of schizophrenia in immigrant groups'. *Int. J. Social Psychiatry* **17**, 292-304.

Bailey, R. and **Brake, M.** (eds) 1975: *Radical social work.* London: Edward Arnold.

Baker, L. and **Husband, C.** 1979: 'Social work for a multiracial society: how has social work education responded?' *Social Work Today* **10(25)**, 24-6.

Balbernie, R, 1966: *Residential work with children.* London: Pergamon.

Ballard, R. and **Holden, B.** 1975: 'The employment of coloured graduates in Britain'. *New Community* **IV(3)**, 325-36.

Barrett, L.E. 1977: *The Rastafarians.* London: Heinemann Educational.

Barrett, M. and **McIntosh, M.** 1979: 'Christine Delphy: towards a materialist feminism?' *Feminist Review* **1**.

Beaumont, B. 1976: 'A supportive role'. *Probation J* **23**(3).

de Beauvoir, S. 1953: *The second sex*. London: Jonathan Cape.

Belotti, E.G. 1975: *Little girls*. London: Writers and Readers Publishing Cooperative.

Bettelheim, B. 1971: *The children of the dream*. London: Paladin.

Beveridge, W. 1942: *Report on social insurance and allied services*. London: HMSO, Cmnd 6404.

Blackmore, J. 1979: 'Kids in care fight for their homes'. *Women's Voice* **25** (Jan).

Bland, L. et al. 1978: 'Women "inside and outside" the relations of production'. In Women's Studies Group, Centre for Contemporary Cultural Studies (eds), *Women take issue: aspects of women's subordination*. London: Hutchinson.

Bookhagen, C. Hemmer, E. Raspe, J. and **Schultz, E.** 1978: 'Kommune 2: Childrearing in the commune'. In H. Dreitzel (ed), *Childhood and socialization*. New York: Macmillan.

Boss. P and **Homeshaw, J.** 1975: 'Britain's black citizens'. *Social Work Today* **6**(12), 354-7.

Bottoms, A.E. and **McWilliams, W.** 1979: 'A non-treatment paradigm for probation practice'. *B J Social Work* **9**(2).

Box, S. 1971: *Deviance, reality and society*. London: Holt, Rinehart & Winston.

Braverman, H. 1976: 'Two comments'. *Monthly Review* **28**(3).

Braybrooke, G. 1978: 'A new Chinese tongue'. *The Guardian* (Friday 15 September).

Bridges, L. 1975: 'The ministry of internal security: British urban social policy 1968-74'. *Race and Class* **16**, 375-86.

British Association of Social Workers 1977: 'Children in care: charter of rights'. *Social Work Today* **8**(25).

Brooks, D. and **Singh, K.** 1979: 'Pivots and presents: Asian brokers in British foundries'. In S. Wallman (ed), *Ethnicity at work*. London: Macmillan.

Brown G. (ed) 1979: *The Red papers on Scotland*. Edinburgh: EUSPB.

Broyelle, C. 1977: *Women's liberation in China*. Sussex: Harvester.

Bruegel, I. 1978: 'What keeps the family going?' *International Socialism* **2**(1) (July), 2-15.

Burgoyne, J. N.D.: 'Imagery of the ideal nuclear family: the contribution of the royal family from Queen Victoria to the present day'. Unpublished paper, Sheffield City Polytechnic.

Burney, E. 1967: *Housing on trial*. London: Oxford University Press.

Burns, M. 1965: *Mr Lyward's answer*. London: Hamish Hamilton.

Campbell, T.D. 1978: 'Discretionary rights'. In N. Timms and D. Watson (eds), *Philosophy in social work*. London: Routledge & Kegan Paul.

Callaghan, J. 1978: Speech to the National Conference of Labour Women at Southport, 14 May. London: Labour Party Information Unit Press Release.

Charlton, V. 1974: 'Patter of tiny contraditions'. In XX. S. Allen, L. Sanders and J. Wallis (eds), *Conditions of illusion*. Leeds: Feminist Books, 166-83.

Chetwynd, J. and **Harnett, O.** 1978: *The sex role system*. London: Routledge & Kegan Paul.

Chibnall, S. 1977: *Law and order news*. London: Tavistock.

Clarke, A.M. and **Clarke, A.D.B.** 1976: *Early experience: myth and evidence*. London: Open Books.

Clarke, J. 1979: Critical Sociology and Radical Social Work: Problem of Theory and Practice. In Noel Parry, Michael Rustin and Carole Satyamurti (eds), *Social work, welfare and the state*. London: Edward Arnold.

Clarke, T. and **Clements, L.** (eds) 1977: *Trade unions under capitalism*. London: Fontana.

Cockburn, C. 1977: *The local state*. London: Pluto Press.

Cohen, S. 1973: *Folk devils and moral panics*. London: Paladin.

— 1975: 'It's all right for you to talk: political and sociological manifestos for social work action'. In Bailey and Brake 1975.

Comer, L. 1977: 'The question of women and class'. *Catcall* 5.

— 1978: 'Ideology of child care'. *Humpty Dumpty* 9.

Commission for Racial Equality 1978: *Multiracial Britain: the social service response*. London: CRE.

Committee on Local Authority and Allied Personal Social Services 1968: *Report* ('The Seebohm Report'). London: HMSO, Cmnd 3703.

Community Relations Commission 1974: *Unemployment and homelessness*. London: HMSO.

— 1977: *Some of my best friends. London: CRC*.

— 1977a: *A home from home: caring for under-fives in a multiracial society*. London: CRC.

— 1977b: *Urban deprivation, racial inequality and social policy*. London: CRC.

Connolly, J. 1979: 'Resisting the run-down of Docklands'. In G. Craig,

M. Mayo, and N. Sharman (eds), *Jobs and community action*. London: Routledge & Kegan Paul.

Corrigan, P. 1977: 'The welfare state as an arena of class struggle'. *Marxism Today* (March).

Corrigan, P. and **Leonard, P.** 1978: *Social work practice under capitalism: a marxist approach*. London: Macmillan.

Critcher, C., Parker, M. and **Sondhi, R.** 1977: 'Race in the provincial press: a case study of five West Midlands newspapers'. In *Ethnicity and the media*. Paris: UNESCO.

Croft, J. 1978: *Research in criminal justice*. Home Office Research Study 44. London: HMSO.

Cross, C. 1978: *Ethnic minorities in the inner city*. London: Commission for Racial Equality.

Counter Information Services/Institute of Race Relations 1976: *Racism: who profits?* London: CIS/ IRR.

Curno, P. (ed) 1978: *Political issues and community work*. London: Routledge & Kegan Paul.

Dahl, T.S. and **Snare, A.** 1978: 'The coercion of privacy'. In C. Smart and B. Smart (eds), *Women, sexuality and social control*. London: Routledge & Kegan Paul.

Dalla Costa, M. and **James, S.** 1973: *The power of women and the subversion of the community*. 2nd edn. Bristol: Falling Wall Press.

Daniel, W.W. 1968: *Racial discrimination in England*. Harmondsworth: Penguin.

Davey, I. 1977: 'Radical social work — what does it mean in practice?' *Social Work Today* **8(23)**.

Davin, D. 1976: *Woman-work: women and the Party in revolutionary China*. Oxford: Clarendon Press.

Davis, D.B. 1970: *The problem of slavery in western culture*. Harmondsworth: Pelican.

Delphy, C. 1977: *The main enemy*. London: Women's Research and Resources Centre.

Demuth, C. 1978: *'Sus': a report on the Vagrancy Act 1824*. London: Runnymede Trust.

Dennis, N., Henriques, F. and **Slaughter, C.** 1956: *Coal is our life*. London: Eyre & Spottiswoode.

Department of Health and Social Security 1978a: *Social assistance: a review of the supplementary benefits scheme in Great Britain*. London: HMSO.

— 1978b: Papers from the 1978 Conference of the Social Work Services of the DHSS. *Social Work Services* **18**.
Dockar-Drysdale, B. 1968: *Papers on residential work: therapy in child care*. London: Longman.
Dummett, M. and **Dummett, A.** 1969: 'The role of government in Britain's racial crisis'. In L. Donnelly (ed), *Justice first*. London: Sheed & Ward.

Edholm, F., Harris, O. and *Young, K.* 1977: 'Conceptualizing women'. *Critique of Anthropology* **3(9/10)**.
Ehrlich, H.J. 1971: 'Notes from a radical social scientist: February 1970'. In J.D. Carfax and J.L. Roach (eds), *Radical sociology*. New York: Basic Books.
Engels, F. 1962: 'The origin of the family, private property and the state'. In K. Marx and F. Engels, *Selected works*. Moscow: Progress Publishers.
Evans, P. 1977: *Publish and be damned*. London: Runnymede Trust.

Ferard, M.L. and **Hunnybun, N.K.** 1962: *The caseworker's use of relationships*. London: Tavistock.
Firestone, S. 1972: *The dialectic of sex*. London: Paladin.
Fishman, W. 1975: *East End Jewish Radicals*. London: Duckworth.
Fitzgerald, M., Halmos, P., Muncie, J. and **Zeldin, D.** 1977: *Welfare in action*. London: Routledge & Kegan Paul.
Fletcher, R. 1962: *The family and marriage in Britain*. Harmondsworth: Penguin.
Foot, P. 1965: *Immigration and race in British politics*. Harmondsworth: Penguin.
Foucault, M. 1977: *Discipline and punish: the birth of the prison*. London: Allen Lane.
Freire, P. 1972: *Pedagogy of the oppressed*. Harmondsworth: Penguin.
Frost, S. 1977: 'Mothers in action, 1967-1975'. In M. Mayo (ed), *Women in the community*. London: Routledge & Kegan Paul, 71-81.

Gagnon, J.H. and **Simon, W.** 1974: *Sexual conduct: the social sources of human sexuality*. London: Hutchinson.
Gardiner, J. 1975: 'The role of domestic labour'. *New Left Review* **89**.
Garrard, J.A. 1971: *The English and immigration 1880-1910*. London: Oxford University Press.
Garrett, M. 1973: *Case Con* (April 1973), quoted in J. Goldup, 'How the

radicals are kept in check'. *Community Care* (14 September 1977).
Goffman, E. 1968: *Asylums.* Harmondsworth: Penguin.
Goldup, J. 1976: 'You're only going away for a little while ... '. *Case Con* 21, 16-17.
Gooden, A. 1976: 'Who cares?' *Case Con* 21, 6-7.
Gooden, L and Hunter, A. 1977-8: 'Sex family and the New Right: Antifeminism as a political force' *Radical America* 11(6)-12(1) November to February.
Gramsci, A. 1971: *Prison notebooks.* London: Lawrence & Wishart.
Greer, G. 1971: *The female eunuch.* London: Paladin.
Gurin, P., Gurin, G., Lao, R.C. and Beattie, M. 1969: 'Internal-external control in the motivational dynamics of negro youth'. *J of Social Issues* 25(3), 29-53.

Hackney Community Health Council n.d.: *User's guide: health in Hackney.* London.
Hall, A. 1978: ' ... And to a life free from care'. *The Observer* (8 October).
Hall, S., Critcher, C., Jefferson, T., Clarke, J. and Roberts, B. 1979: *Policing the crisis: mugging, the state and law and order.* London: Macmillan.
Halmos, P. 1978: *The personal and the political.* London: Hutchinson.
Hammersmith Sub-Office 1976a: *Community work and community social work.* London: HS-O, Free Press.
— 1976b: *The Wedgwood Club report.* London: HS-O, Free Press.
— 1976-7: *The Burne Jones Clinic report.* London: HS-O, Free Press.
— 1977: *The bed and breakfast report.* London: HS-O, Free Press.
Harris, N. 1978: *The mandate of heaven: Marx and Mao in modern China.* London: Quartet.
Hart, J. 1979: *Social work and sexual conduct.* (Library of Social Work.) London: Routledge & Kegan Paul.
Hartmann, P. and Husband, C. 1974: *Racism and the mass media.* London: Davis-Poynter.
Hatch, S., Fox, E. and Legg, C. 1977: *Research and reform: Southwark CDP 1969-72.* London: Home Office Urban Deprivation Unit.
Hechter, M. 1975: *Internal colonialism.* London: Routledge & Kegan Paul.
Her Majesty's Stationery Office 1977: *Policy for the inner cities.* London, Cmnd 6845.
Higgins, J. 1978: *The poverty business: Britain and America.* Oxford: Blackwell.

Hill, M.J. and **Issacharoff, R.M.** 1971: *Community action and race relations.* London: Oxford University Press.

Himmelweit, S. and **Mohun, S.** 1977: 'Domestic labour and capital'. *Cambridge J of Economics* **I(3)**.

Hinton, W. 1966: *Fanshen.* USA: Monthly Review Press. Reprinted 1972, Harmondsworth: Pelican. (Page number refers to the Pelican edition.)

Hoghugi, M. 1978: *Troubled and troublesome.* London: Burnett Books/André Deutsch.

Holmes, C. 1978: *Immigrants and minorities in British society.* London: Allen & Unwin.

Holbrook, D. 1971: *Human hope and the death instinct.* Oxford: Oxford University Press.

Home Office 1969: *The Community Development Project: a general outline.* London: HMSO.

— 1978: *North Shields: organizing for change in an industrial area.* London: HMSO.

Humphries, J. 1977: 'Class struggle and the persistence of the working class family'. *Cambridge J of Economics* **I(1)**.

Humphry, D. 1972: *Police power and black people.* London: Panther.

Humphry, D. and **Ward, M.** 1974: *Passports and politics.* Harmondsworth: Penguin.

Humpty Dumpty 1978: *Radical Psychology Magazine* **8**, 'Politics and therapy' (32 Parkholme Road, London E8).

Hunter, G.K. 1967: '*Othello* and colour prejudice'. *Proc. British Academy* **L111**. London: Oxford University Press, 141-63.

Husband, C. 1975: 'Racism in society and the mass media: a critical interaction'. In C. Husband (ed), *White media and black Britain.* London: Arrow, 15-38.

— 1978: 'News media, language and race relations: a case study in identity maintenance'. In H. Giles (ed), *Language, ethnicity and intergroup behaviour.* London: Academic Press.

Institute of Race Relations 1979: *Police against black people.* London: IRR.

Jacoby, R. 1977: *Social amnesia: a critique of conformist psychology from Adler to Laing.* Sussex: Harvester.

Jäggi, M., Müller, R. and **Schmid, S.** 1977: *Red Bologna.* London: Writers and Readers Publishing Cooperative.

John, G. 1977: 'Blaming the victim'. *Times Educational Supplement* (1 July).

— 1978: *Social and community work in specific settings*: Unit 23, *Black people*. Milton Keynes: Open University, DE 206.

Johnson, P. 1975: *The offshore islanders*. Harmondsworth: Penguin.

Joint Docklands Action Group 1977a: *Rebuilding Docklands*. London: JDAG Resource Centre.

— 1977b: *Docklands: the fight for a future*. London: JDAG Resource Centre.

— 1978: *London's docks: an alternative strategy*. London: JDAG Resource Centre.

Jones, C.J. 1977: *Immigration and social policy in Britain*. London Tavistock.

Jones, H. 1975: *Towards a new social work*. London: Routledge & Kegan Paul.

Jordan, W.D. 1969: *White over black*. Harmondsworth: Penguin.

Katz, D. and **Kahn, R.** 1966: *The social psychology of organizations*. New York: Wiley.

Kiernan, V.G. 1972: *The lords of human kind*. Harmondsworth: Pelican.

Kollontai, A. 1972: *Sexual relations and the new class struggle*. Bristol: Falling Wall Press.

Krausher, R. 1976: *Policy without protest: the dilemma of organizing for change in Britain*. Paper presented to Centre for Governmental Studies Conference on Urban Change and Conflict (January 1976).

Lambert, R. and **Millham, S.** 1968: *The hothouse society*. London: Weidenfeld & Nicolson.

Lee, P. and **Pithers, D.** (forthcoming): *Radical residential work*.

Lees, R. 1972: *Politics and social work*. London: Routledge & Kegan Paul.

Leighton, J. 1979: 'Fighting for better health services: the role of the Community Health Council'. In G. Craig, M. Mayo and N. Sharman (eds), *Jobs and community action*. London: Routledge & Kegan Paul.

Lennhoff, F.G. 1960: *Exceptional children*. London: Allen & Unwin.

Leonard, P. 1975: 'A paradigm for radical practice'. In Bailey and Brake 1975, 46-81.

Lessing, D. 1962: *The golden notebook*. Harmondsworth: Penguin.

Lyons, C.H. 1975: *To wash an Aethiop white*. Columbia University, New York: Teachers College Press.

Macintyre, S. 1976: 'Who wants babies?' The social construction of "instincts" '. In D.L. Barker and S. Allen (eds), *Sexual divisions and society: process and change*. London: Tavistock.

McIntosh, M. 1978: 'The state and the oppression of women'. In A. Kuhn and A.-M. Wolpe (eds), *Feminism and materialism*. London: Routledge & Kegan Paul.

McIntosh, M. 1979: in S. Burman (ed) fit work for women. London: Croom Helm.

Marcuse. H. 1941: *Reason and revolution*. Oxford: Oxford University Press.

— 1969: *Eros and civilization*. London: Sphere.

Marris, P. and **Rein, M.** 1975: *Dilemmas of social reform*. 2nd edn. London: Routledge & Kegan Paul.

Marsh, A. 1976: 'Who hates the blacks?' *New Society* (23 September), 644-52.

Marx, K. 1939: *The German ideology*.

Marx, K. and **Engels, F.** 1970: *Selected works*. London: Lawrence & Wishart.

Mathiesen. T. 1974: *The politics of abolition*. London: Martin & Robertson.

Mayo, M. 1975: 'The history and early development of CDP'. In R. Lees and G. Smith (eds), *Action research in community development*. London: Routledge & Kegan Paul.

— 1977: *Women in the community*. London: Routledge & Kegan Paul.

Millham, S., Bullock, R. and **Cherrett, P.** 1975a: 'Socialization in residential communities'. In Tizard et al. 1975.

— 1975b: 'A conceptual scheme for the comparative analysis of residential institutions'. In Tizard et al. 1975.

Milligan, D. 1975: 'Homosexuality: sexual needs and social problems'. In Bailey and Brake 1975.

Mills, C.W. 1959: *The sociological imagination*. London: Oxford University Press.

Moore, R. and **Wallace, T.** 1975: *Slamming the door: the administration of immigration control*. London: Martin & Robertson.

Moreau, M. 1979: 'A structural approach to social work practice' Canadian Jounnal of Social Work Education **5(1)**, 78-95.

Munro, A. and **McCulloch, W.** 1969: *Psychiatry for social workers*. Oxford: Pergamon Press.

National Community Development Project 1975: *Tate & Lyle*. London: NCDP.

— 1975-6: *Forward plan, 1956-6*. London: NCDP.

— 1977a: *The state and the poverty experiments*. London: NCDP.

— 1977b: *Gilding the ghetto*. London: NCDP.

National Council for Civil Liberties 1977: *Homosexuality and the social services*. Report of an NCCL Survey of Local Authority Social Service Committees. London: NCCL.

Neill, A.S. 1962: *Summerhill: a radical approach to education*. London: Gollancz.

Packman, J. 1968: *Child care: needs and numbers*. London: Allen & Unwin.

Page, R. and **Clark, G.** (eds) 1977: *Who cares? Young people in care speak out*. London: National Children's Bureau.

Paine, C. 1976: 'Residential care: changing the workhouse image'. *Social Work Today* **8(7)**, 16.

Peach, C. 1968: *West Indian migration to Britain*. London: Oxford University Press.

Pearce, F. and **Roberts, A.** 1973: 'The social regulation of sexual behaviour and the development of industrial capitalism in Britain'. In R. Bailey and J. Young (eds), *Contemporary social problems in Britain*. Farnborough: Saxon House/Lexington, Mass: Lexington Books.

Pearson, G. 1973: 'Social work as the privatized solution to public ills'. *B J Social Work* **3(2)**, 209-27.

— 1975: *The deviant imagination*. London: Macmillan.

Phillips, M. 1977: 'Homes for children'. *New Society* **79(753)**, 493-4.

— 1979: 'Council pays for fire started by boy in care'. *The Guardian* (3 April).

Pinchbeck, I and **Hewitt, M.** 1973: *Children in English society*, vol. 2. London: Routledge & Kegan Paul.

Pinder, R. and **Shaw, M.** 1974: *Coloured children in long-term care*. University of Leicester School of Social Work.

Piratin, P. 1978: *Our flag stays red*. 2nd edn. London: Lawrence & Wishart.

Postgate, R. and **Vallance, A.** 1937: *Those foreigners*. London: Harrap.

Pritchard, C. and **Taylor, R.** 1978: *Social work: reform or revolution?* London: Routledge & Kegan Paul.

Ragg, N.M. 1977: *People not cases: a philosophical approach to social work*. (International Library of Welfare and Philosophy.) London: Routledge & Kegan Paul.

Ramdhanie, R. 1978: 'Black boy in the ring', *New Society* (21 September), 623-4.

Red Therapy 1978 (28 Redbourne Ave, London N.3.)

Reich, W. 1972: *The sexual revolution*. London: Vision Press.

Reiche, R. 1970: *Sexuality and the class struggle*. London: New Left Books.

Responsible Society, The (founded 1971): Quotation taken from Introductory Literature. 28 Portland Place, London W1.

Righton, P. 1976: 'It's a battleground: residential care today'. *Social Work Today* 8(3), 9.

Rooney, B. 1980: 'Active mistakes: a grass roots report'. *Multiracial Social Work* 1(1).

Rose, E.J.B. *et al.* 1969: Colour and citizenship. London: Oxford University Press.

Rossetti, F. 1978: 'Politics and participation: a case-study'. In Curno 1978.

Royal Commission on Population 1949: *Report.* London: HMSO, Cmnd 6404.

Saifullah Khan, V. 1979: 'Work and network: South Asian women in South London'. In S. Wallman (ed), *Ethnicity at work*. London: Macmillan.

Salmon, H. 1978: 'Ideology and practice'. In Curno 1978.

Sartre, J.-P. 1963: *Search for a method*. New York and London: Random House.

Scull, A. 1977: *Decarceration: community treatment and the deviant: a radical view*. New Jersey: Prentice-Hall.

Schragg, E. 1977: 'Social workers, social services and the state'. *Intervention* (Autumn), 30-36. Canada.

Secombe, W. 1973: 'The housewife and her labour under capitalism'. *New Left Review* 83.

Sharman, N. 1979: 'A year into partnership'. *New Society* (February).

Sharpe, S. 1976: *Just like a girl: how girls learn to be women*. Harmondsworth: Penguin.

Shaw, O. 1965: *Maladjusted boys*. London: Allen & Unwin.

Simpkin, M. 1979: *Trapped within welfare*. London: Macmillan.

Sivanandan, A. 1976: 'Race, class and the state: the black experience in Britain'. *Race and Class* XVII(4), 347-68.

Smith, D.J. 1977: *Racial disadvantage in Britain*. Harmondsworth: Penguin.

Smith, J. 1978: 'Hard lines and soft options: a criticism of some Left attitudes to community work'. In Curno 1978.

Socialist Child Care Collective 1975: *Changing child care: Cuba, China and the challenging of our values.* London: Writers and Readers Publishing Cooperative.

Statham D. 1978: *Radicals in social work.* London: Routledge & Kegan Paul.

Stedman Jones, G. 1977: 'Class expression versus social control? A critique of recent trends in social history of "leisure" '. *History Workshop* **4** (autumn).

Tajfel, H. 1974: 'Social identity and intergroup behaviour'. *Social Science Information* **13**(2), 65-93.

Tasker, L. and **Wunnum, A.** 1977: 'The ethos of radical social workers and community workers'. *Social Work Today* **8**(23).

Taylor, I. (forthcoming): *Crime at the end of the welfare state.* London: Macmillan.

Thomas, D and **Shaftoe, H.** 1974: 'The patch system'. *Social Work Today* **16**(16).

Thorpe, D., Paley, J. and **Green, C.** 1979: 'The making of a delinquent'. *Community Care* **261** (April).

Tizard, J., Sinclair, I. and **Clarke, R.V.G.** (eds) 1975: *Varieties of residential experience* (Introduction). London: Routledge & Kegan Paul.

Trotsky, L. 1972: *Women and the family.* New York: Pathfinder Press.

Troyna, B. 1978: *Rastafarianism, reggae and racism.* London: National Association for Multiracial Education.

Turner, J. 1978: 'Children not cattle'. *New Society* (24 August), 402.

Vaneigem, R. (n.d.): *The revolution of everyday life.* Situationist International.

Wallman, S. 1975: 'Kinship, a-kinship, anti-kinship: variations in the logic of kinship situations'. *J. Human Evolution* **4**, 331-41.

Walvin, J. 1971: *The black presence.* London: Orbach & Chambers.

Wardman, G. 1977: 'Social work: a communist view'. *Marxism Today* (January).

Webb, K. 1978: *The growth of nationalism in Scotland.* Harmondsworth: Pelican.

Williams, G. (ed) 1978: *Social and cultural change in contemporary Wales.* London: Routledge & Kegan Paul.

Wills, W.D. 1941: *The Hawkspur experiment*. London: Allen & Unwin.
— 1947: *The Barns experiment*. London: Allen & Unwin.
— 1965: *Spare the child*. Harmondsworth: Penguin.
Wilson, E. 1977: *Women and the welfare state*. London: Tavistock.
Woddis, J. 1976: 'The state: some problems'. *Marxism Today* (November).
Wright, P.L. 1968: *The coloured worker in British industry*. London: Oxford University Press.
Wright, R. 1977: *Expectations of the teaching of social work in courses leading to the Certificate of Qualification in Social Work*. Consultative Document 3. London: Central Council for Education and Training in Social Work.

INDEX

INDEX

A code, 22
Alinsky, S., cited, 125, 153
Althusser, Louis, 28-9
anarchy, 205
Anti-Nazi League, 22
apathy, 202-3
Asians *see* ethnic minorities
Assistant Chief Probation Officers (ACPOs), 139
Association of Community Workers, 192
Association of Directors of Social Service, 83
Australian Builders' Labourers' Federation, 126
authority: management as, 200-201; personal conflict with, 198-201, 214; questioning of arbitrary, 203; and self-help, 207-10; theory of, 205-6
Aycliffe School, 120

Bagley, C., cited, 74
battered children, and residential care, 102; responsibility for, 211

Beauvoir, Simone de, 35
Benwell CDP, 191
bed and breakfast project (Hammersmith), 163
Beveridge Report, 29
Birmingham, 115
Bishop Creighton House Settlement, 173-4
blacks *see* ethnic minorities
blind, services for, 207-8
Bookhagen, C. Hemmer, *et al*, cited, 98
Bottoms, A.E. and W. McWilliams, cited, 143
bourgeoisie, hegemony of, 18, 28; and individual against society, 39; and mystification of symptoms, 41; and social control, 101
Brecht, Bertolt, quoted, 109
Britain: black immigration and employment in, 69-70; and minority cultures, 73, 76-7, 81; racial identity and tolerance in, 66-8, 75, 78-80
British Association of Social Workers, 90
British Council of Churches, 22

settlement patterns, 70; *see also* ethnic minorities; race
industrial policy, 184-5, 187
Inner Area Studies, 187
inner cities: class struggle in, 16-17; and CDP cuts, 182; government policy on, 182, 184-5, 187; social deprivation in, 187; in USA, 185
Inner City Urban Programme, 174
Inner Urban Areas Act, 1978, 184
institutionalization *see* child care, residential
intake, 158, 180
Israel, 96

Jewish Board of Deputies, 22
John, G., cited, 67, 85
Joint Docklands Action Group, 192-3
Jones, C.J., cited, 75

Katz, D. and R. Kahn, cited, 178
kibbutzim, 96
Kingsthorpe Home (Woodford, Essex), 115
Klein, Jo, 162, 175

labour: and coloured immigrants, 69-70, 72; and women, 93-6; *see also* employment
labour movement, 10
Labour Party: and CDP in inner cities, 182, 184-5; and employment of women, 94; on immigrants, 76
law centres, 190
lesbianism: and feminism, 92; and male oppression, 35; and motherhood, 97; among social workers, 46-54, 56, 59, 62; *see also* gay liberation; homosexuality
Lessing, Doris, 41
Liverpool, 81-2
local authorities: and CDP, 188-90; and departmentalization of social services, 11; and partnership schemes, 188; powers, 16
Local Authority Social Services Act, 1970, 216
London, 15, 192-4

McIntosh, Mary, 30
management: as authority, 200-202, 204, 210-14; and probationary dismissal, 200; and self-help groups, 209-11; in sub-office team, 177, 179-80
Marcuse, H., cited, 107-8, 111
marriage: and feminist aims, 37-8; and sexual relationship, 54-5, 60; state sanction of, 36; and woman's family role, 54; *see also* family
Marris, P. and M. Rein, cited, 185
Marx, Karl, 17-18, 26, 86, 92
marxism: and authority, 197; and childhood, 97n; and class position, 34; and class struggle, 91; on family, 26, 92-3; and role of state, 27; and social work practice, 12-13; and welfare state, 186
Maternity and Child Welfare Act, 1918, 30
Mathieson, T., cited, 103
meetings, conduct of, 137-8
middle classes, 10; *see also* bourgeoisie

DATE DUE

AUG 29 1995			